RELIVING GOLGOTHA

RELIVING GOLGOTHA

THE PASSION PLAY
OF IZTAPALAPA

Richard C. Trexler

HARVARD UNIVERSITY PRESS
Cambridge, Massachusetts
London, England
2003

Library of Congress Cataloging-in-Publication Data
Trexler, Richard C., 1932–
Reliving Golgotha : the passion play of Iztapalapa / Richard C. Trexler.
p.   cm.
Includes bibliographical references and index.
ISBN 0-674-01064-7 (alk. paper)
1. Pasión de Iztapalapa. 2. Passion plays—History and criticism. I. Title.

PN3299.M6 T74 2003
792.1'6—dc21   2002032743

For Bill, Carlo, Ed, Natalie, and Peter

PREFACE

In the course of my scholarly and personal life I have often been drawn to the study of the various phases of life, especially as they are experienced by dependents—children, the poor, the old. Perhaps this pull of human compassion best explains why, in advanced middle age that may look toward dependency, I found myself in 1997, 1999, and 2001 traveling to Mexico City to witness the reenactment of the passion and death of Jesus presented in the streets of Iztapalapa (previously spelled Ixtapalapa), that capital's largest and perhaps poorest borough. Once a distinct pueblo located at the southern tip of an ancient lake surrounding the old Aztec center of Tenochtitlán, today Iztapalapa is on a subway line from the center completed in mid-1994. That mode of transportation supplements bus and car traffic that brings *capitalinos* and tourists from all parts to the Iztapalapan rites by the tens of thousands, while countless others view the proceedings on television across Mexico and the rest of Latin America, in Europe, the United States, and even in the Philippine Islands.

I soon discovered that this pueblo's annual spectacle offered an excellent venue for studying the celebration of suffering and death. At the end of the nineteenth century the population of Iztapalapa, mostly of Aztec origin, had fallen as low as 10,000. Today, however, this single borough (Delegación; one of twelve) of the Federal District, now as mestizo and urban as any other, houses more than a million struggling souls who, as the preachers have so often said, are themselves crucified daily. In the course of time, the size of the passion proceedings there has grown from humble beginnings to become one of Mexico's (and the Catholic world's) greatest and most important religious events. Iztapalapa is certainly the biggest and most ambitious annual passion play in the world today (Oberammergau, to which the Iztapalapans have often compared their play, is produced only every decade), dwarfing in size and scope even the Way of the Cross that the pope himself, cross on shoulder, has traversed in Rome since 1964. To study these transformations seemed a doable and rewarding undertaking, especially given the fact that the newspapers of Mexico City, most especially *Excelsior* and *El Universal*, offer an almost unbroken written and visual report of the proceedings for the better part of the last century.

When in 1916–17 these newspapers first hit the streets and soon after began their coverage of the Iztapalapan passion, no one could have imagined that the passion play of Iztapalapa would prove so durable, and so resistant to the massive changes of the last century. So we must wonder how and why this play has proven so enormously popular. How is it that real or feigned public mortification–so central to the reenactment of the passion of Jesus–has become such a major part of late twentieth-century history? That is a question I am left with, half a decade after I first saw the three crosses on the Hill of the Star over Iztapalapa.

ACKNOWLEDGMENTS

I wish to thank my esteemed colleague and friend, Jean Quataert, for a complete reading of the manuscript. It helped me immensely, as did Louise Burkhart's more limited, but just as appreciated effort in this regard. For assistance along the way, I am further indebted to Jorge Avila Dominguez, Elizabeth Boone, William A. Christian, Jr., Giles Constable, Katharine Dawson, María José del Río, Nicolás Echeverría, Cristina García Rodero, Carlos Garma, Rafael Gutiérrez, Ramón Gutiérrez, the Guzmáns, Max Harris, Graciela Iturbide, Cecelia F. Klein, Miguel Moraita Mendoza, Julién Morales Guillén, Thomas O'Connor, Eduardo Ontiveros Nevares, the Osmonds, the Sheltons, Dexter Trujillo, the students in my seminar on historical reenactments, and my former colleagues at the National Humanities Center. During the course of this work, I was at that Center; at the University of California, Los Angeles, as an Art Council Professor; at the Wissenschaftskolleg in Berlin as a fellow; and at the John Paul Getty Foundation as a senior research grantee in the History of Art. All these institutions aided my research financially, as did, of course, the State University of New York at Binghamton. I am grateful to all of them.

CONTENTS

RELIVING GOLGOTHA

INTRODUCTION

There's this thing that art does, where we witness death and
loss but we survive it. We experience it vicariously through performance, but we survive it.

Mary Zimmerman (of her *Metamorphoses*)

The show must go on, the show must go on. . . .

Baz Luhrman, *Moulin Rouge*

The passion of Jesus may have been reenacted more often than any other
event in human history. I speak not of Christian priests or ministers who
recall and even claim to reenact this historical event in performing their
churches' liturgy, but rather of historical reenactment in the common
sense of the word: the actual physical and emotional replaying of past history. By focusing on Jesus, I do not mean to suggest that reenactments of
other profound culture-shaping events, such as the annual Shi'ite commemoration of the 680 A.D. massacre of Hussein, the grandson of Mo-
hammed, are any less worthy of attention.[1] This inquiry, however, limits
itself only to the ancient and unbroken imitation of the execution of Jesus, which stretches back in some form to the beginning of Christianity.

It should not be surprising that a religiously uncommitted modern
like myself would be interested in this phenomenon. Partly as a result of
visual technologies beginning with moving pictures, continuing with
television, and reinforced today with virtual images, modern popular
culture across the globe has exploded with reenactments of historical
events. To be sure, these histories are usually of a secular character, so
scholarly literature about reenactments and the popularizations by hundreds of organizations have centered on stories with heroes and villains,
muskets and airplanes, military uniforms and antiquarian artifacts.[2] Indeed, the oldest instances of historical reenactment I have been able to

document were secular in character. Herodotus tells how Athens forbade the dramatist Phrynichus from repeating his *Battle of Miletus* (c. 500 B.C.) because its citizens had burst into tears at the sight of that great Ionian defeat, and in 472 B.C. Aeschylus presented his play *The Persians,* which commemorated the battle of Salamis just eight years before.[3] Furthermore, the secular character of much collective memorialization throughout the European Middle Ages and far into the modern age is apparent in the inveterate Western habit of reenacting past victories and defeats through mock battles during the profane festival of Carnival.[4]

The reenactment of the passion of Jesus and other mystificatory events to which the Christian clergy makes claim, is, to the contrary, reserved for sacred feast days. But just as priests have commonly played Jesus in their commemorative liturgical services—as if he were born and died again in their services—so in popular reenactments the secular event that is recalled, far from being merely past, can in some sense be relived. Actors impersonate their past heroes in the hope of living the past. In their reenactments, the passion of Jesus and other portentous events in the religious pasts of different peoples are not wholly different in kind from past secular events. Here too the past is remembered in order to relive it, in this case through the sacrifice that links the human community with that allegedly still-living God on the cross.

Living a Christian life has historically been referred to as the *imitatio Christi.* If one lives like Jesus, it has been said for almost two millennia, one at least honors the suffering of the innocent man / God and may even earn heaven. The problem historically has been that while Jesus essentially killed himself on Good Friday by obediently sacrificing his guiltless self, few ministers have wanted to encourage their flocks to follow Jesus's passion into self-torture or death, and indeed the Christian clergy has historically warned Christians against such self-imposed suffering.[5] To put it pithily, only the priest and not the laity could change bread and wine into Jesus. Thus already in the High Middle Ages, curates of souls in advising the faithful tended to substitute for the imitation of Jesus's physical suffering, which they decried, a type of moral or mental flagellation that was a quite adequate imitation of Jesus. The "holy athletes" or saints of the past, who had inflicted great bodily suffering on themselves in imitation of Jesus, were to be admired but not imitated. This commonsense clerical position was then reinforced by a doctrine according to which, given Jesus's total innocence, his suffering and death had

produced a grace that was more than sufficient to redeem all the world's
sinners. There was, in short, no real need for ascetic self-punishment.
This of course ran counter to the widespread popular notion that Jesus
continued to suffer for the sins of the faithful, pain which they, in turn,
could mitigate through their good actions.[6]

The Protestant Reformation reinforced the established theory that the
only imitation of Jesus that was incumbent on the Christian was good
living, and throughout the early modern centuries, Protestant divines
regularly pointed to the "superstition" of Catholics who insisted on torturing themselves in imitation of the passion. It was positively uncivilized to do so, many Protestants believed.[7] And indeed, among the polarities that separated Protestantism and Catholicism in these centuries, was
one that some have called triumphalism as opposed to an emphasis on
the passion. In this conceptual framework, elect Protestants, who were
in general opposed to the doctrine of works and thus to the idea that one
saved oneself through asceticism, were devoted to the triumphant feast
of Easter or the Resurrection of Jesus, whereas Catholics remained dedicated to the celebration of Lent and to the asceticism which kept them
in tandem, so to speak, with the living lamb of God.[8]

This modern polarization has served as an instrument of power, both
within particular cultures and in the realm of politics. On the one hand,
the European lower classes were drawn to the realistic reenactment of
the passion of Jesus, while the middle and upper classes in celebrating
Easter tended to vaunt their own upwardly mobile or risen selves. On
the other, the European colonial powers abroad represented to their new
subjects the suffering Nazarene as the sum and substance of the natives'
own guilt for their pagan past, which they had to continually regret if he
was one day to bring them, too, to the table of eternal triumph. Just as in
Europe the lower classes mourned their own poor lives in the glory of
Jesus's redundant suffering and death, so should the natives in the colonies, one and all.

It is this rich legacy of social and political meaning that makes
the *imitatio Christi,* that is, the actual physical and emotional
copying of the experience of a past, present, and future man/
God, such a worthy object of study. It is not news, to be sure, that European historians have long recognized the theme of *imitatio Christi* as be-

ing of the essence of late medieval religion, a period in which the Mendicant friars and the laity developed a more participatory religion that
positioned them nearer the center of meaningful religious action than
such "fools" and "idiots" had been in a previous era.[9] One has only to
think of Peter Damian with his sanctifying flagellation, Francis of Assisi's
effective downplaying of liturgical forms, Mary of Oignies rending her
flesh, and Heinrich Seuse nailed to his own cross to capture the spirit not
only of this European age, but of Christianity transported to the New
World by those same friars. Laid over rich foundations of various indigenous religions across the newly encircled globe, the passion-centered,
popular nature of late medieval religion was eventually so well drilled
into many of the indigenous peoples of the world that, in the end, the
very reenactment of the Good Friday passion of the Levantine savior
would form a firm line of native defense against the colonizers and their
church's assaults on the natives' own cultural heritages.

Understanding how Mexicans came to imitate Jesus in his passion requires some knowledge of the European background
of Holy Week events. Chapter 1 provides it, with a sketch of
passion theater in the Old World up until the end of the fifteenth century. It pays the greatest attention to those elements that will prove of
particular importance to the subsequent American theater. Chapter 2 in-
troduces us to such imitation in the New World. Here I trace the process
by which representations of the passion of Jesus became established in
colonial New Spain (Mexico) and defined during the nineteenth century.
The goal is certainly to describe the historical development of passion
performances in their political and social contexts, but I also aim to identify some of the basic *topoi* that inform the native celebration of that passion in a dominant mestizo society that was slowly marginalizing its re-
sidual native populations.[10] The most important fact I want to establish
in this chapter is that, curiously, the passion came to be a quintessential
means by which indigenous populations in Mexico identified their own
cultures and marked them off from the abuilding mestizo majority.

In Chapter 3 we turn to the passion play at Iztapalapa, in the southern
part of the City of Mexico, a theatrical production that in its present
form dates to the end of the nineteenth century. I examine how the play

developed out of an earlier tradition of passion theater in the Valley of Mexico, when it was brought to Iztapalapa, and when it adopted the all-important texts that to this day are at the base not only of this town's performances but of many other Latin American passions. I look into the various legends that have grown up about the origin of the play. Before all else, I intend to show that the very identity and nature of the Iztapalapan passion play, and indeed of all modern Mexican passion plays, only make sense in the context of Mexican church-state relations during the last century and a half.

The subsequent chapters of the book offer a thematic history of the Iztapalapan pageant during the twentieth century. Divided into blocks of years according to significant changes in the character of the performances, each chapter highlights the main characteristics of its period of time as they emerge from the rich newspaper accounts which are my main source for the history of the modern Mexican passion play. Thus Chapter 4 displays the Iztapalapans' intermittent imitations of Jesus's passion in the age of Emiliano Zapata and the civil war of the Cristeros, during which political disorders and a Mexican church hierarchy in crisis repeatedly forced its suspension. Based largely on newspaper reports from only three years, 1919–1921, this first, tentative description of the Good Friday performances reveals a spectacle that remained tenaciously traditional in character, replete with indigenous actors who still occasionally employed their ancient Nahuatl tongue, may still have worn masks, and who indulged in formal rites of carnivalesque ridicule. Before these images disappear forever, they leave some sense of that other time when a shifting moral stage offered the choice between Barabbas and Jesus, good and evil.

From 1930 until today, the Iztapalapan passion has been performed each and every year in one form or another. In Chapter 5 I describe for the first time not only the rites of Good Friday, but of Holy Thursday and Holy Saturday as well (for 1930–1945), and the details reveal a distinct new period in the history of the Iztapalapan passion. It began with the crucifixion of Jesus being performed at the facade of a church—and thus under the influence of the clergy. It ended with the Iztapalapans erecting three great permanent crosses there where the Aztecs had once renewed the sacred fire on the top of the Hill of the Star overlooking Iztapalapa, where we still view them today. Not a church in sight! Within

this period, we first encounter a central theme of the Iztapalapan passion, the annual interaction or rather confrontation during the Way of
the Cross between the "Jews" and "Romans" accompanying Jesus and
the mass of the audience, either blaspheming or defending the so-called
savior of the world, and we discover that these contacts were often managed so as to provoke religious feeling or disorder, two variants, it appears, of a common behavioral universe. At the end of this period, the
triumph of Christianity seems assured, and the marked dualism of the
previous period is somewhat muted.

The post–World War II years, described in Chapter 6, saw the emergence of the Iztapalapan passion as a significant tourist event encouraged
now not just by the political authorities but at times even by the previously antagonistic religious authorities, *pro bono publico.* Indeed, it is the
politicians' wish to use the clergy as dramaturges, who alone might produce a "decent" spectacle for "honest" tourists, and the clergy's determination to exploit that civic need so as to recapture control over religious
expression here and elsewhere in Mexico, that makes the play at mid-
twentieth century so fascinating. These were also years of structural reforms. New streets were built to bring visitors down to Iztapalapa from
central Mexico City in ever increasing numbers. And while the dust of
ancient Iztapalapan paths slowly yielded to asphalt pavements, the town
fathers decisively changed the city image from a market to a theater. Dis-
placing the old central market, they raised a great hollow space in its
place. For three hundred and sixty-three days of each successive year,
only children used this vast orchestra to play. On Holy Thursdays and
Good Fridays, however, the esplanade became the capital of the world
(in the minds of the town's eager boosters), where the Last Supper, the
trial, flagellation, and sentence of Jesus were carried out.

Chapter 7, centered in the crucial years 1963–1970, implodes the
theme of local passion by describing Iztapalapan reality as increasingly
the product of immense new forces pressing in on the *pueblo* from
abroad. New media were certainly the most decisive. If enclosed theaters
and motion pictures had long challenged Iztapalapa's street theater of
the passion, now television entered the fray, on the one hand allowing
the pueblo to have its product seen worldwide, on the other hand per-
mitting newer passions from across the world *and* across the Valley of
Mexico to attract customers to their performances, thus potentially di-

minishing the number of those willing to trek to sweltering Iztapalapa to witness the extravaganza live. Perhaps the most important of these competitors were the pope and Roman curia themselves, who now began to perform elements of their own passion play in Rome, before the cameras, of course. One of the central phenomena of this new world of passions, both in the Valley and abroad, was the increased use of violence by thespians competing with each other for attention in a passion play that had always featured latent violence. This chapter, in short, documents the growing ferocity employed in the modern media world, in a passion narrative whose essence has always been the demonstration of how the innocent can be made to suffer.

In the decade before 1982 surveyed in Chapter 8, Iztapalapa approached the pinnacle of its grandeur, in terms of the number of its actors, visitors, and police. Not surprisingly, these years also witnessed the most serious attempt to present the spectacle as a unified aesthetic whole, when local and perhaps national political figures allegedly tried to sell exclusive photographic rights for the extravaganza to a foreign firm. The attempt failed, resulting in embarrassment for all involved. In fact, however, the underlying forces at work on the spectacle were leading this increasingly recognizable Iztapalapan package in another direction. As the theatrical aspect of the work became ever more evident, reporters turned their attention to individual players, who now found themselves at times the objects of separate articles in the newspapers. Indeed, individuation is the word of the day in these years. In view of more government funding, the old families that for so long had run the passion had increasingly to yield, in part, to the neighborhoods of Iztapalapa, which demanded their federative say in the spectacle. This chapter shows, if showing needs be, that an expanding collective image of a festivity is commensurate with a growing individuation of its different parts. In this decade, the Iztapalapan passion became a civic image project.

As we shall see in Chapter 9, from 1982 till 2001 Iztapalapans were forced to question whether their deeply traditional opus would have a future in the new millennium. Everything had been done to insure its continued longevity, a new subway now reaching the pueblo-city from the heart of distant downtown Mexico City. Yet dwindling numbers of visitors later in this period suggest that as a tourist beacon, the passion play may have passed its zenith. Still, the religious dynamics that had long an-

imated this spectacle continued to produce novelties. Perhaps most striking, in recent years the Iztapalapan passion has taken on the aura of a
children's play, even if leadership and the major roles remain in adult
hands. Indeed, certain developments since the millennium year suggest
that an unannounced generational struggle was underway for rights of
representation, a festive struggle that eerily echoes the great national
turning point of 1968, when through bloody repression the PRI (Partido
Revolucionario Institucional) political bosses one more time tried to
crush a national reform movement led by university students.[11]

In fact, as this chapter describes the open competition for votes between the established Party of the Institutionalized Revolution (PRI) and
the challenging National Action Party (PAN) in the midst of the passions
of these years, today's reader, aware that the dictatorship of the PRI has
finally ended, will intuit that this passion play has always been a representation, in some way, of national history. Now the citizens of Iztapalapa
may be ready to reckon with the true origins of their great play rather
than with a myth, just as liberated Mexicans have now to reexamine so
much received political wisdom. In 2001, just months after the end of
the old political order, devotees of the Iztapalapan passion looked on almost in disbelief as a bishop representing the cardinal-archbishop of
Mexico took his place alongside the head of Iztapalapa's government in
the reviewing stand of the esplanade to witness the laical reenactment of
the passion of Jesus—a play that more than a century earlier Mexican
history had thrown up as a living protest against the power and influence
of the same church!

The conclusion of this work necessarily restates some of the results
and at least asks about the larger historical and conceptual significance of
reenactments of the death of a savior. But it will also reflect upon the
practical future of reenactments such as the Iztapalapan passion, in
which—and this remains its primary characteristic—not virtual, but real
citizens of a town come out into the streets and relive the humiliation
and redemption in death not just of their eternal lord, but of their neighbors as well.

I

PASSION THEATER:
THE EUROPEAN BACKGROUND

After all, what does it mean to follow, if not to imitate?
Augustine of Hippo, *De sancta virginitate.*

"Do this in commemoration of me," said Jesus to his apostles at his last supper (Luke 22.19; 1 Cor. 11.24). Christians certainly have. From the earliest days of the church until the present, not only has the sacramental clergy repeated its lord's words at that dinner, asserting that, like cosmic actors, they could truly clone the miracle of that banquet, but across history individual Christians have attempted to imitate the actions of their man/God, and especially the terrible events of his passion. One example of that rage for imitation is the subject of this book: the passion play of the Mexico City borough of Iztapalapa.

But if we are to comprehend a passion play that is still performed today, we must first slice into the European past and that of its colonies to observe the various ways in which men and women have attempted to reenact their savior's last days across these two millennia. The majesty of the Iztapalapan spectacle stems to no small degree from past traditions. These roots go beyond the Iztapalapan past, further than the missionary plays of the Spanish Conquests that the friars used to subordinate the native peoples; yes, they go deeper even than the practices monks and some laity adopted for remembering Jesus's passion in the very beginnings of the Christian church.

In the first Christian millennium, the imitations of Jesus most worthy of being recorded were those centered on individuals rather than groups. At the beginning of the second millennium, however, collective imitations of Jesus appear and proliferate alongside a continuing authorial delight in recording individual attempts to replicate the suffering of the savior. This period includes early theatrical representations of the passion in which several actors together portrayed a plurality of biblical characters, aided as often as not by texts of the passion. The development of a European theater of the passion in these late Middle Ages did not, however, reach deeply into the Iberian peninsula. Castile-León, much more so than neighboring Catalonia, was a distinct laggard in the development of passion theater. This means that when the Mendicant friars began their mission work in New Spain in 1524, they did not have an established theatrical tradition of the passion at their disposal.

During Christian pilgrimages to the so-called holy land, devotees did indeed walk more or less in the footsteps of the lord, often with a cross on their shoulder so as to imitate him. One of the earliest extensive records we have of such a pilgrimage was left by a Spanish (probably) woman named Egeria, who in the early fifth century (?) found her way to Jerusalem during Holy Week.[1] She assiduously visited all the places her guide and the local clergy associated with the notable events that had occurred during the days of that week, and was gratified by the experience. Still, Egeria throughout followed the liturgical lead of the churchmen who conducted the program, so that her report is, with rare exceptions, an account of clerical actions rather than of religious discovery. Egeria's experience was, in addition, rare enough in these centuries wracked by civil disorder. That changed at the beginning of the twelfth century, once large numbers of Western knights and provisioners began to stream into Palestine. The imitation of Jesus now emerged as a customary devotional practice, the echoes of which were soon heard back in Western Europe itself. The celebration of Jesus's short-lived triumph on Palm Sunday, the slow establishment of the Stations on what would soon be called the via Dolorosa (Castilian: *calle de amargura*), and the opening of Jesus's (empty) tomb on Holy Saturday, all flickering if not blazing narrative reflections of the Jesus story, date to the twelfth century.[2]

These crusaders' processions are far from the type of theater that tells the passion story from beginning to end. And except for them, the imitation of Jesus in the early centuries of Christianity was something usually done by individual athletic monks to prove they were like the God/man Jesus. Giles Constable, for instance, calls the imitations of this time attempts at self-deification rather than moves to share in the humanity of the man/God, a much later development.[3] The lives of the desert fathers are full of stories of single monks who dwelled upon the physical sufferings of Jesus and in their behavior replicated various actions of his passion: some stretched out on crosses (as if about to be nailed to them), others carried heavy crosses about in imitation of their lord, who, after all, had directly commanded eventual followers to "take up [their] cross and come, follow [him]" (Matt. 16.24).[4] Indeed, we owe to these creative living martyrs the invention of new ways to imitate some non-biblical but presumed suffering of Jesus. Finally, from these early days as well comes the henceforth conventional reaction against violent bodily imitations, with John Cassian protesting such patristic literalism.[5] Much later, Caesarius of Heisterbach (d. 1224) would take up this critique, insisting that Christians needed to distinguish between interior and exterior crucifixion. The former was the Christian way of leading the good life, the latter was not.[6] After all, had Jesus by his immensely charitable self-sacrifice on the cross not saved humanity once and for all? It was unnecessary for the individual Christian to punish himself in this way.[7] This song has been sung from the earliest centuries of Christianity right down to the present.

Yet the historical record documents as well an important number of Christians who have used Jesus's sufferings for their own varied individual purposes, such as restituting or paying back stolen goods to other humans or supernaturals, and second, as a vehicle for manipulating to one's own ends the re-suffering Godhead by playing on the latter's vanity. In turn, it was only a step for such Christians to assume, in the teeth of the church's sacramental doctrine of confession, that by imitating Jesus's suffering during the passion, they could obtain forgiveness and absolution not only for their own sins but for those of others. Beginning with Peter Damian (d. 1072), who first established flagellation as a strategy for salvation instead of letting it stay as merely an involuntary administrative punishment, the names of such sinners in this new age of "Passions-frömmigkeit" are legion. So are the names of those who, beginning in this second millennium, were called upon in visions to punish themselves as Jesus had been punished.[8] Bonaventure, for example, tells of Francis of Assisi, too charitable by half, wanting to be crucified.[9] And Jesus on the cross appeared to a Cistercian monk in the same era, telling him to "do everything that has been exemplified for you on the Mount" [Calvary].[10] The examples of this individualistic imitation know no end, nor any gender barrier, even if women were not made in Jesus's image and likeness. Chiara Agolante of Rimini (d. 1326) had herself bound to a column and whipped every Good Friday, while perhaps the most sensational athlete of self-mortification of this epoch, Heinrich Seuse (d. 1366), considered himself the very image of Jesus through some sixteen years of Christ-like whipping inflicted on his person, or so it is said.[11] It is worth noting that such individuals usually did not develop a narrative of self-mortification following the story of the passion, but tended to dwell on sensational single acts like the above.

All the examples cited to this point have involved religious persons, but in the late Middle Ages the laity made massive inroads into the folklore of imitation. Thomas More tells a story about a man who would have killed himself on Good Friday precisely to imitate Jesus if his wife had not succeeded in talking him out of it.[12] Thus the same emphasis on individual imitation of the passion that had so long been current among the clergy now entered the laity. But when did this lay religion come to the fore? The answer takes us into a new realm of imitation. Beginning in the eleventh century, it produced a culture of passion imitation that slowly but surely took on collective and public dimensions.

Individual laypersons emerging as bona fide imitators of Jesus are known to us because of a literary trope that was used from the eleventh century forward, one involving a religious person cautioning individual laity not to go so far in their self-punishment that they seriously hurt or even kill themselves. Peter Damian warns "noble women" to that effect, while slightly later the archbishop of Arbrissel warned the countess of Brittany in 1108 not to kill herself through self-mortification, "since whoever kills flesh kills the inhabitant."[13]

The appearance of this trope is significant because it implies that in the eleventh century, at least aristocratic lay women were watching the monks and priests beat themselves. That is, some members of the clergy were performing self-mortifications rooted in the passion not only for the eyes of other monks, but for the laity as well, who then sought to replicate their religious betters. What is here only implicit in the evidence, however, is clear elsewhere. Beginning in the late eleventh century, primitive elements of what would one day become medieval theater were scattered about, waiting to be assembled, and elements of Jesus's passion were among them. De Boor, for example, has discovered that, for the first time, the passional person of Jesus was played by a live actor in the late eleventh century Norman liturgy, whereas previously actors had assumed the roles of angels, Marys, apostles, and the like, but not of Jesus, who had remained a sculpted figure.[14] Clearly, at this date and place, small moments of the story of Jesus's passion had taken on a representational character, even if the thrust was liturgical and most elements of true theater were apparently missing—text, persistent narrative line, spoken rather than sung parts, the desire to confound the viewer into believing that what was represented was real, and so on.

Specialists in medieval religious drama have traditionally traced the appearance of passion plays back to earlier established re-creations of Jesus's resurrection. Thus the risen savior's question to Mary Magdalene, "Whom do you seek?" *(Quem quaeritis?)* (Jn. 18.4), proper to the liturgy of Easter, is often assumed to be the point from which, backwards, a passion play was eventually crafted.[15] This approach evidently does establish the fundamental distinction between the *passion* of the living lord and what happened after his death, beginning with his descent from the cross. Thus it is often argued that, historically, the first theatrical elements of a passion re-creation may have been the Harrowing of Hell—Jesus's post mortem actions in that region today called limbo—followed by the idea of performing a procession after Jesus's death bearing his body to the tomb, from which it would soon rise. That processional burial of Jesus was, so goes the argument, linked to the ceremonial demonstration and honoring of Our Lady of Sorrows, that is, Mary suffering in solitude because of the death of her son. The nub of this historical reconstruction is that liturgical action is paramount in addressing questions of the origins of popular cult. A prime proof of this chronology is the Latin Passion of the Italian monastery of Monte Cassino, written in mid-twelfth century.[16] Though obviously composed by and perhaps only for a clerical body, it nonetheless contains some remarkably realistic scenes highlighting the humiliation of the living lord—including Romans who spit in the face of Jesus and beat him—as well as Judas's suicidal hanging, suggesting a bow to an eventual lay audience.[17] Thus the spectacle is said to have developed from top down: clergy who controlled the date and visualization of Easter eventually added on a passion representation to its established resurrection representation, perhaps because the laity, unable to share experientially in the abstract and largely colorless notion of resurrection, increasingly required a representation of Jesus's human suffering to match its own.

Christians have, of course, ever been taught that the miracle of the resurrection and not the death of Jesus was the single decisive moment in their religion's history, the very lynchpin on which its truth depended. And yet there can be little doubt that generally speaking, for all the clergy's millennial efforts to make it important, across medieval and modern Europe traditional peoples paid and pay little heed to Easter. In such cultures, the Christian year in fact culminates with Jesus's violent death on Good Friday, and until very recently, the new Christian year effectively started on the morning of Holy Saturday, when the choirs burst into the great *Gloria!* and the dim covers came off church statues, transforming sacred space from somber grey to brilliant light. Already in the early fifth century Augustine of Hippo had told his audience not to criticize festive activity inside churches, asking his listeners if they would otherwise come there at all.[18] The old German custom of the *risus pascalis* or Easter Laugh was also inspired by this popular lack of interest. Desperate to get people to attend church on this so important dogmatic feast, medieval and early modern parish priests often told dirty jokes during their Easter sermons so as to attract the faithful.[19] Wherever we look in the history of church festivals, modern scholars find repeated indications that despite all the clerical and liturgical emphasis on Easter, the feast was little honored by the flock itself, which rather turned to the celebration of the savior's narratively and experientially much more gripping passion.[20]

Recognizing this state of things, Johan Drumbl has developed a line of historical explanation that wisely abandons a top-down, Easter-based explanation of the origins of the passion play, even if the theory with which he replaces the older view does not as yet rest on the strong evidence that will be necessary to establish its authority. Drumbl's view is that passion plays were essentially the creations of laymen acting largely independently of clerical influence, a laity he misleadingly describes as immersed in private rather than liturgical devotion.[21] Drumbl does not dispute that, acting in the wake of such laical creativity, the clergy did at times attempt to keep the laity in its pocket, so to speak, by itself inventing elements of passion representations. Indeed, he identifies the Latin Passion of Monte Cassino precisely as a reaction to an (undefined) lay initiative. Yet this author does not believe that the inspiration for this great body of work can be said to have come from the clergy, or that passion theater can be understood as merely a sacerdotal catechetical instrument. It arose from the people of Europe, he believes, in an age when the laity was increasingly watching clerical self-mortifications and, I would argue along with Drumbl, from there developed as an independent theater expressing the real-life human experience of suffering and death. Aldo Bernardo once remarked to me that it was his strong impression that in his native Italy, Easter has remained the possession of the clergy, to be sure, but also of the upwardly mobile or rising bourgeoisie and aristocracy. Holy Week, with its unsparing portrayal of a man who cannot help himself, thus always belonged to the poor, who like Jesus die young and often violently.

Other aspects of the question of the origins of passion plays are also important; for instance, attention should be paid to the fact that already in the twelfth century, accusations of Jewish ritual murder sometimes contain the claim that Jews paraded "Jesus" to his death as an imitation of the Christian story.[22] Still, it was not until the second half of the thirteenth century that the first undisputed signs appeared of what would in the fourteenth century develop into passion plays performed by the laity. Thus 1260 marked the appearance in the Umbrian area of Italy of mass public flagellation by the laity and, near the end of that century, of lay confraternities dedicated to the commemoration of Jesus's passion through self-flagellation.[23] As is well known, this corporative innovation spread quickly through Italy, as did the practice of singing lauds to statues of both Jesus and Mary, the latter taking the form of a mournful commiseration (planctus) for Mary's great loss. These were songs done after Jesus was dead and about to be buried. At first these lauds were merely narrative in character, but by 1330 dialogues between characters in the passion had made their appearance in Siena, while at about the same time a confraternity of the Illuminati at Assisi obliged its members to represent the passion to the people each Good Friday.[24]

This proto-theatrical impulse had legs, and in 1375, some lay devotees founded the Confrérie de la Passion in Paris, whose stated goal was to represent Jesus's passion to townspeople annually.[25] This group did not feature self-flagellation as a devotional practice, as did many Italian *Laudesi*, concentrating instead on the performance of all elements of the passion narrative. From this time forward, indeed, across Europe we find the passion of Jesus performed in almost all European lands by groups of devotees. To be sure, through most of the fifteenth century the majority of these groups were not called "Of the Passion" or the like. Rather, our limited evidence suggests that most passion players belonged to confraternities or civic groups named after a local saint, standing alongside other groups that performed other Judeo-Christian stories.[26] For from the later fourteenth century forward, the feast of Corpus Christi slowly became for most of Europe the chosen vehicle for the representation of a total history of Judeo-Christianity, culminating in the eucharist or, what came to the same thing, the sovereign prince usually associated with that host. In as many as four days, images from Adam and Eve up to and including, say, the coming of the friars, were laid out before the faithful, and of course, the passion was a significant though usually not the culminating moment in that history.[27] Within that total historical presentation, the guild or confraternity or small-time theatrical group that traditionally presented the passion stood alongside other collegial groups responsible for performing other moments of Christian history.

For many viewers, the victory of Corpus Christi must have meant a victory of history over experience. Presenting the passion as only one moment in a total cycle of salvation, even if that history at times began, say, with John the Baptist rather than with Adam, meant that audiences were more liable to view the passion as one among the many stories they witnessed rather than as that transforming story that made Jesus's experience identical to their own history of humiliations and dashed dreams. Of course, playwrights of the passions that were performed as part of a total *vita* of their lord must have sought to counterbalance this deadening of audience affect by depicting the punishment and humiliation of Jesus during the passion as particularly brutal and memorable, and historians of various national theaters have remarked how far playwrights went in accommodating this presumptive desire for visualized brutality.[28]

Such a tactic could, however, have had only a limited effect, for reasons of climate. Like all theater, the success of performing Jesus's passion depended upon the empathy the play evoked in the audience. But the liturgical anniversary of these dramatic events was Holy Thursday and Good Friday, two days before the movable feast of Easter, which always fell in late March or in the first two-thirds of April. Thus the faithful in transalpine Europe, for example, were required to be in mourning at a time of year when cold weather did not allow for an open-air passion play and would discourage its performance even inside a church. This had the double effect of discouraging passion plays in non-Mediterranean Europe and fostering the feast of Corpus Christi, which usually fell in June. And in fact, most transalpine passion plays whose performances can be dated were carried out well after the Passion and Easter season.[29] In the Mediterranean world, by contrast, contemporaries in the late Middle Ages performed their passion plays on the very anniversary of Jesus's death, Holy Thursday or Good Friday. Needless to say, a strong association between liturgical mourning and the theatrical vision of their savior in the throes of death did help to anchor the experience of sorrow and solidarity in a way not available to Northerners.

Despite this calendrical limitation, passion plays do begin to appear across Europe as we approach the end of the fifteenth century. Several of them bear the names of professional playwrights, and many were used to attract people from areas and towns roundabout.[30] Further, different regions now acquired reputations for passion plays that have individual characteristics. Most noticeable, perhaps, is the case of Germany, whose many plays, perhaps especially in the Bavarian and Tyrolian areas, were particularly noted for a strong comedic and even ribald strain, an element, as one writer has noted, strikingly absent from the Italian realm.[31] For instance, a gospel passage to the effect that the apostles Peter and John ran to the tomb of Jesus Easter morning was developed into a foot race that gave a hint of sports competition to the Easter story. Still better is what the French, but then massively the Germans, did with the biblical statement that the so-called Three Marys brought unguents to salve Jesus's body. Out of it came the figure of an oil merchant, who features in many plays as a focus of comedic inventiveness.[32] In many European passions of the late Middle Ages, in fact, the dead seriousness of the trial and death of Jesus was calculatedly leavened by apocryphal elements that kept people's attention and even made them laugh.

What is most remarkable in any overview of medieval passion plays is their rarity in the Iberian peninsula, leading one scholar to aver that no performed passion play can be thoroughly documented at any time in the sixteenth century, long after, be it noted, the date the friars' evangelization of the New World had begun.[33] The matter has, to be sure, been bedeviled by some imprecise scholarship, and even by some primary sources that heedlessly label as plays dealing with "the passion of Our Lord Jesus Christ" representations that deal only with the descent from the cross, the Harrowing of Hell, or the meeting of the three Marys at the tomb, all events that happened after Jesus's passion was complete.[34] In attempting to push back the origins of passion plays in Spain, however, one scholar does give us a clue to the social dynamics that were slowly but surely leading toward the type of passion plays already in place elsewhere in Europe. Susan Verdi Webster points to a mandate in the synodal statutes of Seville dated 1511 and reiterated in the following year. Because the laity misbehaved, this synodal decree forbade "representations *in our churches and monasteries* of the passion of our redeemer Jesus Christ *and other acts and commemorations of the resurrection*"[35] (my emphases). From this text, Webster surmises that passion plays, and not mere liturgical actions, must have existed back in the fifteenth century as well. But what was in fact being represented? In the first place, note that the archbishop thought of these "passions" as acts commemorating the resurrection, in short as part of the clerical production that was Easter. Conceiving of the passion as part of the resurrection may explain, in fact, why the prelate repeatedly prohibited such representations only within churches and monasteries, that is, inside clerical precincts. Once readers have read my subsequent account of the 1582 Good Friday representation within the church of Santo Domingo in Mexico City, they will understand what the Seville prelate was referring to in 1511. Given that in Spain, as elsewhere, theatrical manuscripts of the descent from the cross, the Harrowing of Hell, and the meeting of the Marys are significantly older than passion plays, and given the absence of any evidence that Spaniards of this time publicly performed the story of the passion strictly speaking, we may presume that these early sixteenth-century, the "passion" representations unearthed by Webster refer to Jesus's descent from the cross, and perhaps to other postpassion narratives.[36] The descent from the cross was a representation that was conventionally done at the high altar of a church, whereas elsewhere in Europe the actual passion of Jesus had by then been propelled outside by just such clerical prohibitions against plays in church. In short, these early sixteenth-century Sevillan synodal mandates date from a moment in time when prelates may have aimed to crush lay religious theater, before they realized that Jesus's passion was as if made for the decidedly unclerical roads and streets.

But the picture in the peninsula does need further refinement. A distinction must be made, for instance, between Catalonia and Castile, the former historically influenced by the Italian peninsula while the latter was the departure point for the Indies after 1492. In the Catalan region, a liturgical piece commemorating the resurrection was dramatized at Gerona in 1360, but the evidence for a passion here is sparse: the so-called Pasión Didot from the second half of the thirteenth century, which did feature at least the instruments of the passion, survives, alas, only in fragments.[37] Nor is Castile completely blank. Archpriest Talavera speaks of a passion (or descent from the cross?) performed in an otherwise unidentified church around 1435. A text by Gómez Manriga of mid-fifteenth century is a Holy Week lament, but not a representation.[38] Two "representaciones" of Juan del Encina before the duke of Alba have fictional characters describing the death of Jesus. The first is set next to Jesus's tomb, with two hermitaños joined there by Veronica, doubtless bearing the image of Jesus she had apocryphally procured during the via Crucis. She and an angel assure the brothers that Jesus will rise again. The second features a cast of characters telling of their individual experiences of how Jesus had appeared to them after his resurrection.[39] Then, about 1500, Lucas Fernández produced an Auto de la Pasión, but the best guess is that it too was not staged.[40] Shergold does, however, document an anonymously printed 1520 "passion play" that features prophets sentencing Jesus to death, reflecting the particularly strong Iberian notion that Jesus's suffering was predetermined and unavoidable.[41] Then an Ecce Homo (sculpture?) with a rope around the savior's neck was shown to the audience to repeat the moment when Pilate uttered those famous words before sentencing Jesus. Finally comes a scene in which Mary, not having recognized her son because of his disfigurement, cries out in anguish when John the Evangelist insists it is he. Though evocative, this so-called passion is not after all a representation of the narrative of Jesus's last days, and it does appear that even at this late date, Spaniards positively avoided performing the passion. Needless to say, when a peninsular tradition of actual passion plays did develop later in the century, its elements quickly made their way to New Spain and influenced its theatrical development. But for some decades after the Conquest of Mexico, the missionaries in New Spain had no written peninsular models for showing the native Americans how Jesus died.

On the other hand, flagellation, as well as the confraternities that practiced it, were quite well established in Iberia, both behaviorally and institutionally, at the time of the geographical discoveries. According to the Spanish historiographic tradition, the practice of flagellation, obviously intended to have the penitent reproduce on his own body and spirit the experience of Jesus, was introduced into the peninsula by Vincent Ferrer (1350–1419), a Dominican preacher of English extraction born and reared in Valencia. Surely Ferrer's fascination with his and others' public self-mortification did much to encourage this form of behavior in Spain, but it was certainly in place well before Ferrer, if for no other reason than that public flagellation was widespread in Italy by 1300 and must have been carried to the Mediterranean litoral of Spain by that time. Catalonia was, after all, part of the Mediterranean commercial universe of the time, with fourteenth-century Italian merchant companies establishing themselves along that coast just as Catalan merchants had spread east across the Mediterranean in the second half of the thirteenth century.

The conviction of some Spanish writers that flagellation was bad and thus imported has led other writers to blame the foreigners among them for importing such whippings. Llompart has found that in 1487 the Genoese got the right to form a confraternity of flagellants (*disciplinantes*) in Valencia,[42] a date that melds fairly well with the historian Gonzalo Fernández de Oviedo, who in his *Memorias* of c. 1546 says that the Genoese living in Spain now beat themselves "like others of our Spaniards."[43] Indeed, in his encyclopedic work on the confraternities of Seville, Sánchez Gorillo (fl. 1630–32) states that the Sevillian confraternity of Santa Cruz, previously called the Confraternity of the Blood (of

Jesus), had been the first to practice public flagellation on one Holy Thursday night a century and a half earlier. This and other information makes it appear that, though the excitement around Vincent Ferrer certainly included public self-flagellation, the end of the fifteenth century marked the point at which this practice became an accepted and necessary part of the Spanish celebration of Holy Week.

The significance of Genoa in our story deserves attention, because this city did indeed play an important role in the expansion of corporate public flagellation in the Mediterranean which has only recently been recognized. From the city chronicle of Genoa written by Jacopo da Voragine (d. 1298), the famous author of the Golden Legend, we learn of the velocity with which flagellation spread through that populace. At first, in the 1260s, citizens mocked those who went through the streets beating themselves, but soon enough everyone joined in. They went from church to church while flagellating, and those who had ridiculed the initiators now led the city in this behavior.[44] The resulting flagellant confraternities of Genoa were called *casacce*. Probably beginning about 1260, they were certainly in place by the time of the flagellating members of the Bianchi in 1399. They numbered 21 by 1528 and remained crucial to that city's confraternal life for centuries after.[45]

Being the sea power that it was, Genoa exported overseas the city's model of flagellant confraternities to those areas of Europe where the city's merchants lived in colonies. Thus in Sicily certain passion processions came to be called the *processioni di Casazza,* a name which, according to Pitré, probably derived from the influx of Genoese into the island, and in fact in 1591 a Palermitan diarist described "a very beautiful procession of the *Casazza* of the Genoese nation," which represented the whole passion by means of *misteri* or figured representations of the passion's various parts, each carried by children dressed as angels.[46] Thus the activity of the Genoese in founding flagellant confraternities in Valencia and Seville is part of a larger cultural expansion of Genoese merchants in the Mediterranean.

The evidence that the Genoese were founding flagellant confraternities in Spain at the end of the fifteenth century matches that of recent scholarship showing that at this same time, and across the Hispanic kingdoms, peninsulars were founding many new confraternities dedicated to scourging members if not throughout the year, then certainly on the Fridays of Lent, or at least during Holy Week. As we have noted, in this part of the world such activity could be performed publicly during Holy Week itself, allowing for a fusion of calendrical and theatrical emotional power. From that time until c. 1770, public flagellation would reign supreme in Spain as a central behavior of this time of year, and indeed it has not yet completely vanished from the Holy Week scene.[47] The many confraternities instituted in the period 1490–1550 can broadly be organized according to whether they were supervised by the Franciscans or the Dominicans. Usually, Franciscans sponsored those entitled *de la (Santa) Vera Cruz* and Dominicans those labeled *del Santo Sepulcro.*

Beginning with the earliest groups' statutes, it is clear that most confraternities featured certain institutional categorizations of those who processed under their banners. What I quickly recognized, as a former historian of medieval Italy, was that these "brotherhoods" were defined by a de facto class distinction between rich and poor *hermanos,* labeled respectively as brothers of light *(de la luz)* and brothers of blood *(de sangre),* the former carrying candles or torches in the processions but not flagellating, while the latter, carrying various scourges, did whip themselves. From the beginning a class—indeed, in one rare case, even a gender basis for this division—was notorious. Composed just a few years after its founding in 1521, for instance, the statutes of the Vera Cruz confraternity at Cáceres distinguished between brothers who were *"caballeros* and were expected to lead the processions and carry torches," and those who were *disciplinantes.*[48] And in Lorca a century later, the confraternity of the Sangre de Cristo proclaimed what was clearly customary. If a *caballero* or other person of quality wanted to become a brother but did not want to flagellate on Holy Thursday, he had to pay 15 reales and carry a torch in the procession.[49] Nor did things change much before Charles III's effective suppression of these confraternities in 1777. Earlier in that century, the famous fray Gerundio described those *de la luz* as "the bosses *(amos)* of the brotherhood, who are content to instruct the *penitentes de sangre* so they are fired up to consume themselves with lashes."[50]

A knowledgeable French traveler in 1765, shortly before the suppression, characterized the flagellants he saw in Spain as "rented and from the dregs of society."[51] The latter characterization is open to dispute,[52] but the former was undoubtedly true: from the earliest records until the end of public flagellation after 1777, and in the teeth of formal prohibitions, renting men to lash themselves at different times of the year and specifically on Holy Thursday and Good Friday was a commonplace of Spanish confraternal practice, and was doubtless considered a charitable activity to employ these poor self-whippers in this deeply unequal social body. Puyol, for instance, shows how individual flagellants sometimes rented substitutes to suffer for them, while the mayordomos responsible for organizing the whole spectacle would at times hire those willing to beat themselves so as to add to the pomp and ceremony of the representation. Men in this category were sometimes called Simons of Cyrene, after the person who helped Jesus carry the cross.[53] The repeated emphasis on these Cyrenians around 1604–05 suggests a practice that was indeed medieval in its origins.[54] It was not unusual for medieval confraternities and guilds in general to distinguish between major and minor members, and that had carried over to flagellation. Thus at the end of the fourteenth century, such substitutes were regularly hired by Italians involved in the movement of the Bianchi.[55]

Less is known about female *cofradas*. Maureen Flynn did find one rare reference to sisters *de luz*, women whose main task appears to have been to wipe the sweat from the brows of flagellating men.[56] From the sixteenth century forward, synodal laws regularly forbade women to flagellate, at least in public, and it is plausible, as Flynn argues, that in Spain as elsewhere in Europe, women's right to publicity had been in decline since the Middle Ages.[57]

Flagellation was therefore the one part of an eventual passion play that was undoubtedly firmly in place during Holy Week at the time that the Mendicant friars began the immense, and immensely unjust, attempt to convert overseas natives to Christianity. In the almost four centuries from that point in the early sixteenth century until the Iztapalapans began their famous passion play in the 1880s, the Spaniards would develop a rich and varied tradition of passion plays that did indeed impact upon the passion plays of New Spain.[58] But our focus now moves to the Valley of Mexico in the wake of the Conquest.

THE PASSION PLAYS
OF NEW SPAIN

Holy Week is dead.
El Mundo Semanario Ilustrado, 10 April 1898.

[This Jesus] will bear the heaviest cross of all time. . . .
Excelsior, 14 April 1979.

The Franciscan friars who arrived in Mexico City in 1524 brought no passion play tradition with them, as there was none in Spain at the time.
This fact, and not their fear that showing Jesus's sacrifice might confirm
the natives in their own traditions of human sacrifice and cannibalism, is
why in 1530 the friars limited themselves to public representations of
most of the other edifying moments in Christian history—the fires of
hell being a particular favorite—but only later in the century began to
show the passion of their lord.[1] It also helps explain why the passion
plays that were ultimately developed reveal no manifest traces of the native inhabitants' pre-Christian mutilative traditions. Yet if the friars did
not bear passion texts and traditions, they did bring with them the practice of flagellation, which they immediately and personally performed
first for the native Americans, then later for the peoples of the Philippine
Islands, Japan, and China. The internationally consistent content of the
clergy's reports on the subject of flagellation was that, after they learned
how from the friars, the natives loved to beat themselves so much that
the friars had to step in to prevent the locals from hurting themselves by
excessive flogging. The missing link of this story is, of course, that the
friars had encouraged the natives to practice what they saw the clergy
doing, and that the subsequent popularity of flagellation owed much to

the natives' desire to please their new masters. No one knowing the sources will doubt the witness of the Protestant Thomas Gage, who, visiting the Americas in 1648, rightly observed that the friars "ma[d]e the Indians whip themselves the week before Easter, [just] like the Spaniards,"[2] or that converts to Christianity would whip themselves to convince their relatives to convert.[3] It is customary for scholars to cite missionaries' claims that they had baptized some large number of natives as proof of their success, but, as everyone knew, sacramental reception did not guarantee that the natives had in fact converted. Still, reports to superiors of flagellating natives were a clearly persuasive proof of that conversion, for who would whip themselves like the friars but those who imitated them? What these self-congratulatory sources really express is the missionaries' confidence that an account of the extent of native flagellation would convince their superiors that the missionaries had indeed converted the natives. Inversely, the natives convinced themselves that their public self-mortification was what the missionaries most wanted to see as evidence of conversion.

The earliest evidence of Christian flagellation in the New World comes, however, not from the clergy but the laity. Describing for emperor Charles V his long march to discover the mysterious Colhuacan, Nuño de Guzmán wrote on July 8, 1530, that his troop had stopped to celebrate the Holy Thursday just past as much as was possible in this rude land. They first erected the mandatory *monumento* (made of bird feathers!) to showcase the host, then installed five other tiny chapels *(hermitas)* for as many large crosses. Here were the rudiments of the Spanish custom of the Seven Houses *(Siete Casas)* or churches that subsequent creoles and Mexicans would visit over the centuries each Holy Thursday. Following that, "a devout procession of more than thirty flagellants was carried out."[4] Surely the Spaniards' own Holy Week practices in America must have taught the colonized natives acceptable ceremonial behavior.[5]

Still, it was the clergy that came with a strategy, and it was their calculated displays of self-mortification that had the greatest effect on the aborigines, from that day well into the eighteenth century.[6] Without any doubt, the Franciscan Martin of Valencia (d. 1548), leader of the so-called Twelve Apostles of the Indies, stands out in this respect. His pilgrimages to Amecameca at the foot of the volcanos southeast of Mexico

City, where he visited a sepulcher holding the dead Jesus, became the occasion for sustained self-flagellation that was the wonder of the native population. In the annals of the 1590s by the native Chimalpahin (d. c. 1650), for instance, we find the fascinated annalist gleaning from his own "ancients" the story of the sensational and exemplary flagellation this man carried out, often within view of everyone.[7]

But Chimalpahin does not relate such Franciscan flagellation to theater, and for that connection in these early years of the evangelization we must look elsewhere, to an impressive document that shows precisely the symbiosis between the friars' and their flocks' flagellations. The Augustinian friar Juan de Grijalva (d. 1638) penned his account of the deceased fray Antonio de Roa within the *Crónica* of his order to convince his superiors that the friar was nothing short of a saint because of his asceticism. Significantly, Grijalva's laud of Roa appears in the description of a rudimentary passion play whose partly allegorical format still reflects the underdevelopment of the peninsular passion drama. Roa lived in the (Otomí) Augustinian missionary area of Xilitlá and Molango on the western perimeter of the Sierra Madre Oriental, some 60 kilometers north of the capital. The time frame is 1537 to 1563, the year of Roa's death. Let it be said at once that Grijalva's account of Roa's passion activities is not above suspicion, precisely because the author was making a case for beatification or sanctification. Further, we must also note that padre Roa stood at the exhibitionistic extreme of his order's religious devotion, which is why he so interested Grijalva. Indeed, during his life Roa's sensational displays met with opposition from a party of devotees who instead followed fray Juan Bautista, who was ostentatiously famous for avoiding devotional publicity.[8] Nonetheless, Roa's activities do give us a clear insight into an ideal Augustinian missionary, and the practices attributed to him may be taken as normative for the early days of religious conversion, a model that combined Mendicant with lay flagellation.

Because of the "guileless and vulgar" nature of the natives, who would be moved "more by example than by doctrine," says Grijalva, Antonio de Roa decided "to demonstrate on his body everything he preached." The author describes the religious actions Roa performed in his daily life, and those that he carried out particularly during Lent. The daily practices the author further divides into two parts, those carried out in the presence of the natives but far from the eyes of Spaniards, and those executed in Augustinian hermitages, where he might be seen by his Augustinian brothers but normally not by the natives.

According to Grijalva, Roa always went about accompanied by a group of native familiars whom he had instructed in Christianity. Besides protecting his person, this group's main task was to interminably "torment" Roa's body. Clearly, the friars and their native retinues were in some way to be viewed as equal to each other. The attendants practiced violence to such an extent, says Grijalva, that they appeared to be Roa's enemies, whereas in fact the friar had taught them to act out this part on command. Thus the "holy man" went along Jesus's via Dolorosa or *calle de amargura*, that is, the Way of the Cross, "trying to emboss himself with that meekness and suffering with which the redeemer of souls is said to have processed." As he proceeded, Grijalva says, he would pray Jesus to give him some hint of his charity by making him ready to suffer for humanity as had Jesus, and by allowing him to participate in Jesus's feelings and pain, continuing in this vein until he came to one of the myriad of crosses that natives had erected in the mountains not only for devotion, but to ward off the devil, "who lived in this mountain fastness." At that point and at each cross he encountered, his company of natives would then shower blows on him. "There he would fall to his knees in profound sadness and feeling, and they [the natives] would spit in his face, strip him of his habit, and whip him fifty times with both hands, so violently that he would splash blood about." Obviously, this is nothing less than a rough recreation of the Way of the Cross, with the locals as Jews and Roa as the one and only victim. He would then say a prayer. There being many such crosses, there were many stops or Stations where he would undergo precisely this punishment. Thus he would come away from such a walk so full of wounds that the "Indians" who saw him "stood in wonder, in such pity that they would give him their shoulders to help him stand up after such whippings, just as Simon of Cyrene helped Christ carry the cross."

Grijalva tells us that at that point, Roa would turn toward one of the mountain pueblos and preach Jesus's innocence to the natives. Turning to the cross (crucifix?), he would tearfully proclaim that he and not Jesus was the sinner, that he and not the savior merited such penalties, all this with such fervor that "these barbarians could understand the two most important points of our faith, which are the innocence of Christ and the gravity of our guilt, followed by what we have to do to satisfy Christ" for our sinfulness. Once in the pueblo, he would spend the rest of the day caring for the natives.

When evening fell, Grijalva has Roa perform "another wondrous spectacle." In the local church, he undertook "a general discipline [or flagellation], to which everyone would come." The converted Indians whipped themselves, obviously mimicking the behavior of their spiritual master. After that, Roa left the church, naked from the waist up, with a cord around his neck, barefooted. The Indians had already covered the streets with live coals around four bonfires located at the four corners of the patio, so that they would have enough live coals for the occasion. "The holy man now walked over the coals so calmly and with such devotion that the Indians thought him to be more than a man."[9] In this way he went around the whole patio, "and on arriving at the church, he made a great sermon about the pains of hell, in comparison to which these [in the bed of coals] were nothing." At the end of the sermon, he held a "cauldron of boiling water, and with it they bathed his whole body, already so wounded. Then the Indians went home and he to the contemplation in which he spent most of the night, with no more covering than the soil to relieve such a charred [body]."

These spectacular exercises carried out only before the "rude" natives were not, according to Grijalva, like those done while he was at his convent, which were so secret that no one other than Roa's companions saw them. Still, Grijalva knew that at these secret places, Roa was bound to a column like Jesus, while his same Indian "confidants" whipped, slapped, spit upon, and roasted his body in fire. Indeed, the blood Roa shed on these occasions had survived as well, and visitors could still inspect it, said the author, acting for the moment like a tourist guide.

Roa carried out still "more awful" disciplines every Monday, Wednesday, and Friday of Lent. On each such day, he would go out to an oratory in the convent garden at Molango, where he initiated his contemplation of a picture of Jesus in the Garden of Gethsemane; we find ourselves, that is, at the beginning of the passion of Jesus. After he had said a long prayer,

> some Indians would arrive and, laying hands on him, they hit him repeatedly and insulted him verbally, in imitation of the *prendimiento* or arrest of Jesus. Then stripping him down to his waistline

and violently ripping off a penitential grater that he had tied to his skin, they tied his hands, and put a rope around his neck. In this condition his retinue took him to another oratory, where there was a painting of the Magdalene oiling the feet of Christ our lord. There stood an Indian at a tribunal, representing divine Justice. The Indians pulled him [to that spot], and introduced him by saying that they had brought a bad man, an ingrate, full of defects and sins, proud, deceptive, false, with other faults as well. It being [Lenten] tide and pricked by his conscience, [Roa] offered himself. The judge asked how he would plea. Then the holy penitent, with profound and true humility and without saying a word, kissed the feet of that Indian who represented divine Justice, and watered them with tears, imitating the holy Magdalene. He stood there quite a while sighing so deeply that [his tears] penetrated the heavens, and softened the stones themselves. At the end of this pause, in a loud voice he confessed his sins, his defects, and his ingratitude, and finally everything that most bothered his conscience, asking pardon for all his guilt. At this point other Indians appeared from across the way, accusing him of false testimony. The saint [!] did not respond, so as to imitate that most innocent lamb [Jesus] who fell silent when they accused him.

The theme of passion imitation emerges again.

Then the judge [divine Justice] let it be understood that he found the accusation justified, and that it was truly and well proved, and that the accused [himself] was convinced. [So he] ordered him stripped of all his vestments till he was stark naked, so as to imitate in this also his master [Jesus], who stood [painted] there at Mt. Calvary. Here the saint poured out so many tears, [thus] being in concord with that which Christ our savior felt seeing himself naked in the presence of such a multitude. And so standing there naked they held him down on the ground, and beat him so valiantly and contentiously that his blood ran across the ground, and his whole body remained excoriated.

Breaking into the first person, Grijalva says: "I could not pass by here without much pity, and without thanking God for the infinite grace he knew to bestow on such a weak subject as the flesh and such grand [Augustinian] friends he knew he had on earth." Roa's body being so excoriated, with wounds so deep that they went straight through his body, the Indians "now brought up some *ocote,* as they called it, a torch made of pines. They lit the tea and melted it over his body, the resin catching fire as it fell, so that they burned his whole body from the shoulders to the base of the feet."

Grijalva then comments: "The pious may think that these penances were imprudent. . . . I say that the penances are like those of the anchorites of Thebes, as well as those mentioned by Nicephorus, Calixtus, Lippomano, and other ecclesiastical historians." "Such [penances], they say, are more to be admired than imitated."[10] The pious should therefore thank God for "so rare a spectacle, since it is inferior to the [aforementioned] ancients in no way." Returning to his narrative, Grijalva now recounts how the natives "put a heavy cross onto [Roa's] shoulders, and [then,] pulling him by the rope, they took him out in procession around the garden." By this point the Indians had seeded the soil with lit grease, which erupted with the flowers over which one walked. And going barefooted as usual, he crossed those coals, "contemplating along the via Dolorosa."

The Indians pulled him with the rope so that he fell to his knees every minute; he let it happen. His totally wounded body, weighed down by the cross, his feet on the coals: little was required to make him fall for minutes at a time. He arrived in this condition at another hermitage, where the whole passion was painted. There Roa left the cross, Grijalva continues, whereupon they tied him to a column, which still today, he says, is preserved with great devotion and tenderness by those who visit it. There they tied him and left him until the following morning, when the Indians came and freed him. Putting on his clothes, they raised him up quickly so that he could say prime with his companion.

Grijalva concludes by expressing amazement at the speed with which Roa could heal, so that between Monday and Wednesday or Wednesday and Friday in Lent, he could repeat the whole exercise again. We, on the contrary, may marvel at the writer's extreme if limited imagination. If we assume for the moment, however, that things happened much as Grijalva describes them, we may first observe that this friar, like a mime, essentially constructed a passion play without words, one in which he played Jesus while the natives, though unlabeled as such, effectively played Jews and Romans. It is a role-assignment that the clergy would often use throughout the early missionary period, and it can still be found at the present day.[11] Most of the words in Grijalva's description are nonbiblical, like a prayer he attributes to Gregory of Tours and the words the native Americans uttered to divine Justice, at what was clearly an allegorical moment in a play dominated by Roa's historical imitation of Jesus.

While Grijalva obviously wished to show Roa teaching about Jesus dying in far-off Jerusalem, he just as surely intended to document Roa's own suffering space as a worthy goal for pilgrimage. Writing about 1623, not only did he note that religious tourists could still view the very blood Roa had shed and the pillar at which he, like Jesus, had been scourged, but reported just how much he, Grijalva, had been affected by seeing such things. As I have remarked elsewhere, this is a type of rhetoric proper to a land that, at the time of Roa, still had no Christian relics to speak of. Grijalva thus describes a Mexico-based Jesus figure who might command reverence well after his death.[12]

A third point to notice is that in his quotidian as distinct from his Lenten activity, Roa pursued a two-stroke procedure that certainly imitated Jesus, but not narratively so. He would submit to violent beatings of various types, to follow them up by sermons in which, equating his own suffering to Jesus's, he would emphasize how innocent Jesus had been and how guilty humanity was, incidentally pointing to his own suffering as that of another innocent.

A fourth point is no less interesting: the intimate link between Roa and his native inferiors, called his "confidants" at one point, who went about whipping the friar. This is an important feature of missionary evangelism in the Americas and probably elsewhere that has not received much attention. Here we have it among the early records of the conquest. This practice, comparable on its face to the long-established practice of a Mendicant lay brother wielding the whip against his associate friar-brother, was also long lasting. In the late seventeenth and eighteenth centuries, the Congregation for the Propagation of the Faith, centered in Querétaro, still had natives, like so many helpful Simons of Cyrene, beat them.[13] Obviously, Roa's humility was the cardinal virtue demonstrated by this practice, but what theatrical role if any did these "simple and vulgar" natives play? Did they in some way function to build down rage at the friars by disempowered natives? Or did such whippings of the conquering yet innocent friary by humble, if guilty, natives encourage native communities to take up flagellation as their debt to the Mendicants?

A fifth observation leads directly to the core of this book. At the time of Roa's performances around mid-century, the Augustinians had erected various chapels with painted parts of the passion, and these paintings were the focus of seven passion-like activities. These behaviors were:

1. The imitation of the Prendimiento or arrest of Jesus at the garden of Gethsemane.
2. The imitation of Mary Magdalene. This oratory scene is combined with a variant of an *auto sacramental* in which Roa, or rather Jesus, is presented to the allegorical figure of divine Justice, played by an Indian whose feet Roa kisses in imitation of the Magdalene.
3. In the same setting, by his silence he imitates Jesus's lack of response when the Jews accuse him.
4. Again in the same oratory, he imitates the flagellation of Jesus.
5. In a decidedly unbiblical motif, Roa walks over burning coals, imitating the desert fathers.
6. At this point, Roa begins his imitation of Jesus on the Way of the Cross by assuming the cross itself. Armed with it, he then proceeds to walk again over hot coals.
7. After this procession, Roa arrives at a second oratory, which is painted with the whole passion. At that point he leaves the cross, is tied to a column, and is left for the night, before returning to his normal observance of the canonical hours the following morning, to repeat the whole passion on the next day.

By the time Grijalva wrote, textual passion plays and performances were well established across most of Europe. Yet obviously neither Antonio de Roa nor the creole Juan de Grijalva, mixing allegory with history, was familiar with any established tradition of passion plays cum text, and that is not surprising, since this form was not yet well established in Spain itself. On the other hand, it is equally probable that, whatever the truth of Grijalva's Roa story, these Augustinians understood some of the fundamental elements that would eventually end up in such theater: Jesus played by a priest, and native Americans playing Romans and Jews beating white friars, giving rise to the notion that natives would owe self-punishment payable to the very foreign authorities who so readily demanded the lash. Precisely by such subordination mixed with aggression against the friars, the natives, with such a central role in the missionaries' theater, may have contributed to preserving their own cultural autonomy, even in the new religious medium of Christianity.

For their part, Roa and his fellow friars through such activities clearly meant to imitate an apostolic past, reproducing in these Americans the guilty Semites and Latins who had once tortured the lord. In short, a type of macrohistorical theater was in the making. But while these natives were familiar enough with impersonating their Gods,[14] what might they make of the strange and exotic roles of Jews and Romans they were now made to play? And what kind of colonial community could be envisioned that was rooted in such mutual self-mutilations? Perhaps the future of the Spanish imperial experiment will yield answers to some of these questions.

If we are to believe an eighteenth-century copy of a lost manuscript allegedly written by the native cacique Toribio de Sandoval Martín Cortés in the sixteenth century, the author as a child had witnessed a passion performance of some type in Cuernavaca.[15] Fernando Horcasitas translates Sandoval's Nahuatl into Spanish, rendered in English as follows: "Here begins how one did the passion of our God. It was not just an entertainment (*diversión*), but [an account of] how they humiliated him. It was ordered that this be done so we would remember how our God died." The editor thus includes this play among the "first *neixcuitiles*" or example plays that the missionaries used to teach the natives Christian stories and doctrines.

Yet with only this evidence to go on, the identification of this scene as a passion play must remain questionable. And even if it was one, it must have been rare indeed, for the author to have remembered and recorded it in writing. In his chronology of such plays the authoritative Horcasitas himself does not come upon the text of any other passion play until the eighteenth century, suggesting the same paucity. Moreover, the very exiguousness of the text as published by Horcasitas dampens enthusiasm. And finally, there are other claimants for the role of earliest passion performers at the end of the sixteenth century: Franciscans, who, along with the Dominicans of Mexico, were the undoubted leaders in developing the passion genre. Doubtless, there are still discoveries to be made in this area of research.[16] But the wisest course is still to assume that even if Sandoval were to prove a reliable sixteenth-century source, the passion performance he seems to refer to was surely rare.

From the time of the conquest until nearly the end of the sixteenth century, therefore, we have to register not a tradition of passion plays,[17] but rather a pattern of widespread native flagellation during Holy Week, with friars at times playing Jesus-figures, both triumphing (as on Palm Sunday) and being beaten themselves. Thus the Franciscan Toribio Motolinía (d. 1565), one of the so-called Twelve Apostles, sets the tone in describing events around 1540.[18] Men and women, both cofrades de la Cruz de Cristo though separate from each other, whipped themselves not only on Holy Thursday night, but three times a week during the rest of Lent and, indeed, every Friday of the year. Though it would disappear subsequently, women's public flagellation was a feature of this early period of the conquest, when the friars needed to employ females against recalcitrant males.[19] Without naming the ceremony, Motolinía then describes the Thursday evening procession later known as that of the Seven Houses, when flagellants went from one church to another to see the monuments. Once these tinieblas were over—for this is what Motolinía called the overnight events of Holy Thursday night and Good Friday morning—the sermon of the passion and another procession of flagellation followed, featuring both bloodless and bloody, that is, dry and wet, scourging.[20] Throughout Motolinía inflates the great numbers that were present at these Holy Week events, conscious though he was that "people arranged in procession appear to be greater in number than they [really] are."[21] As we shall see, the Iztapalapan reporters to this day know no limits in describing the numbers who visit their procession.

In these early decades of conversion, there is precious little to report about native passion activity beyond flagellation. The second council of the Mexican church in 1565 warned natives not to hold processions during their feast days unless a priest was present, an indication that the Americans were in fact beginning to carve out their own world of syncretic religious practices.[22] But most of the ecclesiastical legislation concerning religious behavior through the middle of the century rather consisted of admonishing Spaniards not to set a bad example for "ignorant persons."[23] Alternately, we encounter admonitions that are race-neutral, such as the significant warning of the same year that the famous monuments in the main churches on Holy Thursday were not being visited—the reference is to the so-called Seven Houses visits—because the people were out in the streets watching "the procession of the flagellants."[24] Undoubtedly, this is very early evidence that the church's prerogatives were being challenged by the lay flagellants who performed mostly in public. The archbishop ordained that the figures of Jesus in the churches were always to be accompanied during that night.

In the year 1596, the Dominican friar Agustín Dávila Padilla (d. 1604) recorded the first extensive description of a Good Friday in Mexico.[25] These pages cannot do it justice, not only because of its length but because, at bottom, it is largely lacking in theatrical elements, and because only Spaniards, lay and ecclesiastical, participated.[26] Dávila is essentially writing confraternal history at this point in his *Historia*. He documents the founding of the confraternity of the Descent and Sepulcher of Jesus, meeting in the church of Santo Domingo, in 1582.[27] The author makes clear that at this date, the confraternity of Mary in Solitude (the Soledad) was already in existence, its cult and procession supporting one of the most important nunneries in the city.[28] Despite or perhaps because of the fact that the Soledad was already at center in the ceremony of the burial of Jesus, the Dominicans, Dávila explains, decided to push for the immediate representation at Santo Domingo of Jesus's descent from the cross and the processing of his body to its grave (the so-called Santo Entierro) by its homonymous new confraternity in the very same year 1582. And so it was, with great success. "Even if I can only represent [it] with dead letters," our author pleads, "perhaps I can after all help explain what type of performance took place."

Dávila first describes the scene within the church, where everything regarding the crucifixion of Jesus transpired. In the midst of the main chapel stood a stage *(tablado)* 20 by 12 feet that rose up almost to the steps of the main altar. Up over this stage rose three crosses, some seven feet high. It was a Mt. Calvary, and its like can still be seen at Atotonilco, where the whole altar end of the eighteenth-century chapel of Calvary is taken up by three moments of the Crucifixion in more than life-sized figures.[29] The figures of Jesus and the thieves were made of reed (caña) as were many such figures in colonial Mexico.[30] Mary stood to Jesus's right, made "so that with some cords placed at the bottom of the litter, [her] image could raise its hands and habit to its forehead, bow its head, and also incline the body."[31] In this most fashionable church of the capital, our lady was a mannequined puppet, cast in that mode for the evident purpose of invoking pity and wonder from the audience.[32]

Dávila then turns to the events of Good Friday itself, so it is immediately clear that there was no representation of the passion story previous to the crucifixion, for the author begins his account by saying that at two in the afternoon the preacher gave what is usually called the sermon of the Seven Last Words while the flagellants whipped themselves in accompaniment. Just as promptly, Dávila moves on to the scene in the church where five priests and five acolytes removed Jesus from the cross. As quickly, the account turns to the burial procession of Jesus, or the Santo Entierro, on which the author dwells at length. Four priests carried the *Christo iacente* from Santo Domingo to the cathedral, then to the church of San Francisco, and finally to the nunnery of the Conception of Mary, where the body was deposited, the procession returning to Santo Domingo. It had been accompanied by two *pasos* or statues on litters surrounded by flagellants, the one wood *bulto* being of St. Peter and the other of the Magdalene. Dávila almost apologizes for the grandiosity of this quasi-monarchical spectacle, replete as it was with coats-of-arms and two heralds, explaining that Jesus after all was a king and had to be treated as one.

Indubitably, the removal of Jesus from the cross was a theatrical moment, but little else is of representational interest.[33] In this whole account of Good Friday, 1582, there is no reference to a single spoken word by any save the preacher. Indeed, the focus of both the descent from the cross and the Santo Entierro was rather to demonstrate to the audience the sundry Instruments of the Passion, beginning with the nails and ending with the cross itself. This was a spectacle which knew nothing of the suffering statue of caña, but rather was a more or less liturgical exposition of each thing associated with the crucifixion, comparable to an anonymous sixteenth-century drawing of a Santo Entierro procession (see fig. 1). Still, Dávila recalls vividly and at different points in his account the emotional impact that the passion activity had on those present at Santo Domingo, and there is every reason to accept his account.

Indeed Chimalpahin, who had not yet been born when the event took place, confirms the events of 1582 (he mistakenly says 1583) as a breakthrough in Mexican historical representation. "It was a marvelous thing," he said, "to follow the sufferings endured by the lord our savior, for never had the equal of such a thing been carried out in the churches of Mexico."[34] The more prosaic truth was that historical reenactments of the passion itself, that is, the events before Jesus's death on the cross, were still in the future. Yet just as surely, the events at Santo Domingo did have an impact. The same Chimalpahin reports the Santo Entierro at his hometown of Amaquemecan in 1584, and then notes that the southern Mexico City suburb of Coyoacán witnessed a representation of the passion on Good Friday 1587.[35] In fact, the chronicler again got his information from Dávila, who says that the Dominican confraternity of the Descent and Santo Entierro spread from Mexico City to Dominican convents in these two towns, adding without elaborating that the natives in these towns responded favorably to these new cults.[36]

At almost the same time that Dávila's work was being published in Madrid, Motolinía's student, the Franciscan Gerónimo Mendieta, wrote his *Historia eclesiástica* (1595). He copied his master's description of Holy Week, adding some interesting details. To Motolinía's description of Jesus's triumphant entry into Jerusalem on Palm Sunday, for instance, Mendieta adds that the native *principales* and "even more, the women," threw their wraps on the ground "so that the priest and his ministers, who represented Christ and his apostles, would walk over them."[37] Then on Holy Thursday, Mendieta continues, the Franciscan friar guardian "who . . . stood in for Christ our Redeemer," instructed the natives that the Washing of the Feet, which the guardian (as Jesus) carried out on twelve poor natives, was an excellent example of Christian charity. The identification of the Christian priests with the man/God obviously continued apace. Mendieta then mentions, as had Motolinía, the flagellant procession of the Vera Cruz confraternity on Holy Thursday, but now also that of Mary Soledad, which included "more than 7,700 flagellants by count."

In little more than a decade, the last of the triad of Franciscan chroniclers, Juan de Torquemada (d. 1624), completed his monumental *Monarquía indiana*. To be sure, Torquemada duplicated Motolinía and Mendieta, telling again how the priest and his ministers represented Jesus in the latter's triumph of Palm Sunday, but he added information as well.

Describing the 1609 events, he said that the Jesus who rode on an ass into Jerusalem was a figure of the man/God rather than a living person. Thus Jesus was represented in both live and sculptural forms on that day, as he still is today in Iztapalapa.[38] Further, Torquemada confirmed for the first time the existence of a confraternity of the Nazarenes.[39] The word "Nazarene" was customarily applied to an image of Jesus carrying his cross, and, by extension, "Nazarenes," then as later at Iztapalapa, were defined as those who bore crosses. It is therefore probable that this confraternity specialized in bearing crosses on their shoulders in penance.[40] Thus we may suspect that from the early seventeenth century on, "the processions of the flagellants" had grown to include those of the cross-bearers.

But Torquemada considered that a breakthrough in *native* theatrical history came out of the innovations that he attributed to his close associate, the Franciscan Francisco de Gamboa, a man Torquemada characterized as "desirous of imprinting devotion to the passion of Christ into the hearts of all Christians." And indeed, it seems to have been Gamboa (d. 1604) who introduced a quasi-theatrical cult of the passion into the Mexican cultural gestalt.[41]

Torquemada states that during his first stint as vicar of the native American chapel of San José, Gamboa began a procession through that church of the statue of the Soledad, that is, of Mary who had lost her son; it was the revenues from that procession, we recall, that were threatened in 1582 by the new Dominican cult of the descent and burial of Jesus. Then in his second round as vicar, Gamboa extended his interest to the passion proper, ordaining Friday Stations for the natives, in each of which was "executed a representation of one scene of the passion during the sermon in progress."[42] Scholars are surely right in thinking that while the preacher spoke, the native in question on command performed the apposite passion scene in what could only have been a mute pantomime, a type of dramatic action well known in the European homiletic tradition.[43]

This rudimentary Friday theater would appear to be the first certain theatrical representation of a passion scene in the Mexican tradition. But Gamboa was not finished with his innovations. Torquemada tells us that the friar also instituted, on Sunday evenings after sermon, some "representations of examples, in the manner of Comedies," *which were per-*

formed in Nahuatl. This was definitely theater, with voice exemplifying through thespian action the tale that had just been spun by the preacher. We shall presently see that these Sunday example plays certainly told stories congruent with the ecclesiastical calendar, and so we may already suspect that passion themes were prominent among these *neixcuitiles* in Lent, though Torquemada does not specify this fact. Indeed, he does not locate Gamboa's Sunday evening representations in time at all. None of these plays, many written by one fray Juan Bautista, has survived, but we may suspect that some form of written passion play, performed in church and thus very much under ecclesiastical control, had been established by then.[44]

Clearly, the dominant element of passion activities during the sixteenth century is processions constructed and led by the clergy in the city of Mexico. The one certain theatrical imitation of Jesus during Holy Week was public flagellation, carried on by several different confraternities, to which must be added the Washing of the Feet on Holy Thursday, a long-established, quasi-liturgical activity called into being and effected by priests, who played Jesus in that foot washing. Isolated indications of theatrical moments occurred within churches, where mute actors seem to have played out moments (Stations) of the passion to accompany the preacher's declamations. Finally, the first sign of truly theatrical activity relative to Holy Week, the Descent and the Burial of Jesus or Santo Entierro, was under the control of the clergy, and the latter rather a procession than theater. They are also post-passion events. Since it is commonly said that the modern passion plays like the one in Iztapalapa descend from the missionary plays of the sixteenth century, our finding is sobering. The famous play of the *Tres Caídas* or Three Falls of Jesus on his Way of the Cross, in which some modern laity go through town and village streets playing out the passion until they reach Calvary, is still nowhere on the horizon.

At first sight, the seventeenth and first half of the eighteenth century seem to promise little more by way of background to the modern plays, so sparse are the primary sources and scholarship dedicated to this period. Yet, surprisingly, this century and a half will after all furnish us with some important markers on the way to the modern performances. And no single phenomenon leads the way in this respect more than the decision early in the seventeenth century to build the fourteen Stations of the via Crucis or Way of the Cross into the urban fabric. From this time on, Mexico City boasted an outdoor route through the heart of the city mimicking the via Dolorosa traveled by Jesus.[45]

Though unmentioned by Torquemada writing in 1609, Jesus bearing his cross (that is, a statue of Jesus Nazarene), made his way along a *via sacra* already in existence in 1612. That is, a longitudinal axis for and eventual reenactment of Jesus's Way of the Cross existed at that date.[46] The route "from the house of Pilate up to Mount Calvary" began at the church of San Francisco and moved west toward Mount Calvary, which was a chapel alongside San Diego. Today this former church houses the Viceregal Art Gallery, at the west end of Alameda park. But in the year 1612, the Franciscans erected a chapel half way along the route, which later came to be called El Calvario, and obtained an indulgence for those who would pray their way along the route to this point. Soon thereafter, patrons of the Franciscans, an order that claimed a historic right to the cult of the Way of the Cross across Europe, began to erect fourteen separate chapels along the route representing the fourteen Stations of the cross, that is, the events of Jesus's passion from his arrest in the Garden of Gethsemane till his burial. For purposes of orientation: the first of these was at San Francisco itself; the third was just opposite the church of Corpus Christi, which until the recent earthquake housed the Artesanal Museum of the Pueblos; the fourth and fifth Stations were on present-day Avenida Juárez, which was called at the time Calle de Calvario. Similar rows of passion Stations, each originally housing a painting of one particular moment of the passion, are still to be seen in many Mexican cities, even if the *via sacra* in the capital was dismantled in the nineteenth century, when the chapels were used more for garbage storage than anything else.[47] But for the period that interests us, this Way of the Cross was important indeed. It is true that no direct evidence of theatrical activity seems to survive in the capital's sources, even if other sources indicate that such Stations did become stops for actors in tableaux vivants inspired by the painting in each chapel.[48] As customary at such moments, the veil covering the image in each chapel was probably lifted at the peak of the Station homily.[49] In any case, Jesus now had his own outside route in Mexico City, an urban formation that was bound to be copied in other Mexican towns and villages.[50] And by now, Jesus Nazarene under his cross was being carried about on this outdoor route by confraters, while individual devotees were being urged to join the Way of the Cross not only inside, but also outside churches.

If it proves difficult to document some sign of theatrical activity linked to the *via sacra* established in Mexico City, the same is not true to the north, in Querétaro, where the Colegios of the Propaganda Fide of New Spain held sway. Citing one Antonio Frontera, the historian of the Colegios, Isidro Espinosa, describes a 1683 procession of "so many penitents" performing "so many penances" when "passing the chapels of the *via sacra.*"[51] And in the same year, we find the brothers themselves observing the Stations in the cloister of their friary, carrying around crosses, being pulled by ropes around their neck and wearing crowns of thorns. As the author says repeatedly, these were religious persons who continually "dreamed up new ways to copy into their very selves the sad image [of Jesus] being so affronted."[52] Nothing had changed, it seems, since the time of Antonio de Roa. Yet it is important to note that the locale had, for the laity was now following these clerical exemplars in their mortifying practices in urban Mexico.

The best evidence is that at the very time that the Franciscans were constructing chapels along the *via sacra,* the secular authorities in Mexico City were attempting to put an end to public flagellation by confraternities of laymen, a goal that was not permanently achieved until 1777. Thus one surviving decree of 1612 unearthed by Chávez prohibits all scourging and all processions during that Holy Week, an extreme measure indeed, whose cause at present remains a mystery.[53] For another example, an internal ordinance forbade the Franciscan Third Order, founded in 1615 and dedicated to flagellation, from doing so in public except with the permission of a superior.[54]

Our next primary source, the 1696 *Crónica* of the Franciscan Agustín de Vetancurt, represents a landmark for the student of Mexican passion plays, because it mentions for the first time the *Tres Caídas,* or Three Falls of Jesus, which unequivocally refers to the reenactment of the actual passion of Jesus, that is, to the horrible events before his death when he was judged, bore his cross to Calvary, and was crucified. Vetancurt's information is sketchy but important. Describing the chapels of the great church of San Francisco, he dwells on the chapel of St. Joseph, called "of the Spaniards." It has an office

> where are kept a quantity of crosses that are used in the procession
> of the Nazarenes, which departs at three in the morning on Good
> Friday with the devout image of Christ weighed down by the cross.
> More than 600 persons march silently in it with crosses and torches
> intermixed. This edifies the pueblo. On its return, to the accompa-
> niment of the preacher one does the Station *(paso)* of the *Tres
> Caídas,* that of Santa Verónica cleaning the face [of Jesus], and the
> encounter with his most holy mother. This incites [the people] to
> tender tears, and to many acts of contrition among the numerous
> people attending.[55]

Let us have no expectation of a play similar to what is performed today; what is important in this quotation is simply the verification of a
cult to the Three Falls. For the actual performance of the Three Falls was
obviously not done as part of the procession of Nazarenes bearing their
crosses, but separately, upon their return to the patio of San Francisco. In
any case, from this point forward the expression "Three Falls" will recur
frequently in the sources, and still today stands as the name of the performance staged in the city of Iztapalapa.

Vetancurt also recounts activities in the other chapel of St. Joseph, *de
los naturales* (of the natives). He says that on the Fridays of Lent (it is not
clear if Good Friday is included), after having done Stations, the natives
hear a sermon in Nahuatl, at the conclusion of which a representation of
the Station or *paso* is unveiled, before which the natives then make an act
of contrition: "Then the *paso,* which represents what happens in [what is
represented], goes into the streets. To make it effective they have articulated carvings of Jews and soldiers, carrying them about to the sound of
trumpets, with lights and music. On their return they sing the Salve and,
if it is somewhat dark, they beat themselves."[56] This is a first reference to
quasi-theatrical figures that move their limbs, statues (at times also called
pasos), dressed up as Jews and Roman soldiers, features that till today, *mutatis mutandis,* remain central to many passion performances. Though no
hint of any text is given, we must say that most of the other elements of
the modern play are now in place in some form, even if the various parts
are still, so to speak, only partly animated.

At this point Vetancurt turns to the activities of Holy Week proper, spelling out which confraternities engage in what processions. It is something of a surprise that he lists all the processions of each day but gives no hint of theater other than the traditional descent from the Cross and the Santo Entierro, which was more like another procession than a theatrical representation. Thus in 1696 there were signs of passion theater apparently on the Fridays of Lent, but not, it would seem, on Holy Thursday or Good Friday, the anniversary of Jesus's agony and death, and the days on which, in modern times, the passion is in fact performed. What might explain this curiosity?

Vetancurt does not keep us waiting. After assuring readers that the *neixcuitiles* or example plays were still performed each Sunday evening, he notes that the example play performed on Palm Sunday was the passion of Jesus. On reflection, it seems obvious how this day of triumph had come to harbor the sad representation of the passion. Palm Sunday was the last Sunday in Lent, and thus the last opportunity for Sunday plays to recount Jesus's passion. Easter Sunday was clearly not an option. Thus the first written passion play, "in the manner of comedies" as Torquemada had said, was performed in the patio of San Francisco in Mexico City. This does not mean that a theatrical form would not develop out of the proto-theatrical street processions we have already documented on Good Fridays; that is, after all, what we do encounter in modern times. But the first persuasive evidence of written passion plays does in fact begin with the Sunday evening plays first documented by Torquemada. That evidence is confirmed at the end of the seventeenth century in Vetancurt, who specifies that the whole passion was the subject of the Palm Sunday evening plays. And we shall presently see that exactly this form of passion presentation was alive and well in the second half of the eighteenth century just south of the capital. But we are not finished with this chronicler. Vetancurt's account is certainly rich, and fills in still more spaces between the performances of his time and the modern play:

On Palm Sunday, [when one represents] the passion of Christ our savior, the person who plays the role [of Jesus] takes communion with much devotion. Present at this and the remaining representations is such a crowd that there is no space in the patio or on the balconies. It is a day of great tenderness. This is especially the case when the lance is [thrust into Jesus's side], for they put a vessel of red liquid into the wound of a Santo Cristo. At this moment the preacher intones the act of contrition for having seen such a tender spectacle. Women are moved to heart pressures and men to tears.[57]

Vetancurt is surely describing a native production, in which Jesus himself was played not by a priest but by a layman; the actor who took an especially devout communion can only refer to a layman because it goes without saying that a priest would "take communion with much devotion." Further, the role of Jesus was usually the last role to be consigned to a living person rather than to a statue, so the fact that Jesus was impersonated certainly means that he was accompanied in this play by other living actors playing the various roles of the passion. Again, Vetancurt makes no mention of a text, but this account definitely has the ring of a textual performance of some type. The age of the texts of passion plays that have survived was not far into the future.

Another contemporary account appeared in the *Gaceta de México* compiled by Castoreña y Ursúa during Lent, 1722.[58] In the history of the Mexican Holy Week, this account stands out as the first description of a combined ecclesiastical and governmental display. Its description of the Santo Entierro procession on Good Friday tells of "the Company of Infantry of the Palace, led by its Captain and military chiefs," that is, viceregal soldiers. They accompany and guard the coffin of Jesus, as Roman soldiers *(armados)*, playing a role that will soon move them to the center of the indigenous passion plays.[59] But this report also documents another small but significant presence: that of the confraternity of Nazarenes, which Torquemada had mentioned in 1609. Now Castoreña y Ursúa, who otherwise records only processions and provides no true theatrical information, reports that on that same Good Friday the confraternity "de las Tres Caídas de Jesús Nazareno" issued from the church of San Francisco, accompanied by the Franciscan Third Order. Alas, there is no telling if this was the very group mentioned a century earlier by Torquemada. All our author reveals is that "in memory of the *Tres Caídas* of the lord, the confraternity made many genuflections and diverse penances." One must assume that this confraternity marched as had unnamed brothers in Vetancurt's time alongside the litter carrying Jesus Nazarene. It is at least possible that the "genuflections and diverse penances" refer to choreographed moments in which that figure of the Nazarene "fell" and rose from the ground during its way of the cross. Thus a quasi-theatrical procession copying Jesus's via Crucis stands alongside an evidently theatrical production on Palm Sunday in the patio of the Franciscans in Mexico City, two distinct representations of the Way of the Cross.

Moving away from the city of Mexico and toward the towns and villages well southeast of the center, clear evidence emerges in the 1750s and 1760s of a number of passion plays performed by a population whose majority was probably still made up of native Americans. The legal context of these events is interesting. In 1765, the archbishop of Mexico, Manuel de Rubio y Salinas, issued a decree forbidding native Americans from doing religious representations, and this was followed in the same year by a notice to the same effect by his subordinate, the bishop of Puebla.[60] Then in 1769 the new archbishop, Francisco Lorenzana, issued another edict whose purpose was "to eliminate the idolatries, superstitions and other abuses of the Indians."[61] Lorenzana, a reformer who was a trusted aide of Charles III and would soon be called back to Spain to assume the archbishopric of Toledo, listed several such abuses, of which the most important were the *neixcuitiles,* which he significantly defined as "representations *al vivo* of the passion of Christ, our redeemer." These the prelate outlawed, "no matter in what language, including Castilian, they are performed." The claim used by some that the natives learned about Christianity through these plays was out of line, Lorenzana said. Perhaps two and a half centuries earlier that argument had weight, but not today. Ecclesiastical judges were to seize all the texts of roles used to try out for the examples of the Sundays of Lent, *neixcuitiles,* dances, and the rest.[62] Thus from this decree if from nowhere else, we learn that the Sunday plays were still the main vehicle for example plays, and that it was not uncommon by the eighteenth century for natives to represent the passion theatrically and *al vivo,* both in their own language and in Castilian.

In the wake of Rubio y Salinas's edict, the Inquisition was importuned by various parties to look into such native performances of the passion, and it was certainly the documentation piled up by the Inquisition that led Lorenzana to compose his edict. The sources at our disposition are some well-known Inquisition documents preserved in the *Archivo general de la Nación*. They contain records of hearings held between 1765 and 1770 by inquisitorial commissioners in an area that includes Huejotzingo to the east of the volcanos, but is concentrated west of them, to the northeast of the city of Cuernavaca.[63] In the proto-theatrical materials we have already studied, a clear distinction can be drawn in Mexico City between processions that had come to have some rudimentary theatrical elements, and set theater pieces done in church patios or cemeteries. Occasionally, contemporaries performed such set pieces at the conclusion of processions, but as we know from Vetancurt, they did the whole passion on Palm Sunday evenings, probably in relation to passion sermons preached in the church of San Francisco that day and evening.

The records from the area between the capital and Cuernavaca were directly related to the latter constellation. All the passion plays described consist of set pieces performed only on Palm Sunday on stages usually erected in cemeteries. The very word "procession" does not occur even once. Thus the passion plays referred to in these 1765–1770 records must be viewed as contextually similar to the Palm Sunday passion pieces described by Vetancurt three quarters of a century earlier. Speaking still more generally, we may surmise that the first Palm Sunday passion plays were documented through Torquemada's account of 1609, even if the author did not state that the passion was done on that day. They thus continued at least until the end of the third quarter of the eighteenth century in these rural areas southeast of Mexico City.

The judicial facts have been examined by others, and a brief summary will suffice. The suit was brought to the Inquisition by disgruntled priests, who condemned passion theater as indecent: the person who played Jesus was presented naked; he repeated the exact holy words of the consecration of the host; the figure of Judas irreverently kept everyone in stitches, and so on.[64] In the end the Inquisition, following Lorenzana, did again outlaw the natives' performances, but in the meantime one inquisitorial commissioner actually rejected the suit, pointing out that passion plays were at least as old as the 1402 Parisian *mystère*, that there was something to be said for passion plays that were not all solemn but instead contained a diversion, and that anyway there was little evidence that the natives had meant to be impious.[65] The charge that those who played Jesus in these representations were treated badly by the plays' Jews and Romans left one commissioner cold: in his view, these miserables were beaten much less severely by the players than they were by their actual lords or *curacas*.[66] As far as this commissioner was concerned, the plays could continue.

At a deeper level, however, the authorities revealed some concern that the Spanish-speaking *gente de razón*, who had grown accustomed to watching the passion, had themselves produced a comical Castilian version when the Indians were no longer permitted to perform it.[67] In their drive to collect all the texts and tryout records they could, the authorities often asked about translations, and especially about ones from Nahuatl to Spanish.[68] They describe not only a world in which it was easy to observe one passion play in Nahuatl and another in Castilian in the same town (as did a Jesuit in Tepoztlán),[69] but, more intriguingly, one in which a Nahuatl text close to the Bible was converted into a Castilian text full of comedic derision, which was then sometimes performed by the natives for Spanish speakers. Indeed, while these records make it clear that the natives had written texts in their own language (see the text from Amecameca) and used that language for performances, as at Huejotzingo, the three passion texts that survive in these inquisitorial records are all in Castilian. That was what most worried the commissioners about these plays, which were said to be performed throughout Mexico.[70] Now, it was feared, the Spaniards would be exposed to more carnivalesque versions of the passion and death of Jesus, versions, in short, that reflected the irreverence that had suffused the historical Holy Thursday and Good Friday.

The Inquisition's records reveal a good deal about the actual performances, all of which seem to have started at 4 P.M. on Palm Sunday. Tryouts for roles began halfway through Lent, and according to one source, the local curate cleared the texts for these roles.[71] The performances themselves were carried out in the church cemeteries, on the very stage, one offended cleric complained, which was used at other times for secular comedies.[72] While they counted on Judas to keep audiences amused, elders trained the local children to play the Jews expected to beat Jesus, a custom that the erudite commissioner compared favorably to the inversions of the medieval boy bishops.[73] When Palm Sunday arrived, the various actors donned clothing from the statues in their churches. They did this, the erstwhile actors explained, not only in the interest of realism—the statues obviously showed the supernaturals as they really were—but because they themselves were poor and could not personally afford such finery.[74] Thus while confraternities and churches in the city of Mexico might be able to afford statues and clothing for their litters, or were at least able to rent clothing to dress up in, in the countryside the church statues themselves were stripped to accouter these living actors. People came from all around to see the play in Huejotzingo.[75]

Who then were *los pasionarios,* as they are called in these sources? Especially in the records from Huejotzingo, we meet several of them, including the seventy-year-old town cacique don Antonio Guevara, who played the roles of Jesus and of an apostle, his widowed forty-five-year-old sister who played Mary, and another relative who played St. Peter, as well as Lorenza Dorada, who played Veronica.[76] Antonio assured the Inquisition that all the roles, including that of Jesus, had been played by Indians, indeed by the caciques and principales of these small towns. Guevara asserted that in fact the Huejotzingo play had not been performed for some thirty or forty years, after Bernabel Bustamante had died of drink, because they had been unable to find anyone to replace him as Judas. Not surprisingly, the natives of several towns appeared anxious to convince the authorities that they had stopped performing the passion in the moment archbishop Rubio y Salinas had forbidden them from performing it.[77]

Just as strenuously, the natives repeatedly claim that the texts of the roles for these plays had also been lost. As we have said, three Castilian texts have survived, one undated from Ozumba,[78] a second, dated 1753, from Amecameca,[79] and a third, dated 9 May 1768, containing glosses with thespian instructions.[80] The Ozumba text begins with a group of jealous devils who get together after Jesus's triumphant entry into Jerusalem so as to plot the lord's downfall, but the main subject matter of all these texts is the oratorical meetings in "councils" of the Jews, led by Caiaphas and Annas, to plot Jesus's execution by the Roman authorities; the Amecameca text, for instance, begins directly with that assembly. The parts of the passion actually involving Jesus, from the Last Supper through the crucifixion, command relatively little text, and I have been unable to come up with an explanation for this fact. It is important to note that the natives clearly defined the passion as only the events stretching from the prayers in Gethsemane to the crucifixion.[81] Thus it is not surprising that nowhere in these records is there reference to the deposition of Jesus and but one to his interment, both of which were, of course, post-passional events.

Some of the peculiarities of these plays can and must be traced directly to the relative poverty and limited population of all these rural centers, as well as to the paucity of clergy in them. I have elsewhere described the inherently thespian role of clergy, which gave cities "a separate processional identity, a technical apparatus maintained by citizens and professional religio-thespians appointed to protect, expand, profit, and honor the commune."[82] Obviously, Mexico City had that apparatus, but most of the theater towns did not: no easy availability of clergy, no processions. Note, too, that the records of all the stage plays described above make no mention whatever of statues being taken out of the churches for use in the theater performed outside, whereas the records of processions in Mexico City of 1722 mention many statues indeed.[83] Poverty and the technical simplicity of small towns explain that omission. Conversely, in the contemporary diocese of Córdoba in southern Spain, the bishops repeatedly demanded that the small towns of their diocese cease and desist from performing the passion each year with live actors and use sculptures (as the big cities had done) to theatrically represent the lord's passion.[84] There may in fact be other factors that entered into the decision to use actors or statues to play the passion, but there can be little doubt from these contemporary records that the simplest consideration was the relative wealth and population of the municipality that wished to imitate Jesus in his passion.

In the history of Mexican passion theater, the time frame for this particular type of performance had apparently reached its climax and its end. If we are to trust these sources, across the eighteenth century we may imagine native Americans south of the city of Mexico, surely inspired by the capital, interacting with *gente de razón* to produce on Palm Sunday evening a staged life of Jesus from his prayers in the garden till his crucifixion. References to the celebration of Easter do not emerge in these native accounts, so that we may postulate that earlier urban Easter representations of the Resurrection had been driven overwhelmingly by the clergy. But after 1770, the Palm Sunday plays of the whole passion themselves apparently end. From 1770 onward, our sparse Mexican sources make no references to passion cycles on that day. Perhaps after all the prohibitions of the archbishops had had their effect, or perhaps the king's 1777 prohibition of flagellation had had some effect. In any case, to judge by our sources, from this date forward passion theater was performed only on the appropriate days within Holy Week, that is, on Holy Thursday and Good Friday.

Initially concurrent with, but then outlasting the previous group of inquisitorial documents regarding the Palm Sunday presentations, another set of archival documents deals with the celebrations of the passion of Jesus on the passion's "actual" days.[85] These records do not document the type of theatrical presentations on stage that we have just described from the mid-eighteenth century, but rather mobile processions, which are nonetheless characterized in these sources as "representations of the passion and death of our lord Jesus Christ." And it is indeed in these late eighteenth-century processions that we divine the makings of the modern Mexican theater of Holy Week.

On 10 April 1794, the parish priest of Xochimilco in the southern suburbs of Mexico City, determined to demonstrate how well he had executed his office, sent the archbishop of Mexico a copy of a letter the prelate's office had sent to Xochimilco some thirty-two years earlier, on 15 March 1762. In that mid-century missive, the archbishopric had protested the disorders and scandals in the church of Xochimilco on Holy Thursday nights, that is, at the time of the *tinieblas*.[86] In the very presence of the host exposed in the monument and in violation of the passion fast, the earlier prelate had written, men and women dressed up and drank freely till dawn. The (ethnically unidentified) *armados,* that is, those dressed like Romans who among other duties acted as Jesus's (the eucharistic host's) "bodyguard" around the monument, constrained the Indians to furnish them with beds in the church so that they could relax while they guarded the host. Far from encouraging the people to reflect on Jesus's sacrifice, the archbishop continued, this practice abused the church, and hence he solemnly outlawed it. All *sagrarios* were to close at 9 P.M. The cemetery of the church was to be closed to any gathering of people, as were the gates leading to the church. The *armados* were not to be allowed to sleep either in or around the church. And the priest was to read this 1762 decree to the assembled faithful on Sundays.

The high church authorities' war against late-night gatherings that had begun at the onset of the evangelization of New Spain obviously continued apace. But new in the archbishop's mid-century letter is the earliest evidence I have encountered of clerical opposition to men dressed up as Romans during the passion period, an antagonism that will be remain a central feature of the documents to follow. Interestingly, that opposition emerges in a letter that does not state whether these *armados* were Spaniards or natives, a point of rhetorical conflict around which the individual parishes and curates would resist all attempts to disarm the *armados*.

With this copied letter documenting the bad old days, the Xochimilco priest now proposed to show how admirably he had brought the parish's practices into line since the Franciscans had given the parish over to the secular clergy. Significantly, he was specific on the matter of *armados* where the earlier archbishop had remained vague. "The centurions and *armados* were all Spaniards" and not Indians in his parish, he insisted; the men who dressed up as *armados* on Easter Sunday did so on their own and without any support from the local church. As for the Indians, he continued, they all now went home at 10 P.M. on Holy Thursday night. They did return at 6 A.M. Good Friday morning, he admitted, but that was because their one passion duty was to participate in the procession of the *Tres Caídas* that morning. But they did not, he repeated, dress up as Romans for that procession. Nor did the priest see any reason to suppress this Indian participation. During 363 days of the year these natives were "exemplary drunks," he said, but on Holy Thursday and Good Friday they absolutely do not drink. "I would swear to their honor on these two days only." This letter clearly indicates that the clerical concern at the end of the century was about Indians dressing up as *armados*, even if it was, at least in this parish, an established right and duty for the Indians to stage the specific representation of Jesus's passion procession on the morning of Good Friday. Readers may decide for themselves if in fact a public procession of the Three Falls was conceivable without the accompaniment of the Romans leading Jesus to his death.

On 18 March 1794, at the behest of the confraternity of St. Homobono, the viceroy Revillagigedo had brought this whole problem of the *armados* to a head.[87] He simply forbade any further arming during Holy Week, claiming that it was more of a diversion than a devotional act. Originally intended to apply only to the city proper, the prohibition was soon after extended to include all the *pueblos de contorno*, that is, the heavily Indian suburban towns and villages around the Ciudad de Mexico. Now one after the other, other parishional curates followed Xochimilco in insisting that they too did not allow natives as *armados*.[88] But just as surely, from many other quarters came evidence to the contrary. In fact, subsequent documentation from the pueblos of San Angel, Xochimilco, Tacuba, Tlalnepantla and Azcapotzalco convincingly demonstrates that whatever may have been the ethnicity of these units in times past, now they were in fact overwhelmingly made up of native Americans, not Spaniards.[89] Where once the creole or perhaps mestizo infantry of the viceroy played the *armados,* now that theatrical task and opportunity had passed to native men in the Valley of Mexico and beyond. This ancient native custom of "arming" in Holy Week now "transcended all the Americas," in the words of the curate of Tlalnepantla.[90]

No sooner had the viceroy issued his order in 1794 than the very real economic impact of such a prohibition was felt by those whose livelihood was most immediately affected by it, the clothes renters *(alquileros).* The spread of the custom of companies of *armados* had brought with it a commensurate expansion of these purveyors "to almost all places in the realm, villas and pueblos."[91] They let no doubt exist that it was the Indians "who regularly take part in these functions" of Holy Week, and just as little doubt that these clothes renters would quickly be bankrupted if they were not allowed to arm the companies of Indians in Holy Week, for, as their representatives explained to the officials, the renters met early each year to determine the conditions of the market, and then contracted for their allotments of clothing.[92] No arming, no sales; and thus business failure. Calling themselves at one point simply "the renters of clothes for Holy Week," they made it clear that that season, and those natives, accounted for most of their annual income.[93] The officials were not insensitive to these protests, but in the end were not, it appears, dissuaded from their decision because, as one official noted, the clothes renters did most of their business with the suburban pueblos, so those outsiders would suffer the bulk of the losses.[94]

A second economic consequence of the prohibition, repeatedly mentioned by our sources, was that a number of male natives would leave their home parish where the *armados* had truly been outlawed for some place where they could see a procession during Holy Week. To put it as did two of our sources, if they could not witness "this representation of the passion and death of our redeemer Jesus Christ" in their own towns, they went where they could.[95] That might take the inhabitants of Silao, north of Mexico City, to Irapuato or León, or it might lead parishioners of the parish of San Angel, one of the "external pueblos" south of the capital, to simply abandon their homes and travel east to the pueblo of Coyoacán, where they could witness what was by now obviously if not demonstrably a full-fledged, total representation of the passion. Not only did this mean that the affected pueblos, like San Angel, might not be able to carry out their own Holy Week ceremonies; it meant as well that a town like Silao, whose processions and *armados* were simply suppressed for some years, lost most of the income it had traditionally pocketed from tourists coming to see the Holy Week processions, to the great detriment of both government and trade. Still further, three quarters of this town's confraternities simply ceased to function when they had no processional duties to perform in Holy Week, dissolving this important socioinstitutional glue. For his part, the curate of San Angel demanded either that these processions be uniformly suppressed so that his parishioners had no place else to go, or that his parish be exempted from the prohibition, as were others.[96]

More generally, both these and other petitioners pointed to the moral cost to the Indians as a result of the prohibition of local passion representations. The men who went outside their parishes, ranches, or haciendas ended up gambling and playing all types of illicit games, according to the curates. They wasted their money, then returned home with no provisions for their families. Needless to say, high-minded pleading for weakwilled Indians was not new in the 1790s, and just as surely, these were some of the same reasons that the reformers gave for outlawing the *armados* in the first place: the Indians allegedly drank too much at these gatherings, gambled, spent more than they had to get their arms, and so forth.[97] Indeed, one letter from "the poor" begged the viceroy to suppress the custom of dressing up as *armados* or centurions to guard Jesus, intimating, correctly, that the curates were part of the problem. Sounding very much like a priest, "the poor" said that it would be better if natives gave simple alms rather than arm themselves.[98]

Those favoring the elimination of these representations and those holding to them agreed, in short, that the natives needed discipline. Three social categories—the clothes renters, the curates, and various governmental officials—followed the same script: yes, the natives needed discipline, the kind furnished by the thespo-processional show of Holy Week. Because of their limited culture, native Americans learned only from images, and withdrawing the images furnished by the passion representations assured that they would quickly forget everything they had learned about Christianity.[99] The ideological claptrap the Spaniards had arrived with in the 1520s had not changed, nor would it when they were driven out early in the following century. Thus the curate of Tacuba, while agreeing that "the soldiers of Holy Week cause disorder rather than devotion," favored keeping the rites as, on balance, "good fruit," for the Indians would not come to the parish "if not to see the *sayones.*"[100] The clothes renters warned that without the live representations, the natives would forget the passion story, and anyway, their petition continued, "even in Spain these representations are done, and all the guilds have their *paso,* and such processions have even been printed!"[101] Significantly, in all these representations to the secular authorities, those favoring the *armados* and thus the "representations of the passion and death" of Jesus did not once put forward the standard argument of a traditional culture that without these commemorations of Jesus and these processions, the divinity would be displeased with New Spain and punish it severely (an approach that still flourishes at Iztapalapa, however, near the end of the twentieth century). Instead, the reasoning of these petitions was from first to last driven by practical utilitarian considerations.

Finally, these precious documents of the 1790s offer some important hints as to how the *armados* were selected, an extraordinary bonanza because the same companies of soldiers were indeed the very organizers of the modern passion play, as we shall see at Iztapalapa.[102] While it is clear that the curates had a vested interest in festivities performed in their parish, the most important point is that at this time the "election" of those who would dress up as soldiers was an Indian affair, from which, according to the curate of Tlalnepantla, the curates might be excluded. Indeed, he protested his "humiliation" at one point: the (Indian) governors and principals having "elected" their subjects to be part of the *soldatesca,* some of the latter asked the curate to intervene and personally "elect" the guard. But the Indian *principales* refused to allow such a breach of custom.[103] A document from Zempoala, a pueblo just north of the capital, fills in the picture. In the presence of a royal judge, the neighbors *(vecinos)* met each year at about the time of the "election" to select some of their "subjects" to pay the expenses of the *armados* and the cost of guarding the monument, with different rates for those tasked and those not tasked. That list, with names and appropriate sums, was then posted on the front door of the church.[104] From a third source we learn that upon being "elected," one of the appointed *armados,* wishing to be captain of the squadron, might put out a sum of money to buy drinks all around to achieve that honor.[105] Especially the custom of *armados* guarding the monument was so deeply rooted among the electors and *principales,* the curate of Tlalnepantla said, that it was impervious to change.[106]

From these seductive but sparse indications, we would hypothesize that the appointment of *armados* at this time reflected hierarchical divisions among the natives themselves, with the *principales* fielding a squadron from among their "subjects" much as did a *messere* of an early modern European confraternity. Doubtless, some of these "soldiers" tried to flee this duty because it was so costly, but others reveled at the attention. In any case, the tenacity of the institution of *armados* must be seen at least in part as a means for the natives to maintain their public social organization to the present.

Finally, a document unearthed by David Brading offers some specifics about the dramatic action of these "representations of the passion and death of Jesus" in this period. In 1788, the curate of the pueblo of San Pedro Maracho (Michoacán) complained that his parishioners for Holy Week always chose an Indian to play Jesus. Clearly referring to passion events reenacted on Holy Thursday, the rector says that "these barbarians [meaning the spies of the high priest Caiaphas] went from house to house searching for Jesus." After his arrest, this Jesus was then held prisoner overnight and until noon on Good Friday. At that point he was brought before Pilate and Herod for his trial and sentencing, his body already painted with the instruments of the passion and his "face, shoulders and body bathed in blood."[107] The group of searchers probably ended up in the local church, where the imprisoned Jesus was held. We are now on the cusp of a new century, when the sources for these dramatic actions will be ever more detailed.

These significant if fragmentary sources on Holy Week in the eighteenth century, near the end of the Spanish era in Mexican history, indicate that a staged theater of the passion was well in place in the capital and to its south in 1760. Documents from the 1790s show that native Americans themselves organized and portrayed in procession and in churches the soldiers who guarded the body of Jesus, definitely in the monument of Holy Thursday and probably also when it lay buried in a coffin after the crucifixion, just as had similar Spanish *armados* gathered there back in the late sixteenth century. It was the native Americans, after all, who had as their sole responsibility the procession of the *Tres Caídas* at Xochimilco. Indeed, for all its fragmentary nature, these sources of the 1790s, once combined with the Michocán reference of 1788, leave no doubt that there was a total "representation of the passion and death of Jesus," from the arrest on Holy Thursday to sentencing in the afternoon of Good Friday. Documents yet to be presented reveal that it was none other than the *armados* themselves who organized and presented these representations; thus they were a cultural product of the descendants of the original inhabitants of Mexico. It might be foolhardy to deny the influence of the first missionaries in establishing such representations, even if no document associates them to a passion play. But our meager documentary tradition indicates that the natives, imbibing certain images of Christianity, in effect developed their own cultural product in the face of an unfriendly clerical, if not creole, universe.

The ever-richer documentation of the nineteenth century, until the anticlerical laws of the 1860s and 1870s, confirms our hypothesis while slowly affording us the detail necessary to understand the modern passion play of Iztapalapa, which got underway in the 1880s. At first the documentation is sparse as ever, a governmental decree of 30 March 1836 prohibiting in the city neighborhoods those elements that had already been outlawed "in the pueblos," that is, in the area surrounding the capital: "*armados,* spies, the [caped] *sayones,* centurions, pharisees, and other ridiculous objects with which one claims to represent the said *pasos* of Holy Week." The government was determined to drive these "vestiges of the barbaric centuries" from "such a civilized capital as this one," especially since they did not engender reverence but only derision for the divine cult.[108] In one reading the "objects" could be interpreted as representing the listed figures, but it is more probable that some combination of living and figured persons was intended.

What one pueblo's representation looked like is fleshed out by Guillermo Prieto's description of Holy Week in the nearby pueblo of

Tacubaya in 1840.[109] The action began on Holy Wednesday, when a suspicious group (obviously the spies sent by Caiaphas and Judas to find and arrest Jesus) gathered around the "colossal image" of Jesus the Father under guard in his home *(morada)* . They were met in combat by the lord's defenders. At a certain point Judas himself arrived with his lantern and whistle; he gave the signal, and Jesus's house was assaulted. A merry ruckus of demons followed, till Jesus (surrendering) made his way to the church, where he was put in a prison cell. The building was swarming with "Jews" standing guard over him and profaning the church as much as possible, "just like good Jews," says the author in a stereotypic throwaway. Of course, adds Prieto, the sight of Jesus in that prison (the *aposentillo*) stimulated many prayers and fervent demonstrations of devotion.

From Prieto's words it is not possible to be sure if at any point this Jesus was impersonated by a living person or not, though we do know that many other players were real, having been "elected" to play their roles. The situation is clearer on Good Friday, after the centurion read out Pilate's sentence, "an incendiary libel in which blasphemies of every type and absurdities capable of scandalizing Satan himself competed with each other." The via Crucis proceeded both inside (the Stations) and outside the church, with the role of the Nazarene and Simon the Cyrene played by a large image ensconced upon a magnificent litter. Each moment in the procession of the *Tres Caídas* had its own preacher elaborating on the scene for the people.[110] Finally, the ceremonies of Good Friday finished with "the famous procession of mourning," that is, the Santo Entierro of that evening, in which marched "a rigorous levy of beatas, old women, and timid and pretty little girls." Throughout these events, Prieto concludes, "Jews on horseback and on foot criss-crossed through the pueblo in all directions, crying out." It appears that in Tacubaya's celebration, the points of dramatic action were two, the *morada* and the church, but the whole town was involved in the story in one way or the other through street actions: the various processions and also the "Jews" racing through the streets to find Jesus and proclaim their victory over Christianity. In this way the community defined itself as Christian by its parts, female as well as male, representing the contending forces.

The use of either actors or figures to play the role of the Nazarene is especially interesting in the detailed accounts of Holy Week ceremonies preserved in the memoirs of Frances Calderon de la Barca, the Scottish-born wife of the Spanish ambassador to Mexico, who resided in Mexico from 1839 to 1841.[111] Her first account, in a letter of 21 April 1840, describes what she saw in downtown Mexico City in that year. On Holy Thursday, she paid visits to the *Siete Casas* or churches, and most of her attention was given over to liturgical performances by priests, as well as to the splendid attire of the "proper people" of the capital. Calderon decisively describes a mestizo and creole Holy Thursday rather than one in which the native population had any role other than provisioning the rich and their churches. While she does make the formal distinction between a celebratory Holy Thursday and a more solemn Good Friday, little of what I have described above changes, so there is no need to dwell on the great wealth of detail in her account.

Yet certain of her 1840 observations do deserve attention. She describes a Holy Thursday in which, absent their usual carriages, the ladies "take the opportunity of displaying all the riches of their toilet" and "velvets and satins are your only wear."[112] While these days might commemorate the death of Jesus, the lower classes rather favor Mary at her many shrines. "To the Son," she writes, "their feelings seem composed of respectful *pity*, of humble but more distant adoration, while to the Virgin they appear to give all their confidence . . . as to a kind and bountiful Queen." Mary "condescend[s] to admit the poorest beggar to participate in her woes, whilst in her turn she shares in the afflictions of the lowly, feels for their privations, and grants them her all-powerful intercession."[113] Calderon also mentions the sale of the Judases, which will be exploded on the following Holy Saturday morning, and describes the Good Friday procession as "a long and pompous retinue of mitred priests, with banners and crucifixes and gorgeous imagery, conducting a procession in which figures representing scenes concerning the death of our Savior, were carried by on platforms, as they were the preceding evening."[114] In short, at this date the standard procession in the center of Mexico City consisted of several litters bearing *misteri*. This was the mark of a powerful urban entity that could afford such representations and did not need actors. Instead, a military band hired for the occasion at one point played a piece from the opera "Semiramis," at another, one from "Norma."

Calderon's description of Holy Week in the following year is much more relevant for our purposes, for this time the author observed the ceremonies first in San Angel and then in Coyoacán, neighboring southern pueblos of the city rich with indigenous populations.[115] Here she draws the distinction between "splendor in the churches [of the capital], but in the country a play, a sort of melodrama, in which the sufferings, death, and burial of our Savior are represented by living figures in pantomime."[116] In the period before Holy Thursday, "the country has been overrun with Pharisees, Nazarenes, Jews, and figures of the Savior carried about in procession." Well-dressed Pharisees rode through the streets searching for Jesus, who ultimately appeared, a large figure on a litter borne by four men. On the next evening, a similar procession took place, "always accompanied by a crowd of Indians from the villages," but this time the figure was of Jesus being whipped at the column.[117] What Calderon describes, it seems, is a series of tryouts before the main events.

Early on Holy Thursday, Calderon and her party traveled the short distance east to Coyoacán, where she was greeted by friends. After visiting the main church, where they saw the lovely monument surrounded by flowers and oranges,[118] they soon encountered the drama itself. To the sound of music, an image of Jesus appeared on a litter, followed by eleven (live) disciples. Jesus was placed among trees as if in the garden of Gethsemane, and then a preacher gave a sermon that evoked that lord's suffering in the garden, as he awaited the spies and Judas. Wearing piglike masks, the former made their entry, lurking at first among the trees, followed by Judas, his face covered by a black crepe veil. After him came a band of soldiers. The preacher commented: "Now observe what the traitor does," and when the kiss was planted: "It is done!" The *prendimiento* or arrest and buffeting of Jesus followed, each action a response to the lead of the preacher. That concluded this scene, whereupon Calderon and her party returned to San Angel for the night. There she visited the churches (the *Siete Casas*), ending with the parish church, which was nearly dark, "a few alone of the devout . . . still kneeling before a figure of our Savior in chains."[119]

On Good Friday morning the party returned to Coyoacán. In front of the church they found the preacher, again with a portable pulpit, just concluding the first of the day's three sermons. The second sermon now began, to accompany a procession that was intended to evoke Jesus's journey from prison to the palace of Pontius Pilate, where he would be sentenced. What fascinated Calderon most was that accompanying the figure of Jesus Nazarene (that is, Jesus [already!] bearing his cross) on his litter was Simon the Cyrene who, utterly frozen in place while helping the wooden Jesus, finally revealed, to Calderon's astonishment, that he was not a figure but a live human being. After them came the pharisees, Jews, and Judas in procession, and others with "helmets and feathers, and armor." These are our *armados,* to be sure.[120]

The next sequence was Pilate delivering his sentence, and Calderon's party "now proceeded to search for a convenient place from which to hear the padre's next sermon, and to see the next scene in the sacred drama." It was eloquent but lengthy, and by its end Calderon under the Mexican sun felt "as if my brains were melted into a hot jelly." Again the procession, as it had before, passed by the preacher's pulpit, in effect serving as a reviewing stand. Then suddenly a man with a plumed helmet galloped up with the text of Pilate's sentence, which he handed over to the preacher. He "received it with a look of horror, opened it, tried to read it, and threw it on the ground with an air of indignation." The preacher then addressed Jesus, whose bearers now brought him up to the pulpit, followed by the mournful figure of the Virgin. And so ended that act.[121] From this passage it is evident that in these pantomime plays led by a preacher, that padre too was an actor as much as he was a liturgist.

Unfortunately, Calderon left no account of an eventual Way of the Cross or *Tres Caídas,* if there was one, for she and her party left after the sentence and did not return until later in the afternoon, in order to see the Descent done inside the church. A black curtain covered the altar. The padre began by summarizing all that had occurred, all the agony that not only Jesus but Mary had undergone, evoking tears from all the women. Then all of a sudden the preacher cried: "draw back the veil, and let us behold him!" At that point the curtain fell and the faithful saw Jesus crucified. More tears and wailing and beating of breasts from the women. The figure of Mary was seen to bow her head in grief, but "unfortunately" Calderon was in front and could see how the trick was accomplished. At this point soldiers (not clergy) mounted a ladder and detached and lowered the image of Jesus from the cross. The priests showed the bloody hands of this Jesus to the crowd in the midst of general grief. The soldiers stood below, clashing their swords.[122]

The ceremonies ended that evening with "the funeral procession of the savior," that is, the Santo Entierro, which had now come also to be called the Procession of the Angels, referring to the angels carried on litters in that procession. But the center of the procession was indeed *Christo iacente*, laid in a glass hearse and carried by men chanting a dirge, followed by Mary Soledad. Then Calderon walked out of the pueblo to the church of La Concepción, where she watched the procession go by again and attended the ceremony of the *Pésame*, in which both preacher and faithful consoled Mary for her loss. On reentering Coyoacán, the author summed up the experience in a positive fashion. Despite occasional thefts, the spectacle had been a resounding success. There had been no noise, no mirth, and no drunkenness.[123] So much for protests about native misbehavior in these holy days.

Our sketch cannot begin to evoke the rich atmosphere that this gifted writer has left behind in her text. Yet it is the substance of these descriptions that must be stressed, especially when combined with the contemporary record from Tacubaya. First and foremost, Calderon's accounts show that by this time a clear distinction existed between the largely nontheatrical ceremonies of the city and the more dramatic and native productions of the pueblos. Second, especially at Coyoacán, the whole native production was clearly organized around, and presumably by, the clergy in a pueblo that yet had a strong Hispanic presence, whereas the account of the contemporary play at Tacubaya placed no emphasis on the curate. Third, even though a tradition in which native actors spoke their parts had by now long been in existence, an even more ancient tradition of native pantomime, linked as always to a preacher who uttered the biblical text and freely commented upon it, was still in use in the nineteenth century. Indeed, Calderon states that the dramatic actions of Holy Thursday at Coyoacán were all "enacted in succession, though sometimes the curate was obliged to repeat the same things several times before [the natives] remembered what to do."[124] Fourth, in both pueblos statues of Jesus were used for dramatic purposes even if other personages were played by living actors and, at Coyoacán, a live Jesus was also evident. The organizers obviously delighted in the use of *trompe l'oeil*, tricking viewers into mistaking graphic forms for human vitality. And finally but importantly, a combination of littered processions and stage moments of passion was the rule in these performances.

The 1860s and 1870s would bring many changes to the celebration of

Holy Week; the most important ones were written into the 1857 Constitution and its later glosses, documents through which the Mexican Republic would struggle to bring the Catholic church under its control. These changes will be studied in the next chapter. Suffice to say at this point that the old ways died hard. In 1871, *El Correo del Comerolo* asked its readers who among them had not gone to Metepec, west of Mexico City, to see the *Tres Caídas,* and reminded its capitaline readers of what might still be seen at a pueblo on the nearby western coast of Mexico: some 60 *sayones* plunging into a tiny church, simulating the rabid fury of the Jews, taking an image of Jesus from the altar, binding its hands and then putting it on a litter and taking it to its prison; then, during the Santo Entierro, the same *sayones* guarded the casket after they had adorned Jesus's head with chicken feathers.[125]

Still, when in 1877 Joaquín García Icazbalceta penned his fundamental "Representaciones religiosas en México en el siglo XVI," certain irreversible changes had been decreed by the Mexican secular authorities in the way that citizens could legally memorialize the passion and death of Jesus.[126] García evoked the old days, and knew that his readers had themselves seen at one time or another the pantomime passions with their *Prendimientos, Tres Caídas, Descendimientos* and the like, all "represented *al vivo,* even within the capital and in the surrounding pueblos, the last recollection of those happy and devout solemnities established by the ancient missionaries." He paid tribute to another tradition as well, in which passion scenes were actually spoken by the natives, though none of their texts had survived (the author was unaware of those from mid-eighteenth century we discussed earlier). Referring clearly to the new body of law directed against displays of religion outside the churches, García mourned the passing of this ancient world so regulated by an all-powerful church. "In the end, neither an affected scrupulosity . . . nor the desire to avoid disorders . . . but rather a barefaced persecution of the church ended the discussion and put an end to the religious representations, leaving instead total liberty for profane things to arrive at the rudest immorality."[127]

Looking back on this prerevolutionary world, historians surely recognize that the passion plays were no mere copies of what the missionaries had instituted. For all the pull of custom, under the press of social and political changes they had remorselessly evolved across the centuries into the variegated forms of the mid-nineteenth century. Yet our survey has to date regrettably failed to ascertain who in fact organized these traditional productions. The role of the clergy in all this evidently goes without saying, but by mid-eighteenth century the native authority structure and leading families themselves had played the roles and assembled these plays with the mere agreement, but not the participation, of the curates. And at the end of that century Indian *principales* had made it clear that, time out of mind and in the teeth of opposition from the secular and ecclesiastical authorities, they themselves had organized companies of *armados,* to the end not only of performing the passion, but also of expressing and reforming the political organization of the native pueblos in that passion.[128] In fact, these same "companies of *sayones,*" these mock caped soldiers, formed the organizational nucleus for the Iztapalapan passion plays we will henceforth witness. Struggling as they did to preserve the experience of their ancient crucified, these natives as well fought for the memory of the social forms they had forged to accompany their crucified lord.

IZTAPALAPAN BEGINNINGS

At the end of the nineteenth century, the editors of the conservative Mexico City newspapers *El Tiempo* and *El Mundo Semanario Ilustrado* regularly bemoaned performances of the Good Friday Passion Play of the *Three Falls (Tres Caídas),* which in one way or the other acted out the horrors that Jesus had suffered on his way to Calvary. True, such plays had largely been suppressed in central Mexico City, but in the vast margins of the capitaline area, where indigenous peoples still made up important parts of the population, villagers and townspeople continued the tradition. These journals regularly mentioned Tacuba and Azcapotzalco to the north and west of the center, but they directed their concern and ire most often at the plays put on in the watery *pueblos de indígenas* to the south and east, including Mixcoác, Coyoacán, Iztacalco, and, mentioned for the first time in 1898, Iztapalapa.[1] These performances, said one writer echoing the general view of his colleagues, did nothing but "make the Man-God look ridiculous."[2] Thus from the beginning of the modern record of Mexican passion plays, the elite city dwellers who wanted their God solemn up there above the altar meet in head on conflict those tradition-bound residents of the pueblos who insisted on playing out every year their God's historical debasement in the streets.

The strong stench of status resentments and racism pervades these

early newspaper commentaries, which, aimed at pleasing a conservative lay and ecclesiastical establishment, had little good to say about
these plays at the margins of "decent" society. The editor of *El Mundo
Semanario Ilustrado* compared the serious, mystical, and upper-class character of the already long-running Bavarian passion at Oberammergau
favorably to the plays around Mexico City, which, he said, had been
left "to the last layer of society."[3] For decades after, comparisons to
Oberammergau would register both the perceived "shame" and linger-
ing hope of Mexicans, ever sensitive as they were to their standing in the
world. Everywhere in these reports preceding the Mexican Revolution
of 1910 are denunciations of the natives' denseness, drunkenness, and
superficiality, complaints all but identical to the sixteenth-century Conquest accounts. Still, by now these "conquerors'" accounts are mixed
with the refreshing admission that the people putting on these plays
were not mere "Indians" but "nothing if not mestizos."[4] It was no longer
possible simply to dismiss "our Indians," as the indigenous peoples were
usually labeled, as so much refuse from the past, because a *Mexican* culture had emerged that, alas, still had a powerful indigenous component
that was not going away. Any fair assessment had to recognize that those
who still performed these "ridiculous" plays were racially less and less
distinct from the other Mexicans who denounced them.

Still further complicating any thought of laying blame for these "indecent" plays was the undeniable fact that at the end of the nineteenth century, the passion performances in the pueblos were popular among capitalinos. In Mexico, the week of Jesus's passion and death had evolved
into the common spring vacation period, and subsequent attempts to
weaken the "too religious" status of Holy Week by establishing a thoroughly secular vacation period in May would have little success.[5] Thus
citizens customarily relaxed and grieved at the same time, and before Acapulco became the favorite haunt of metropolitan vacationers, these passion towns and villages around the capital offered urban dwellers that pe-
culiar mix of edification and leisure-time relaxation which often marks
the passage from a traditional to a secular society. Early journalistic accounts reflect this complex reality. In 1895 the editor of *El Tiempo* published the train schedule and then encouraged travelers to go see "the
terrible scenes of the passion of the savior" as they were performed at
Amecameca, in the foothills of the great volcanos to the southeast of the

capital, thereby favoring this capitaline vacation or leisure goal over any other.[6] There in Amecameca, our editor opined, the local pastor had organized a performance of the passion that reeked of propriety. With this short train trip, the decent pilgrim or relaxed vacationer could complete his or her life with religion, all while avoiding the outrages that accompanied these plays in other venues.[7]

If it was clear to the literati of the capital that piety ought to mesh with diversion, the matter was no less obvious to the provincials who performed the plays in these hinterlands. Whatever pious goals they may have pursued, these country Christians knew that visitors from the city wanted "diversion" along with their passion "spectacles," the two terms that recur in these first accounts of modern passion plays.[8] Thus it is not surprising to find in early newspaper accounts often vague generic references to riotous cultural forms, not at all hidden, that have no direct textual relation to the passion of Jesus.[9] Easily the most intriguing documentation of this type is the repeated mention of the *huehuenches* or off-color old-timers' songs, surely in part in Nahuatl, performed not only during carnival but on Good Friday itself. More than once these songs are associated with the figure playing the Jewish high priest Caiaphas, who along with Annas prosecuted Jesus before Herod and Pontius Pilate.[10] There were other practices jarring to modern sensibilities in these early documents, but the early and repeated references to the *huehuenches*—they do not reoccur in the Iztapalapan passion records after about 1920—mark them as favorite examples of indecencies put forward by opponents of these plays. At this date, the live recollection of the passion of Jesus was not yet in danger of becoming a reverent, dull, and orthodox recollection of the death of the Christian savior.

Thus even while admonishing their readers not to attend these performances, the editors of the early periodicals knew that many of their readers did go to them, if only out of curiosity, and they even admitted that truly beautiful moments existed in the midst of such bacchanalian riots.[11] Anyway, it seemed that nothing decisive could be done to eliminate them. Sometime in early 1900, the archbishop of Mexico issued a decree that apparently limited the participation of curates in outdoor passion activities, and one editor was gratified to note that attendance in that year's passion activities had fallen off.[12] Still, everyone knew that whatever the rules of the archbishop, local parishioners could constrain their curates to participate in their Holy Week performances, and they knew as well that the government commonly paid no heed to curates' protests about their parishioners' festive activities, citing the enlightened notion that varied cult activities deserved to be tolerated.[13] The only hope for all right-thinking people, one of our editors determined, was that with time the Indians would become better educated in religion and would themselves abandon these performances.[14]

The roots of the cultural pessimism registered in the Mexican capital's *fin de siècle* reporting about its indigenous peoples' Holy Week performances must be sought in church-state relations. One issue is that of control. Pre-modern New Spain had long been marked by the church's attempt to control passion performances. From the mid-sixteenth century right up until 1769, the archbishops of Mexico had repeatedly tried to limit if not stop the famous *neixquitiles* or mute pantomime "example plays" that the Indians of New Spain, with or without clerical approval, had made their own in the colonial period.[15] Now it was the turn of the secular state, and in the wake of the Constitution of 1857, amidst a series of major reform laws, the national government set about stripping the church of many of its privileges, among which none would prove more important than the right to control the streets.

The purpose of this stream of legislation was to restrain the church by restricting clerically inspired public assembly. Thus on 14 December 1874, enabling legislation with constitutional status forbade the performance of any "religious act of public worship" anywhere other than inside places of public worship; whether the attached atria or large outdoor porches of many churches were to be considered as places of public worship remained open to debate. In practice this far-reaching mandate, in the event of its implementation, meant among other things that religious objects like statues and cassocked priests could not be taken outside churches, for that would make it a "religious act."[16]

To the extent it was enforced, this edict was bound to influence the whole structure and content of the Iztapalapan pageant, especially during the first half of the twentieth century. But it is clear that at the time the ordinance was aimed more generally at preventing clerically controlled outdoor gatherings from being used for political ends, such as protesting anticlerical laws. In 1875, for example, the central authority fined the municipal administration of Milpa Alta, a hillside municipality just south of Iztapalapa, for having permitted the "customary" processions of Holy Week. And in the capital itself in the same year, the police force treated another Holy Week procession, presumably replete with statues and priests, as a mutiny and tried to suppress it. They were met by devotees throwing rocks.[17] Future pages will show convincingly that the history of the passion play in Iztapalapa and more generally in the valley of Mexico at large is decisively linked to control of the streets on the one hand, and to church attendance on the other.

Here then was the context which enveloped pessimists like García Icazbalceta at the turn of the century, here the explanation for one of their numbers' grudging admission that "there is no denying the beauty of such representations, without apparatuses or artifice," that is, without statues or clerical rites.[18] Evidently, the church no longer had full control of its native flocks and festivals, and the locals were in a position to perform their passion rites without, the critics felt, much opposition from "decent people." In his 1900 edict, which withdrew preachers from the Way of the Cross, the archbishop had no recourse but to order the effectuation of the government's will.

A word about the primary sources of the Iztapalapan play itself. During the late 1990s I read all the Holy Week accounts of all the major newspapers published in Mexico City, but my main sources for the previous century are the almost century-long runs of two hoary Mexico City dailies, *Excelsior* (hereafter referenced as *E*) and *El Universal* (hereafter referenced as *U*), both of which started publishing in 1916 and continue to this day, when their respective circulations daily, aimed clearly at a middle-class readership, are 210,000 and 102,000, and on Sundays 220,000 and 145,000.[19] In most of the intervening years, on each Holy Saturday, that is, the day before Easter, these periodicals published their reporters' accounts of the passion plays that had transpired on Good Friday, and unless otherwise stated, all the information we cite from these periodicals regarding Good Friday of any given year appeared in the respective newspapers' Holy Saturday edition.[20] The same rule of a day's lag applies to other feasts: any Holy Thursday information comes from the respective newspaper's edition of Good Friday, details from Palm Sunday on Holy Monday, from Easter on Easter Monday, and so on.

Besides their own personal observations, reporters relied heavily for background information on the play's organizing committee (Comité), which for many years has held journalistic briefings just before and after the spectacle. Curiously, the Comité is also the source of information on when the Iztapalapan play originated. In recent years the story has gone as follows: the play began as a response to the cholera epidemic that swept through the Valley of Mexico in 1833. It originated either in that year or, in the more common account, in 1843 or 1844, when the Iztapalapans (belatedly) got around to thanking God for saving them a decade earlier. The earlier date does concur with a real epidemic, which certainly did decimate Iztapalapa. But no more in this case than in that of Oberammergau, where an epidemic is also associated with the origins of a passion play, is there any evidence linking the one with the other. Here as there, the story is an invention rather than a memory.[21]

On examination, the Iztapalapan story, not to mention the dates on which it rests, proves to be of astoundingly recent vintage. Not only is there no documentation to confirm these dates as relevant to the town's passion play, but the story itself emerged from the organizing Comité at an embarrassingly late date. Believe it or not, the first reference to the passion play's origin in the epidemic appeared only in *Excelsior*'s and *El Universal*'s 1985 accounts. That is, only yesterday, so to speak, did the Comité obviously give this story to the reporters! The year 1833 as the spectacle's point of origin first emerged in *El Universal* in 1976, then in *Excelsior* in 1985, and again in 1988 and 1994. Meanwhile the date 1843, which today is more generally accepted, first appears in *Excelsior* only in 1979, when the representation is said to have been in its 136th year (1979 minus 136 = 1843). That year had a significant afterlife. In 1982 and 1983 *El Universal* says that these were respectively the 139th and 140th years of the spectacle, while *Excelsior* speaks of the 142nd year being in 1985. Finally, a book on the Iztapalapan Passion entitled *150 años* has an introduction dated 1992, and it says that that year was the 150th anniversary of the first performance.[22] Thus 1843 and occasionally 1844 have ruled as the years of origin from 1979 till the present, a mere quarter century ago. All in all, a sustained claim that the play started in the first half of the nineteenth century began only recently.

To be sure, 1833 and 1843 were not the only dates when the Iztapalapa play was supposed to have begun, but it would add needless detail to list them all, especially since none is demonstrable. What is more interesting is the tendency of local boosters to choose a round number, especially 150 years. Thus if the earliest date given without further qualification is the 1805 mentioned by *Excelsior* in 1961, that paper says in 1968 and again in 1975 that the play was 150 years old, yielding dates of 1818 and 1825, well before the lately favored 1833 or 1843 were ever mentioned in the papers. That beginnings were negotiable is all too evident. Since the organizing committee has never documented its declarations, no historical foundation supports the story linking an epidemic to any of these dates, or to any of the several others encountered in the sources.

What does emerge from the record, however, is the organizing Comité's apparently calculated decision to push origins a full two generations back from the actual probable date of origin, as that date, c. 1883, had regularly been given to reporters for years. Thus in 1964, both *Excelsior* and *El Universal* stated that the play had started in 1884, likewise, the first magazine article on the play at Iztapalapa, appearing in the same year, said that it began in 1883.[23] Obviously, all these sources were echoing a statement of the organizing committee, which in this as in other years gave press releases to reporters. In 1967, *Excelsior* says that the representation dates "from the end of the past century"; then in 1970 and 1971 *El Universal* lists 1888 and 1875 respectively as starting dates, while in 1976 *Excelsior* repeats the year 1883. But in that same year *El Universal* went with the new story, according to which 1833 had been the beginning of the Iztapalapan saeculum, and from that year on, that new doctrine has predominated. My research, however, confirms that the Iztapalapan play as we know it today dates back for "only" a century and a quarter ago, to the 1880s.

As has long been clear in the literature, a passion play was performed in Iztapalapa as early as 1867, but that performance was significantly different from the later, modern plays. This early representation is described, at least in part, in a letter of 30 November of that year written by José María Suárez to President Benito Juárez.[24] From it, we may deduce that the representation was carried out in the not-yet completed Santuario or Shrine of the Holy Sepulcher or in its patio. The parish priest of the pueblo, fray Antonio Sánchez, was involved in the services in the Santuario, but his and the pueblo's parish church of San Lucas was not.[25] The Santuario was under construction at this point in time for the purpose of housing Iztapalapa's so-called Lord of the Cave (*Señor de la*

Cuevita), a wooden statue of the supine dead Jesus *(Christo iacente).* As Suárez specifically mentions an Iztapalapan procession for Jesus's funeral *(Santo Entierro),* we may assume that the same *Señor de la Cuevita* was already the centerpiece of this procession. By the early twentieth century, at least, after the wooden Jesus was taken down or deposed from its cross on Good Friday afternoon, the Iztapalapans encased the statue in a glass casket and, in that grand funeral procession of the Santo Entierro, carried it back to its cave in the Santuario, where it would stay at least till Easter morning *(U:* 1921).[26]

Suárez refers to three elements of a passion representation in his 1867 letter. He first mentions the crucifixion of Jesus, telling Juárez that friar Sánchez charged his parishioners 200 pesos "if there are no Jews who crucify the Lord," but 300 pesos if there were, as was the case in that year. This means that the charge was 200 pesos if there were no dramatic "Jews" demanding crucifixion, but 300 pesos if the representation took the form of a true reenactment with Jews and Romans, thus requiring greater participation by the friar. For centuries, passion plays had featured priests who gave a short sermon or interpretation at each significant step of the passion; obviously, a priest charged more for such a service than for an event involving no theater. Secondly, Suárez refers to the deposition of Jesus, and in enough detail to show that here in Iztapalapa in 1867, live indigenous actors played not just the Jews, but the parts of the good and the bad thieves—conventionally called Dimas and Gestas. Jesus himself, however, was represented *de bulto,* that is, by an "articulated" wooden figure, whose limbs moved to permit the crucifixion, deposition, funeral procession, and his burial. Indeed, the mistreatment of the two theatrical thieves was one of Suárez's main complaints. From Good Friday morning until the imaged Jesus was taken down from the cross, these indigenous actors hung under the blazing sun on either side of the wooden Jesus wearing nothing more than underpants and a wig! Once finally taken down from their crosses, Suárez adds, these play thieves had to follow the procession of the Santo Entierro—the third passion element—with their arms tied behind their backs, thus paying their respects to the corpse of Jesus. And for doing all this, they had to pay alms to the curate![27]

The reenactments of the early twentieth century were still performed at the Santuario. But at this later date, earlier parts of the passion which

Suárez does not mention, including Jesus's judgment by Pontius Pilate and his flagellation, took place some four blocks away, at the parish church of San Lucas, a temple unmentioned in the 1867 account.[28] Suárez's wording makes it clear, moreover, that the representation of the passion was episodic rather than annual or periodic in character. Sometimes "Jews" crucified Jesus, sometimes not. Thus at this date, before the anti-ecclesiastical laws of the 1870s, the passion of Jesus in Iztapalapa was apparently neither traditional nor customary. And from 1867 until 1898, there is no further documentation of a passion play at Iztapalapa.

This does not mean that these thirty years are without interest for our study. To the contrary, this period may be regarded as the seed bed of the modern spectacle. Unanimously, previous students of the play have assumed that the passion play of Iztapalapa originated and developed *ex novo* in the town or village itself, as if a genuine product of local culture. The idea is unproblematical. For since 1570 the parish has been under the authority of the archbishop or secular clergy rather than a religious order, and the religious orders historically nurtured sacred theater in New Spain, whereas the secular clergy opposed it. On its face, Iztapalapa would seem to have offered little encouragement for the establishment of sacred theater.

But what if the play we today admire was imported into Iztapalapa from some other site where it had indeed had Mendicant roots? For when individual Iztapalapans and other natives of passion towns moved away from home, they sometimes recreated the play in their new residences, both in the Valley of Mexico and elsewhere. Just one example will suffice: beyond the volcano of Popocatépetl in the state of Puebla, the creators of a passion play at Huaquechula are said to have moved it about 1928 to Atlixco, some 13 miles to the northeast (*U:* 1980). Now, if we are to believe the authoritative word of Santiago Guerra, perhaps the single most important actor, organizer, and spokesman for the Iztapalapan passion play in its history, that is precisely what happened in Iztapalapa. Speaking to a reporter of *El Universal* in 1979, this famous Pontius Pilate "indicated that the representation did not originate in Iztapalapa." "In the last century it was done in Chimalhuacán, and from there our ancestors brought it to this part of the city. Because of the nearness to the Hill of the Star *(Cerro de la Estrella),* which is perfect for the crucifixion," Guerra continued, "[Iztapalapa] is better suited, and so our ancestors brought it to this part of the city."[29] (Iztapalapa is 13 miles southwest of Chimalhuacán.) Thus we have it on the authority of this towering figure that the play's roots reached not back to time out of mind, but only into recent history. It began under the Dominican sky of Chimalhuacán, but would reach its apex in Iztapalapa, a town whose church was under the authority of the secular clergy, which would historically remain the play's most inveterate enemy.

But what did Guerra mean exactly when he spoke of "the representation"? In my view, he must have been referring at least in part to the main literary source of the modern play, Enrique Pérez Escrich's *Mártir de Gólgota,* which Guerra referred to immediately after mentioning Chimalhuacán.[30] We thus come to the key question of the textual basis of the Iztapalapan and other passion plays. Late colonial texts of the passion did exist, and as late as the second half of the eighteenth century, the Inquisition was still trying to keep them out of the hands of the native Americans in the pueblos, obviously in the hope of suppressing the plays themselves. Still, most indications are that by that time, church authorities had resigned themselves to accepting such plays, if not always their texts, as mere theater which was beyond the regulatory authority of churchmen. Now a century later, a genuinely new text tradition surfaced for the Iztapalapa passion celebration, Pérez Escrich's script being one of its two parts.

The first important statement regarding the literary basis of the modern Iztapalapan play occurs in *El Universal*'s 1941 account of the pageant. The reporter implies that the performers have no acting skill because they merely memorize text from the *Librito de los Cuatro Concilios, editado por Vanegas Arroyo.* A fuller picture emerges in 1947, when Ralph S. Boggs and Vicente T. Mendoza reconstructed and published the whole text used in the Iztapalapan passion performance of 1945,[31] all the more important because only rarely had the press bothered to properly credit the written source(s) of the play.[32] Boggs and Mendoza make clear that the text for the play stemmed from two works. The first is the Valencian Enrique Pérez Escrich's self-described novel *El Mártir de Gólgota: tradiciones de Oriente,* and the second is the Mexican Francisco Ozácar's *Los Cuatro Concilios para la celebración de las Tres Caídas en la Semana Santa.* Close attention to these two printed texts shows that they in fact became the canon for passion performances in Iztapalapa at the end of the nineteenth century, that is, at the very time the modern plays began to be performed. *Mutatis mutandis,* they continue in use to this day.

One piece of evidence for this claim is that Pérez Escrich's work, originally brought out in Madrid in 1863, appeared under a Mexico City imprint of J. M. Aguilar Ortíz in 1878. This same (sixth) edition of the work, in turn, was the one used by the organizing committee in 1945 to prepare that year's performance.[33] The supposition that Aguilar Ortíz published this work in Mexico because in 1878 there was a market for it among those organizing passion plays is then confirmed by the very title of the second work, the *Cuatro Concilios*—The Four Councils (of the Jews deliberating on Jesus's fate)—which says that this work was used "for the celebration of the Three Falls in Holy Week." That is, Francisco Ozácar wrote or compiled the *Cuatro Concilios* for those seeking texts for passion plays. The dates of the editions of this work fit this hypothesis perfectly: A. Vanegas Arroyo in Mexico City published identical editions of this work in 1890, 1895, and 1918, at the very point when the Iztapalapa play was becoming a regular production.[34]

Each work covers the whole passion of Jesus from his arrest on Holy Thursday through the consultations of the Jews, the trial, the Way of the Cross, and the crucifixion on Good Friday.[35] But by spending a large amount of time on the council meetings of the Jews leading up to the sentence of Pontius Pilate, the appropriately named *Cuatro Concilios* seems at times to hearken back to the eighteenth century texts mentioned above, which also gave most of the play over to what, after all, was only the buildup to the Way of the Cross and Jesus's crucifixion.[36] Once the *Cuatro Concilios* enters into the proper passion of Jesus, however, it appears to abridge parts of the story Pérez Escrich relates.

The broad social significance of these long-winded speeches of the *Concilios* should not be missed. While the actors who played Mary, Joseph, and the apostles—in short, the proto-Christians—usually executed those roles for a one-time performance only, those who played the roles, such as Jesus's persecutors Caiaphas, Annas, the devil, Judas, various Romans, and the like, had done so for many consecutive years, the roles in effect being inherited. "From now on," *Excelsior* has a father announce to his son in 1961, "you will be the Roman, with the firm hand and proud gesture that I have always employed. Do you understand? And be careful not to hurt the family's reputation!" It was in fact not Jesus or the apostles but these theatrical non-Christians who ran the play, and they constituted themselves as the Comité Organizador, which originally may have been labeled the Concilio.[37] Thus those involved in the Concilios that accused Jesus were by and large the same persons as those in the Comité. The long speeches of Caiaphas and Annas that make up so much of Ozácar's *Cuatro Concilios* were in a sense the performative pay-off for these persons' efforts in organizing the celebration. The original creators of the Iztapalapan canon picked, chose, and then combined into one text sections from both works, a procedure that Boggs and Mendoza deconstructed in their edition of 1945.[38] Ever since, subsequent organizers have selected passages from both these works to construct the text for each year's performance.

Iztapalapa was by no means the only American homestead for the work of Pérez Escrich. The nearby town of Milpa Alta, for instance, whose Good Friday processions were already "customary" in 1875, had probably incorporated both Pérez and the *Cuatro Concilios* into its play's canon by the end of the nineteenth century, but definitely by 1942.[39] Next, a fragment of the passion play at Tzintzuntzán (Michoacán) published in 1925 turns out to be from Pérez's *Mártir.*[40] Likewise, in 1955 the residents of Tepalcingo (Morelos), adopted Pérez Escrich's novel as their text,[41] and it forms the base of the passion play in Cuajimalpa just west of the capital in 1973. And further afield, I have found Pérez's *Mártir* serving as the text for the passion play performed in the city of Granada, Nicaragua.[42] More research will surely determine that many other festive organizers across Latin America have used this work as their passion text,[43] so it is more than surprising that this author's fame in the passion plays of the Americas has apparently escaped students of Spanish literature. The author's character-drawing, his willingness to dramatize the biblical account and to give names to passion players both real and imagined, have all proved suited to the performance stage in a way no other script has done.

Yet whence had come the group that founded the play? We return to our search for the origins of the Comité, and to a report in *El Universal's* 1954 Holy Saturday story. While singular and partially fanciful, it certainly sheds a revealing light on this problem, because the story links the

Council's origins to the emergence of the text of the *Cuatro Concilios*. In the beginning, this report says, what would become the Iztapalapan pageant consisted of nothing more than a procession of images. But then seeing the irreverence with which the bearers treated them, the religious authorities forbade the laity from using them in processions. Soon after that, our story continues, a group called at the time (and still in 1954) "of the soldiers" *(de los sayones)*—headed, we learn in 1944, by Caiaphas (U)—"began to stage some biblical scenes of the *Pasión y Muerte de Nuestro Señor Jesucristo,* according to the original [text] of an author at the beginning of the century." The reference is surely to Francisco Ozácar, author of *Los Cuatro Concilios*. Still later, the reporter concludes, this *comité de los sayones* introduced the practice whereby acting in the pageant was limited to those individuals who swore engagement to a five-year term. During this term and through their thespian participation in the town passion play, they fulfilled a promise or *manda* they had made to a supernatural in exchange for a favor they had received. Besides fulfilling the individual vows made to the divinities, these promises obviously provided the Comité with a consistent group of actors to perform the passion plays.

Surely some of the details of this yarn are false. The Catholic clergy began the struggle to seize control of images from native Americans already in the wake of the conquest. Further, we have seen that in the first documented passion performance in Iztapalapa, in 1867, living thieves and not just images accompanied the sculpted Jesus. Still, this 1954 account of a laity misusing sacred images does evoke recent history after all, once we recognize the ancient clerical bias against the laity. In fact, the local memory of 1954 probably recalls events following upon the law of 1874, which forbade the presence of (church-owned) images in processions. That legal move, once enforced, obviously would over time have encouraged the laity here, as it did elsewhere, to convert the procession of the *Tres Caídas* into a totally live theatrical representation controlled by the laity because the clergy, along with their images, were now confined to their churches. This the 1954 report gets exactly right. The legacy of Iztapalapan lay control over the passion pageant can be traced back to that point, at which neither priest nor church image dared venture ceremonially into the streets.

Just as important for the long-range history of passion theater is what this report tells us about that controlling lay body. Evidence from the second half of the eighteenth century showed that the *sayones,* the cape-wearing "Roman" soldiers, constituted the top layer of native American society in the area around Mexico City. They were elected to their duties by their native fellows each year, and at the end of Holy Week defended their society's right to dress up and parade in fake Roman armor. In short, this quasi-executive body was comparable to and possibly derived from the native *cabildos* for religious festivities so well known to historical anthropologists of Mexico. In 1921 *El Universal* confirms this intimate linkage of the still-young Iztapalapan passion play with such a quasi-military Pretorian guard by characterizing that year's passion performance as "the *Pretorio* or the passion."[44] Subsequently, the 1954 report in the same newspaper definitively traces the Iztapalapan Council or Comité directly to this ancient soldierly tradition. Thus "the soldiers," the organizers of the great Iztapalapan Passion Play, trace their roots back to feigned soldiers, that is, to that unit of native American society which had historically defended the native male right to dress up as warriors against an emasculating colonial power. To this day we still witness this historical assertiveness in late industrial Iztapalapa.

The link that this 1954 report establishes between the play, its organizers, and a text, is certainly significant. Taken all together, the available information argues convincingly for the end of the nineteenth century as the point at which the pageant began to be performed with some regularity. Viewed historically, easily the most common date given for that event in the newspaper accounts of the twentieth century is 1883, although what particular event, if any, might underlie that year's popularity remains unclear. Recall that it was then just nine years after the law of 1874 that legally put an end to images in the streets. Then, in rapid succession, three unchanged editions of *Los Cuatro Concilios* were published: in 1890, 1895, and finally in 1918. This represents a strong circumstantial case that the play as we know it did originate around 1883. I hypothesize that the Iztapalapan ancestors whom Santiago Guerra invokes in 1979 brought precisely the text of Pérez Escrich from Chimalhuacán to Iztapalapa sometime after 1878, the year of that work's first printing in Mexico.

Beginning in 1898, the newspapers *El Tiempo* and *El Mundo Semanario Ilustrado* repeatedly refer to this town as one of the main theatrical sites for Good Friday performances. By then, the government's prohibition of outdoor religious processions with priests and images, for example, of Jesus, had been in effect for nearly a quarter of a century, and the age of the Iztapalapan passion with live actors but no images had begun. Perhaps the archbishop's circular of 1900 had had the claimed momentary success mentioned earlier because some celebrants were ready to enter the churches after the lay procession outside, yet soon enough the church hierarchy used that opening to insist that "curates may not permit staged performances that are full of folklore."[45] The 1921 account leaves little doubt that this archepiscopal decree was understood to prohibit staged performances even in the atrium of a church. In short, it represented the prelate's radical attempt to put an end to the populace's creative performances of the passion of Jesus that had been opened up by the Republic's prohibition of church images and priests in public. This brings us to a still more important, general finding. The same *Excelsior* account of 1921 reported that the Iztapalapans so persisted in their determination to put on the spectacle in the face of archepiscopal opposition that the clerics finally caved, and the performance went forward. This dynamic passage from clerical prohibitions to lay obstinance and victory will remain the rule across a century of pageant history. Time and again in the twentieth century, church authorities claimed the right to forbid these plays, and yet they would repeatedly step aside and let the plays go forward at the last minute.

The legal background of the Iztapalapan passion again—and forcefully—directs our attention to the control of the streets, one key to unlocking its history. In a recent book on the *Semana Santa en Iztapalapa*, the vice-chancellor of the archbishopric of Mexico explains why in Iztapalapa there is so little coordination between the clergy and the people who perform this great festival. "The principal cause," the prelate wrote, "is the constitutional limit that impedes parish priests from preaching in the streets," an obvious reference to that part of the law of 1874 that carried over into the Constitution of 1917 and was still in effect in 1992.[46] He notes that the population of Iztapalapa had grown rapidly in the recent past, so that a passion ceremony that had once been held in the atrium of a church had perforce to be moved outside. But that is a space, he continues, from which the preacher is excluded. Needless to say, the prelate's account is imperfect history. Yet the overall picture is clear. From an early time, the clergy had always tried to encapsulate the passion play within a space it controlled. Later, the Mexican state had in a sense obliged, driving the preachers from the streets. But with a population explosion, the charisma of the people imitating Jesus could not be contained in an atrium or a church. The history of this passion play will always reflect a search for religious authenticity, in the unwalled streets of the profane modern town.

4

fROM NATIVE CULTURE TO POPULAR CULTURE AfTER THE REVOLUTION

The Mexico City newspaper reports from 1914 to 1929 provide the building blocks for an understanding of the Iztapalapan passion play for the remainder of the twentieth century. Yet in tone and atmosphere the descriptions of this period also look back to an earlier period, affording us the opportunity to grasp some of the substance of the play before regular newspaper reporting began. It seems to have been a somewhat different type of play, passion performances dominated at times by what Bakhtin calls "popular festive culture."[1] The reports of this period hint at a folk passion celebration that reveals not only a solemnity that must fold over into ridicule, but also a comedy that is the precondition of reverence. After about 1930 the church, the political authorities, and not least the pretensions of the Iztapalapans themselves will slowly suppress some of these established popular forms, including the remnants of the Nahuatl language of the indigenes. Thus these popular festive forms deserve our particular attention as we enter the streets of Iztapalapa during the earliest detailed plays of the passion.

The evidence for a passion performance in 1914—the only one between 1900 and 1919 for which there is any evidence—is circumstantial; the performances of 1919, 1920, and 1921

are richly documented. In the latter year, *El Universal* for the first time refers to the Iztapalapan passion play as an annual "tradition," yet not before 1930 do the performances really begin to anchor themselves firmly in the communal calendar. Indeed, from 1921 until 1930 there were no spectacles, most likely owing to the aftereffects of the Revolution of 1910 and to the disorders of the Cristeros Wars. In 1926, President Plutarco Calles closed church schools, expelled foreign priests, and ordered the rest to register with the state. The uprising of the Cristeros that began at that point lasted until late 1929.

Relying on the Comité for historical information, the capitaline newspapers later regularly claimed that the passion play was almost uniformly presented throughout these years. To hear them tell it, the pageant was suspended for only a short period during the Revolution, one report specifying the period between 1914 and 1916, when most of the actors had fled (*U:* 1964). The usual story, however, goes like this: in 1914 the popular revolutionary *caudillo* Emiliano Zapata stepped in and again made a performance possible, after which it has been performed each year to the present day (*E:* 1988). Zapata, who has remained a heroic figure especially for rural Mexicans, is said to have procured the horses that the Iztapalapan "Romans" needed for their part in the play. In another account he also lent the actors the money to rent their costumes (*U:* 1985).[2] Zapata's sympathy for traditional religious observances is in fact well known, and, indeed, he was in the general vicinity of Iztapalapa during Lent, 1914.[3]

While there is, as we see, no documentary evidence for the alleged performance of 1914, another oral source, in further validating the Zapata story, claimed that the performance of that year was the first such celebration from almost the beginning of the century! Without any hint of boosterism—the bane of historical research on such civic entities—the 99-year-old Nabor Reyes, on being interviewed in 1992, stated firmly that the play had actually been suspended in 1904, long before the outbreak of the Revolution, and was not resumed until Zapata's intervention in 1914. The obstacle, he explained, was the 1903 law of political and municipal organization that created the prefectures. Firmly and plausibly, Reyes states that from the passage of that law until the intervention of Zapata in 1914, the Iztapalapans could not get permission to hold processions.[4]

Thus it appears that the archbishop's prohibition of 1900 and then this governmental action made for either a very episodic play between 1904 and 1914 or none at all. But there is more. Much the same can also be said for the period after the alleged Zapata intervention of 1914. For in 1919, *Excelsior* notes that in the intervening years, ones of continuing political tension, the passion of Jesus had scarcely been celebrated,[5] and in fact, I could find no mention of performances between 1915 and 1918. The Zapata story itself remains to be verified. It can be regarded as one more of the scores of legends attached to the figure of the great Morelian revolutionary, which sprang up so easily in areas like Iztapalapa and Milpa Alta so famous for their Zapatista sympathies. Indeed, the story of an alleged 1914 Iztapalapan passion surfaces in print only in 1968, in *Excelsior,* in keeping with the world of exaggeration that is such a constant in the Iztapalapan record.

Despite the lack of contemporary documentation for much of the first score of years of the twentieth century, newspaper accounts in the years 1919, 1920 and 1921, when the serial reporting of Iztapalapan performances begins, make it clear that the drama had already become established at some earlier point. Not only does *El Universal* label the pageant "already traditional" in 1921, but at two different points in these three years, the newspapers make references to performances of times now past. In *El Universal's* Holy Saturday story of 1919, entitled "How One Commemorated the Death of Christ in the Old Days" *(antaño),* the reporter dwells on "the famous Three Falls which was carried out in the picturesque pueblos of Santa Anita, Iztacalco, and Iztapalapa." They had by now "passed into history," to be sure, and "these profane ceremonies now belong in the domain of articles and books." Thus to answer the question the article headline posed, the reporter cites Antonio García Cubas's memoirs of 1904, which include a description of Good Friday celebrations in the capital from the time of his youth till the end of the nineteenth century.[6] Clearly, these three contiguous pueblos followed an established tradition that included the allegedly now abandoned Three Falls, a procession which, as we know, was but one element of the larger Good Friday representations at this time.

In 1920 *Excelsior* refers again to this older tradition when its reporter states firmly that Iztapalapa was now the only pueblo in the Valley of Mexico to stage the passion annually. This contemporary performance included not only the procession of the Three Falls (obviously not passed into history!), but other elements as well that differed markedly from those of the old days, as our reporter notes in an addendum to his account. Earlier, he explained, an image of Jesus had been whipped and crowned with thorns after being sentenced, to then figure in the procession of the Three Falls. Now things were different. Now a live Jesus made that trek, a shift we shall explore at greater length in what follows. Clearly, the ceremonies at Iztapalapa were no new thing in 1919; however irregularly, they stretched back to the last score of years of the nineteenth century.

The accounts of the years 1919–1921 afford us a wealth of information concerning both the elemental structures of the celebration and its historical dynamics in these early years of documentation. The first signs of organized tourism to the festival also appear in these reports. The *Excelsior* account of Good Friday, 1920—printed as always on Holy Saturday—states that some 15,000 people came down from the capital area; it is not said how many arrived from the villages and towns surrounding Iztapalapa. Most capitaline visitors arrived by buses and trains which, though they left the Plaza de Armas in the city every four minutes, proved unequal to the task of moving such a crowd. Automobiles brought the better-heeled urbanites, some ten of which broke down on the way. By this point, in short, the spectacle at Iztapalapa had become a tourism attraction for "caravans and trains" (*E:* 1921). From the beginning, that is, cult and trade were as always inseparable commodities.

Visitors reached their destination after passing through Santa Anita, a pueblo to the north of Iztapalapa that was still famed for its own celebration of the *Viernes de Dolores,* the Friday before Good Friday, when Mary first learned of her son's fate. Its waterways packed with barges loaded down with visitors, Santa Anita featured an unending wealth of flowers, many of which had been brought up from the *chinampas* or floating gardens of Iztapalapa itself. In 1921 *El Universal* describes the behavior of those passing through Santa Anita en route to Iztapalapa just one week later: "They buy the indispensable crown of poppies and pansies, for everyone attending [Iztapalapa] either as actors or as simple spectators have to present themselves in character," men *de rigueur* wearing their crown of fresh flowers in the shape of a scarf, women theirs in the shape of a straw hat. On entering Iztapalapa itself, this reporter encountered long lines of people crowned with flowers, and wearing extravagant clothing.

This same account, perhaps the richest of all descriptions of the

Iztapalapan festival of these years, now puts us in the sacred context within which the celebration took place during these years. The reporter states that on arriving in the pueblo, people first went to "Monte Calvario," identified as a small eminence to the east of the Santuario.[7] The spot was famous, the reporter said, because some years earlier *(algunos lustros),* a dead Christ *(Cristo exangelo)* appeared in the trunk of a tree to an Indian with the odor of sanctity. Believers kneel before this tree to pray and, through suggestion, see a crucified Christ crowned with thorns." The significance of this attempt at sacred legitimation should not be ignored. What is charismatically present is a crucifixion image in a tree. What is absent is any mention of a man-made religious image, and most noticeably absent is the erstwhile famous statue of the Señor de la Cuevita, the supine Jesus for whom the Santuario was built in the nineteenth century. In fact, the only direct early indication that this statue had cult occurs in 1931, when it is said to be venerated (U). Not until 1964 in *El Universal* do we read that the Cuevita was making ever more miracles, so that Iztapalapa could become a great pilgrimage site. Once again, another element of today's popular sacred history entered the Iztapalapan book of legends as late as only a third of a century ago. To the extent that any sacred wonder drove the earliest documented history of the Iztapalapan passion, it was not a statue but a vision of the crucifixion in a tree.

After saying a prayer at this charismatic site, the visitors in 1921 came back down the hill in our account and proceeded to the atrium of the parish church of San Lucas, where the Good Friday theater would begin with the judgment and sentencing of Jesus (see fig. 2). The accounts of these three years make no direct reference to any representations before those of Good Friday, but that is certainly because the reporters came down to Iztapalapa only on the morning of Good Friday. In fact, we may be confident that then as now, the passion play had actually started on Holy Thursday with the representation of the Last Supper, Jesus's Washing of the Apostles' Feet, his Prayers on the Mount of Olives or Gethsemane, and his Capture and Imprisonment by the Jews or Romans.[8] In the story Jesus appears in chains at the very beginning of his role in the Friday events; he had obviously been arrested during the show the previous evening.

Erected within the atrium of San Lucas (was that the clergy's space or

the people's?) and decorated with flags and plants were four platforms
that held the various actors involved in the judgment and sentencing of
Jesus: Roman priests, Pontius Pilate and Herod, and the contingent of
Jewish authorities led by Caiaphas and Annas, along with their servants.[9]
In *El Universal's* account of 1921, Pontius Pilate, ensconced on his platform, awaits the arrival of "the court" before the drama proper commenced. Both newspapers describe the cortège as it made its way to the
Roman ruler beginning at 1 P.M., as *Excelsior* informs us, and the details
are nothing if not unusual. *El Universal* has the court led by Cornelius the
Centurion, who raises a ruckus, "half in an accented Spanish, half in a
corrupted Aztec." In that paper's 1919 account, the actors in this same
pre-sentencing procession were Jesus himself, the good thief Dimas, Simon the Cyrene, who would help Jesus carry his cross in the later procession of the Three Falls, Veronica, who would wipe his face, Mary
Magdalene, the Virgin Mary, St. John, who later watched Jesus on the
cross, and the archangel St. Michael, who is nowhere else documented as
a participant in the passion play.

But it is the cast of characters listed in *Excelsior's* 1920 account that
provides the greatest surprise. They included the fabled Three Kings or
magi, who had brought gifts to the infant Jesus, the figure of a pope, a
feigned representative of Spain, another of the (presumably Spanish)
Emperor, and a theatrical representative of Mexico! As they entered the
atrium of San Lucas, our reporter remarks: "Here we should alert readers that in the course of the trial of Jesus there were great anachronisms
and a lamentable confusion of persons. But this is not what matters."

It would be foolhardy to speculate what logic lay behind the presence
of many of these figures in a representation of the passion, other than to
suggest that the "procession of the court" may have brought together all
those actors who had or would put on not just the passion, but all the
representations that might be seen as leading up to the crucifixion. This
company might be seen as a summary of past and present sacred history
in the moment of that history's culmination, the passion and death of
the faithfuls' savior. In any case, this procession served unmistakably as a
form of general introduction to the decisive moments of the passion
of Jesus, which then properly commenced in the atrium of San Lucas,
one of three decisive spaces for the presentation of the total passion.
Impeded by the praetors or Roman soldiers, the crowd that surrounded

the atrium tried its best to prevent the court from arriving there. Meanwhile, the parish priest scurried about the atrium of his church, giving instructions to the various actors (E: 1921). It had been the custom for several centuries in Europe and the New World for the preacher to instruct from the pulpit the actors who mimed the dreadful events of Good Friday.[10]

Piecing together the accounts of these three years brings out a somewhat archaic image of the events at San Lucas, which is nonetheless consonant with the legal strictures already mentioned. Thus in its 1919 and 1920 reports, *Excelsior* notes more than a score of men, the *fiscales* of San Lucas, taking down from their altars in the church of San Lucas statues of "the sentenced" Jesus (presumably an Ecce Homo),[11] and of Mary in Solitude (Soledad). Placed on litters, the statues were then carried "to the entrance of the church, without passing the threshold," so that these images could view the passion scenes in the atrium from that spot. Obviously, at this date the law forbade taking such images beyond the church proper.

Yet at the same time, a particular group of the devout, the Nazarenes, did leave the church and entered the patio, that is, the space of the judgment. The presence of this historically significant group in the passion play must be clearly understood once and for all. The Nazarenes, followers of Jesus the Nazarene, were simply today's penitents rather than actors playing historical personages. They performed no real historical role, serving instead as a devotional group that punished itself for the unjust death of Jesus nineteen hundred years earlier, being theatrically "resurrected" in Iztapalapa on this day. Yet from a different point of view such penitents can be said to have a certain historical character, because since the thirteenth century European groups of this type had been a standard part of such theatrical renderings. Thus these Nazarenes had a history, and it is precisely their conservatism that we glimpse in these early reports, before it disappeared into history. In 1919, *Excelsior* reports that the faces of the Nazarenes who followed behind the image of the sentenced Jesus "were covered . . . with black masks, while they carried heavy whips *(sendos látigos).*" Needless to say, such masks had a rich history in Mexican festivities and are occasionally still to be found in other parts. But never again will the Iztapalapan Nazarenes be said to be masked, or indeed armed with whips, in the local passions. This account is our best evidence that in an earlier age, many of the actors in the passion, for instance Caiaphas, wore masks. In the decades to follow, masks largely vanish from these pageants.

Even if the organizers in these years proved unwilling to obey the archepiscopal demand referred to by *Excelsior* in 1921, namely, that the curates not permit "scenic acts full of tradition" or folklore *(actos escénicos y llenos de convencionalismo)*, it does appear that from 1919 until 1921 the events at the atrium of San Lucas proceeded carefully within the secular framework established by the anti-ecclesiastical law of 1874, as ratified in Mexico's new 1917 Constitution. *Excelsior* spelled out this legal context in 1920:

> Taking the middle road, the authorities could respect the spirit and the letter of the laws as well as the customs and traditions of the Indians. In that way, without violating any legal disposition, [the authorities] could [permit] the representation of the moving scenes that the Catholic church recalls in this week. For their part, the priests and the Indians were able to understand that acts of cult ought only be carried out within church walls. And thus they do not allow images or any objects to be taken outside that could serve as a pretext for labeling [that action] a religious ceremony, instead of what it really is, a representation that they carry out with great enthusiasm.

We turn now to the actual behavior in the representations of these three years, first by providing a frame of two fundamental polarities that inform all the actions in the passion plays. The first is the conflict between good and evil, or between reverence and irreverence. According to *El Universal* in 1921, inside the church of San Lucas, Jesus—whether a figure or a person is not clear—was released from his chains of imprisonment, even while outside, the common criminal Barabbas had his chains removed. Both were then brought before Pontius Pilate. After a series of addresses by the Jewish leaders, several played of course by members of the Comité, the crowd accepted the release of Barabbas as the condition Pontius Pilate imposed before agreeing to sentence Jesus to death. That sentence was promptly announced. The opposition of good and bad— Barabbas, the Jews, and the Romans on the one side, and Jesus, his apostles, and the pious women who followed him on the other—was there for all to see.

A second polarity, that between living actors and inanimate theatrical figures, had of course long been imaged in the historic presence, documented in Iztapalapa as far back as 1867, of a wooden Jesus hanging in the midst of two living "thieves." As we have seen, *Excelsior* in 1920 explicitly states that in the old days, an image of Jesus was the normal means of representing the Christian lord in this play, and indeed in mid-twentieth century Milpa Alta, Jesus was still played only by a statue, "por respeto."[12] In Iztapalapa, however, change had now arrived, the result being an overlap between the real and the figured. The wooden Jesus seems to have watched from the entrance of San Lucas, while a boy playing Jesus took over the thespian role of Ecce Homo on the platforms. In a striking innovation, a lively seven- to eight-year-old boy and a young girl of equal age appeared before the Councils in the atrium of San Lucas, playing respectively Jesus and Mary.[13] Once Jesus's sentence was read— *Excelsior* recorded the text in 1920—the attendants tied the boy child to the column and the scourger set about pretending to whip him. Then the child was crowned with thorns. The real significance of this seemingly awkward presence of two Jesuses at the sentencing and condemnation should not be missed. At stake were two visions of the representation of Jesus's passion: a clerical one harnessed to statues, and a lay one rooted in theatrical imitation.

Not long before 1919 the ensuing procession of the Three Falls had been executed within the atrium of the Santuario, apparently in the form of the 14 Stations of the Cross located in different parts of that atrium.[14] For whatever reason, that had now changed, and after the sentencing and flagellation in the atrium of San Lucas, the procession of the Three Falls, also called the Way of the Cross, proceeded through the streets in the direction of the Santuario. These streets formed the second decisive space (after the atrium of San Lucas) in which the passion was presented in these years. It would take Jesus to Calvary along with his persecutors and followers. No procession of the Three Falls took place in 1919, however. *El Universal*'s story in that year insisted that the *Tres Caídas* had passed into history, and *Excelsior* that same day told readers that after Jesus's sentence was read at the atrium of San Lucas and its rector, a man of *raza pura*, began to preach, people got up and left, obviously because the show was over.

But in 1920 and again in 1921, the citizens of Iztapalapa did participate in the *Tres Caídas,* which brought Jesus from San Lucas to the atrium and facade of the Santuario, where the passion would culminate. In the *Excelsior* description of 1920, one group of *fiscales* carried the cross on which Jesus would eventually be crucified, and another the statue of Jesus which would eventually be attached to that cross.[15] It was covered over with a red cloth, perhaps so that it could not be said to be involved in a "religious ceremony." *El Universal's* coverage of 1921 describes scribes, pharisees, *sayones,* pretorians, and Jews walking in front, "yelling in an Aztec-Spanish jargon," followed by Mary Magdalene and the apostles, all crowned with yellow flowers *(zempaxuxeles).* Then came (an image of) Jesus carrying a heavy cross (that is, a Jesus Nazarene), then the whole court, followed finally by thousands of spectators, all wearing their flowered crowns of thorns.

At that point, according to *Excelsior* in 1920, the two children playing Mary and Jesus joined the procession of the Three Falls. A type of sacrificial victim, the child Jesus, his hands tied behind his back, marched in the midst of a phalanx of Roman soldiers—much as those soldiers still surround a somewhat older Jesus in today's passion plays—and was jerked forward by executioners who pulled ropes attached to the young deity's neck, even as people lining the procession route, the main street of the town, fell to their knees before this "divine victim."[16]

This barest hint of ritual child sacrifice suggested by the very presence of a child amidst all these adults is rendered still more fascinating when we know that the majority of spectators were said to be from the working class, while "the richest citizens of the population" reputedly took on the roles of the major enemies of Christianity in this performance (this would not always remain the case). This observation confirms that the actors were in fact adults, and so does the oral testimony of an old timer referring back to this era.[17]

The marvelous details in *El Universal's* 1921 story complete *Excelsior's* 1920 description of a seven-year old playing the role of a thirty-three year old Jesus. The second account places front and center the non-solemn, irreverential part of the *Tres Caídas,* which our sources usually declined to describe for their readers. This reporter departs the reverential and enters the "profane" realm of his description of the Three Falls by evoking the noise of the great procession. The air was full of discordant yells, he says, with the sighs and moans of the apostles matching the taunts and exclamations of bystanders. At this point in his account, the *El Universal* reporter, or his editor, draws a line under his earlier rendition, to then begin a new subheading, entitled "The Fun Part" (*La Parte Jocosa*). We have here a rare description of clearly defined irreverent threads within a tapestry of Jesus's Three Falls—each one provoking ever greater ridicule—and his ultimate sacrifice.

In this account, the children ridicule Barabbas, who is in charge of this "fun part" of the procession up to Mount Tabor (presumably Calvary is meant), that is, the Three Falls:

[Barabbas] carries a sandal in his left hand, and is armed with a creaking wheel barrow at his right. He tells the grossest jokes to make those around him laugh. Barabbas hurls cruel epigrams at the son of Mary and beats the young and the old. Those around answer by throwing oranges at him, slapping him, even throwing stones at him.

Our journalist leaves us in no doubt as to how important this tomfoolery was in the whole scheme of things:

This grotesque ceremony is definitely the most enjoyable part for the common people, and even their betters. . . . The masquerade moves slowly toward the Plaza de Pueblo, amidst jokes by the pharisees, levites, and legionnaires, sighs from the apostles, and clowning by Barabbas.

It does not take a musician or a painter to call to the mind's eye this moving stream of humanity marked by contretemps of sounds of sorrow and devilish elation, of images that evoke awe and ridicule.

It would be misleading to make this one description stand for all the Ways of the Cross in the early years of this celebration, for doubtless there were variances each year. And yet, precisely this raucous type of Three Falls procession—how shall we doubt it?—must have closely reproduced the actual Jesus event of two millennia earlier. Further, what we read here in 1921 matches the contents of those passion fiestas denounced by newspapermen at the end of the previous century and even much earlier. It matches as well references to the bad old days that we shall repeatedly encounter in the newspaper stories of years to come. Finally, the stark irreverence of parts of the procession in this and doubtless other years easily explains why the episcopal authority, the representative par excellence of all that was solemn, worked so ceaselessly for the suppression of these lay-inspired and executed processions of the Three Falls that showed so vividly how it actually had been.

This *El Universal* account of 1921, I believe, is a classical description of an early twentieth-century Three Falls procession in Iztapalapa and in the areas roundabout. In it, in almost Manichean fashion, the principle of the bad and that of the good are juxtaposed. In it, what is solemn and good is rendered sacred in part by the endless insults and ridicule of the good or reverent by the bad or obscene. In Barabbas and his cohort, the principle of quotidian life and eros conflicts with those other principles embodied in institutions, memory, and unavoidable death. Needless to say, this representational conflict was precisely what in coming years both state and church would be determined to suppress.

It needs be said that contemporaries were clear about the Manichean quality of their passion presentations. Conventionally, Barabbas was viewed if not as Jewish himself, then certainly as the quintessential creature of the Jews. In one reporter's words, the Jewish high priest Caiaphas, conventionally hated by audiences to these spectacles, had been Barabbas's "advocate," obtaining his freedom in exchange for Jesus's crucifixion.[18] Doubtless, this 1921 passion pitted Christians against Jews, and the dualistic sentiment we have observed continued for years. Thus *El Universal* in 1933 tells us that "in the vividly colored clothing of the enemies [of Jesus] there are details of marked grossness, while on him who represents the just [Jesus], one finds a more-than-Franciscan note of simplicity." As late as 1979, the key organizer and performer Santiago Guerra, who had been involved in the passion at least since 1944, told *El Universal* that 400 actors would participate in this year's spectacle: "Half are Jews and members of the Council, and the other half are Nazarenes or followers of Christ. That is, the number of actors is divided between half good and half bad."[19] It would be inadequate, I think, to label such thinking anti-Semitic. It hinted rather that as an elect people, Christians had had a divine right to be welcomed and not persecuted by the ancient Jews.[20] In terms of Mexican society, whose historical anti-Semitism cannot be compared with that of European countries, what is more incisive is to note the dualism in Guerra's statement. No clearer statement of the dualistic thought behind this presentation in this era can be imagined, no more forceful vision of what the clergy had to combat in the coming years can be presented.

The third significant space in which the Iztapalapan passion of these years transpired was the Santuario and its atrium, where the crucifixion of Jesus was staged in 1921 and again in the early 1930s. Even though Suárez's letter to Benito Juárez indicates that the crucifixion might also have taken place at this (unfinished) temple as far back as 1867, the Santuario was not the spot where the modern crucifixion, with its text by Pérez Escrich, had originally been staged. According to Santiago Guerra, the play had come to Iztapalapa from Chimalhuacán precisely because the Cerro de la Estrella or Hill of the Star just outside Iztapalapa was an optimal height for the crucifixion. We may assume, I think, that this hill must have been the terminus of the early modern play. Indeed, in 1934, when the Santuario was still being used for the crucifixion, *El Universal* explained that "in other times" the spectacle had gone from San Lucas "up to the peak of the Hill of the Star." In those days, the reporter continues, the native who played Jesus stopped many times along the way while the faithful said the prayers attached to each of the (fourteen) Stations of the Cross. He was clearly referring to a time when a preacher essentially led an outdoor *liturgical* procession of the Three Falls.[21] This source concludes that upon reaching "the top of the Hill of the Star, [a wooden Jesus] was crucified along with the two thieves."[22]

I suspect that the reason the Cerro had ceased in the meantime to serve as Golgotha was related to the legal reforms of the later nineteenth and early twentieth centuries, which, in theory at least, forbade priests from carrying out "religious services" outdoors and essentially confined them to their churches. One can indeed witness the efforts made to separate the clerks' and the laity's activities in the newspaper reports: in 1920 *Excelsior* bravely describes a neat division of the two estates. On entering the atrium of the Santuario, the procession of the Three Falls ends, "and then began the actual religious ceremony, without any input from the play's actors, or with very discreet intervention." In 1921 *El Universal* presents us with a more complex reality, and it is this description of the Santuario, headlined "On Mt. Calvary," which, *mutatis mutandis,* the folklorist Frances Toor will again witness in 1930.[23] The scene, also preserved in a photograph of 1931 (see figs. 3 and 4), may be synthesized as follows.

In 1919, the crucifixion, "the conclusion of the masquerade" in the words of one reporter (U: 1921), was to take place on a Mount Golgotha that had been constructed on and attached to the church facade, facing out toward the atrium. More precisely, the hill was attached to the elevated second register of that façade, "at the level of the church's belfry" (U: 1921), so that a small path or Way of the Cross led from the atrium proper up the "Mount" to that level. Toor notes that the base for the figures about the crucifixion was a wood platform well above the church entrance proper, with a small path leading to it, the whole apparatus being disguised by a mass of laurel and olive branches.[24] The living Jesus's ascent up the stairs of this path was not at all easy, El Universal assures us in 1921, with Excelsior in 1933 giving one reason why: José Galicia, who was playing Jesus, was ridiculed by the Romans every step of the way. At that point "sleight of hand" came into play. El Universal in 1921 describes how, once the cross was raised into place by ropes attached to the belfry, the flesh and blood Jesus who had climbed the path stepped (through a window) into the upper register of the church and hid behind its choir, while others from that same position produced a wooden Jesus, which was then nailed to the cross at 3 P.M. sharp. Minutes later, the flesh and blood thieves Dimas and Gestas were bound to their respective crosses, to be mocked by the soldiers.

At 6 P.M. on Good Friday of this year 1921, three hours after the wood and flesh martyrs had been crucified, they were taken down from their crosses,[25] to the accompaniment of a musical overture, "the bugles of the legionnaires, the clicking of cameras, [the explosion of] dynamite cartridges, and the sepulchral silence of the spectators." But that was not yet the end of the representation. In the same 1921 account, El Universal follows with a description of another procession that came after the trio's descent from the cross. It was the customary procession of the Santo Entierro, or funeral procession of the (image of the) dead Jesus, followed by the whole court, making its way by an unstated route back to the Santuario. Once arrived at this church, the statue was laid in a glass coffin, which then was "buried" in the rear of the church, to be watched over by Veronica, Mary Magdalene, Joseph (!), and John. A wooden statue of Mary was also there, surrounded by the apostles, and she quickly enough became the object of worship for thousands of the faithful, who one by one came forward, kissed her gown, and left alms. This scene is also easily identifiable. It is the conventional quasi-liturgical wake of the Pésame or Condolences, an honor paid the virgin on the death of her son. A live St. Peter made his presence felt here. Dressed in a bright white mantle and shiningly bald, he tried with his censer "to asphyxiate the faithful," as our source merrily notes. At 8 P.M. the sermon of the Pésame ended, as did the spectacle as a whole. Tired, the Indians headed for home. They had finished their *pasión de bulto, as they call it,"* that is, a representation of events performed in a church with sculpted images.

No overview of these early representations of the passion would be complete without some notice of the participants' clothing. From the little the reporters had to say about masks, for instance, it is clear that they no longer played any central part in the passion representations either at Iztapalapa, or in the whole Valley of Mexico. In the regions along the Gulf of California they can still be found in use, but at the country's center masks had by now been largely consigned to the period of carnival.[26] *El Tiempo*'s Holy Week account of 1900 spoke of "the *huehuenches* and the masks [or "masques"?] they make of Caiaphas, of [Simon the] Cyrene, and of the centurions," used in the Valley, but not by name in Iztapalapa. Indeed, in our pueblo the only possible reference to character masks is in *Excelsior*'s 1921 report, where the person of Caiaphas— the prime object of the audience's rancor—was said to be "truly ugly," and "slightly grotesque" twelve years later (*E:* 1933). The Iztapalapan Nazarenes wore masks, but they may have been no more than penitential face covers. An important collection of old passion masks from Tzintzuntzán has unfortunately been lost.[27]

The reporters have more to say about the clothing worn by the players of these years, often to prove that the plays' content was anachronistic. To the mind of the *Excelsior* reporter, the most out-of-place element of the 1920 passion play was the March of the Dragon played by the local orchestra, but usually it was inappropriate clothing that was viewed as the main violator of decent sensibilities. In addition to the strange apparitions we have already mentioned, in the descriptions of 1919 and 1921 we read of pharisees dressed as diplomats, Hebrew scribes with doublets from the time of Henry IV, rabbis with trousers, centurions wearing Prussian helmets made of gold or silver leaf, Pontius Pilate wearing a magnificent kimono sewn with a gold dragon, and Roman soldiers wearing short capes "of the type used at the time of the Medici."

To be sure, the locals did not know what clothing would be proper to Near Easterners of the first century. And doubtless, they may have favored such outlandish wear to draw an audience. But the simplest explanation for such bizarre costumes is that the Iztapalapans in the first half of the twentieth century rented much of their clothing from the second-hand shops and theaters in town.[28] Clearly, now and later they lacked both the expertise in the history of costume and the money to commission such appropriate threads.

A particular type of clothing which reporters highlighted both now and in later periods was so-called Apache dress. What this was is not always transparent. Thus in 1897 it is said without elaboration that two *sayones* who performed the (feigned) flagellation of Jesus were "dressed like Apaches," and one is tempted to think the author meant simply dressed, embellished perhaps with pieces of animal skin, as one still sees these figures wear today.[29] Yet in 1930 Toor describes Barabbas, another person ranked low on the civilization scale, as "dressed like an Apache"—outfitted in "a short skirt with many ruffles and a shirt adorned with spangles—making the public laugh."[30] "Gauche" may be the best translation for Apache dress.

From these early accounts it is clear that the newspaper men (and later women) approached the Iztapalapan passions with certain preconceptions and thus viewed them through particular lenses, and we must be cognizant of these reportorial stances to avoid being misled. The authors rightly and repeatedly characterize the plays as reconstructions of the Bible story, even as a "complete historical resurrection" of the passion, from which nothing essential was omitted (E: 1920). They then critique any given passion when elements of its presentations were not faithful to the biblical account. We might object that the text the actors followed was, after all, a novel.[31] But the reporters themselves were comparing what they saw to what they remembered from their own upbringing. They therefore sometimes overlaid their observation of the Iztapalapan passion with a particularly old-fashioned, rigid attitude toward this "picturesque spectacle" (E: 1920). At other times this rigidity came from the editor, not the reporter. How else can one explain that in these years

Excelsior reports nothing of the rough, devilish side of the performance of the Three Falls so well documented in 1921 by *El Universal?* Obviously, that rakishness was not what the passion play meant to *Excelsior,* and definitely not what that journal wanted its readers to glean from its reportage. Further evidence of reportorial interpretation is found in that same paper's passion story of 1920, where the writer traces the Iztapalapan play to its missionary past. Iztapalapa was a pre-Hispanic city, he informs us, one of whose glories was that it had been ruled by Cuitláhuac, the successor of Moctezuma. Likewise, the town's passion play was a direct descendant of the Mendicant-inspired theater of the Conquest. "The Indians of Ixtapalapa," he said, "admirably preserve the traditions that their missionaries created among them," and spectators in 1920 got a "firm *(enrocadora)* vision of the plays the sixteenth-century friars had used to illustrate the mysteries proclaimed by the church to those neophytes of the Catholic religion." Thus neither the plays nor the players stood within the currents of history as the actors and products of a mestizo culture. Rather, as the *Excelsior* writer says in 1921, this passion and death of Jesus was "one of the typical manifestations of our civilized aboriginal pueblos."[32] No room for the antics of Barabbas in this interpretation of the Iztapalapan passion!

One last noteworthy convention that the reporters of these years repeated endlessly was their characterization of the Iztapalapan passion as a "curious profane-religious spectacle" (*E:* 1920 and 1933) or a "pagan-religious" spectacle (*E:* 1988). So self-understood was this phrase to readers that I only encountered an explanation in 1983, when *El Universal* equated "religion" with "piety" in the formulation "half pious and half pagan," so that "profane" or "pagan" was equivalent to irreverence, "religion" to "piety," that is, solemnity and formalism. This apparent meaning of the term is, incidentally, in keeping with the Spanish word "religion," which, different from "religiosity," refers only to solemn clerical behavior. Thus the term "pagan" clearly alludes to the indigenous, nonclerical, often irreverent aspects of the passion presented at Iztapalapa. It would have been heresy in this, as in most ages, to suggest that irreverence is in fact the precondition for awe in the presence of sacred persons and things.[33]

Thus despite their lay status, the *Excelsior* and *El Universal* reporters of these years always presumed, as did the clergy, that a solemn recollection of the Christian savior was the only type of memory that was appropriate, even though in the biblical accounts the course of the historical Way of the Cross had in fact been dominated by the derision of Jesus. The days when the Iztapalapan celebrations might come to seem a gold mine for the city and even the country as a whole had not yet arrived, and thus a strongly negative attitude toward the passion play was still in vogue, even in *El Universal*. In 1921, after affording its readers such a marvelously detailed account of the total affair, the newspaper ended the story by calling on the cathedral clergy and the civil authorities to suppress the spectacle. It was less the ridicule heaped on the savior that bothered the writer than the drunken brawls that took place in the atria of both churches.[34] For decades to come denunciations of *pulque* (a beer-like drink made of fermented cactus juice) at the fiesta would emblematize the church and state's determination to render the streets of modern Mexico decorous.

In summary, the outstanding feature of the Iztapalapan passions of the years 1919–1921 is their more or less fixed axis, which ran from the church of San Lucas to that of the Santuario, even if that uniform passage concealed a wealth of shifting details as year by year the citizens attempted to meet or subvert the legal requirements of state and church regarding the use of space and images. Second, and just as important, was the conflict between principled forces of good and evil, or better, of solemnity and profanation, performed by actors whose leading lights played the roles of the enemies of Christendom. Third and last, the emergence of a young boy playing the thirty-three-year-old Jesus (and an eight-year-old child playing his mother Mary), brings together the previous observations. For rather than appointing an adult to play this humiliating role, the Iztapalapans chose a child Jesus to supplant at least in part the established wooden image of an older Jesus that had been customary at an earlier time. Just as a statue was once whipped and derided, so now a young boy would be the object of the derision heaped on Jesus by the adult "Jews and Romans."

After the 1921 play, what had now come to be called an "annual event" was brought to a halt for nine long years.[35] The reasons for this long hiatus were both ecclesiastical and openly political in nature. In 1922, *El Universal* summed up the processions of previous years by saying that the man (or rather boy) who played Jesus "was truly rendered a martyr; only the crucifixion was simulated." But the rigor of these earlier performances had been converted into something like a fiesta, leading to the suspension of the procession of the Three Falls for the current year.[36] (The following year the journal informed its readers that the archbishop himself was the source of this prohibition of Good Friday representations in Iztapalapa.) The *El Universal* writer of 1922 was sure that churches would benefit if such outdoor lay activities were suppressed, and as evidence he claimed that the services within the Santuario on Good Friday 1922 were unusually splendid and the sermons very well attended sans the external events. But the same newspaper's reporter a year later knew better. No popular devotions in Holy Week, he said, no flocks. At Iztapalapa, in neighboring Mexicalzingo, in Santa Anita and at Iztacalco, attendance at liturgical services was low. In general, he observed, "one can say that the enthusiasm that once was present in those places during the 'Holy Days' has disappeared."[37]

And yet there was no turning back, a conservative editorial the next day in the same paper averred. The ecclesiastical authority had necessarily suppressed the indigenous passions of the "outlying parishes" like Azcapotzalco, Coyoacán, and Iztacalco, because of their excesses. It was a new world, he wrote. The archbishop had no choice but to fight back, because all had become speculation and lucre!

In addition to the ecclesiastical prohibition resulting from the clergy's opposition to the plays, the latter part of the decade erupted in a veritable war between the Mexican state and church, that of the Cristeros. That conflict was heralded in Iztapalapa in 1926, as *Excelsior* reported on Holy Saturday. On Holy Thursday, solemn ceremonies in San Lucas had brought to an end extensive repairs made to that church. The rector blessed the church that day, he continued, and on the following day helped carry out the ecclesiastical liturgy of Good Friday. "But the traditional reenactment of the passion and death of the Lord was not done," he said. "Due to the developing severity of the federal authorities in the application of constitutional precepts, the typical representation of the Tragedy of Golgotha was not carried out as in previous years." Those who had come from the city to see the play had nothing to do, alas, but visit Iztapalapa's *chinampas*. The danger of civil unrest was tangible, and three months later, on 31 July, the archbishop, furious at President Plutarco Calles's enforcement of the Constitution of 1917, imposed a clerical strike on the whole country, with grave implications for Holy Week 1927.[38] In the *Calendario*, Galván reports that in that year "for the first time in the history of Mexico the religious ceremonies of Holy Week were not celebrated."[39] Indeed, for three full years thereafter, some of the most basic clerical services were suppressed as the church struggled with the republic. In some cases, the churches were put into the hands of citizen committees that led prayers, responsoria, and singing, and who knows, in some places perhaps even attempted to stage the *Tres Caídas* as well.[40] We hear of a woman directing services from the pulpit of a church in the capital, and of the laity there performing the clerical liturgy of the Washing of the Feet on Holy Thursday. Other churches in the capital, bereft of the great flowered monuments or decorated "sepulchers" of Jesus proper to that day, seemed abandoned, while the customary processions of the Seven Houses that same evening to those different monuments proved a shadow of their former selves.[41]

This general prohibition of cult by both the state and the church in late 1926 and 1927 could not have failed to have an impact on Iztapalapa's rites, especially since the archbishop had specifically recommended that his faithful abstain from "dramatic representations of passages from the passion."[42] And in fact, the nine-year suspension of that pueblo's celebration continued. Indeed, according to *Excelsior* in 1933, the same prelate had in 1928 specifically suppressed any representation of the passion in the atrium of the Santuario.[43] Only in 1930 did the "annual" and thereafter indeed uninterrupted passion play of Iztapalapa begin.

5

fROM DUALISM TO NARRATIVE
IN THE DEPRESSION

In 1933, a seventy-year-old participant in the Iztapalapan passion told the reporter for *El Universal* that after a long period of unrest, the spectacle of the passion and death of Jesus was back on track, "as long as the images are not removed from the churches." His confidence proved indeed justified, for without exception, from 1930 until the present, some or all of the total spectacle has been carried out each year. Writing around 1935, in one of the earliest essays dedicated to the Iztapalapan passion, Higinio Vázquez Santa Ana described the difference between the "old days" and the new by recording elements of the traditional passion that were now on their way out: "In earlier times, there were many pious acts, like that of the Three Falls, in which the priests intervened with sermons that were pronounced in the same atrium [of the Santuario], like the Sermon of the Lance and that of Consolation. There was [also] a devout procession at 9 P.M. with the true Christ [in the Eucharist] and with the Dead Jesus [*el Santo Entierro*], in which all present joined with lit candles."[1]

This observer lived in an age when pressures of various sorts were diminishing the homiletic and ecclesiastical cast of the passion, despite the desires of the clergy. The church might denounce the laity's play, as it did, for instance, in 1942, dissatisfied as usual with the noncanonical character of the texts. But in the end, it always capitulated to the leading citizens of the borough—who still felt honored to assume the principal anti-Christian roles—and allowed the use of the Vanegas Arroyo text of the *Cuatro Concilios* (U: 1941, 1939, 1942). Then, too, visitors impatiently fled the sermons to watch the crucifixion, which was slowly becoming the highlight and thus the *telos* of all Good Friday activity. After it, people tended to go home, and as a result, even the previously important procession of the Santo Entierro, in which the wooden body of Jesus was returned to the Santuario on Good Friday evening, slowly sank into relative neglect. We shall see what precipitated that neglect in the following pages. Needless to say, the spectacle evolved substantially, and it is my goal to describe not just the details of the continuities, but the dynamic changes to which the spectacle was subject.

The span of years in this chapter, from 1930 to 1944, covers the Depression and much of the Second World War, during which Mexico remained neutral. Internally, this period saw the end of the anticlerical Calles regime, the presidency of Lázaro Cárdenas, and the reign of Manuel Ávila Camacho, the first twentieth-century president of Mexico to declare himself a Catholic and the one who began the process of reconciliation of the Revolution with the church.

With regard to Iztapalapa, for the first time information on the planning of the spectacle becomes available. In addition, in these same years the reporters give us the first detailed descriptions of events performed on Holy Thursdays and Saturdays, as well as important new details regarding the judgment and sentencing of Jesus on Good Friday. These stories help to formulate an overview of the whole spectacle during most of the first half of the century. Reporters also provide the first extended descriptions of the interaction of the players with the spectators, allowing us to assess the role of women in the total spectacle. In this period evidence also mounts for a slow but decisive change in the moral thrust of the play: the movement from a dualistic performance of the passion to a narrative in which the actors playing the bad people, though still very much present, are unmistakably rejected, making for a slow, halting victory of solemnity over irreverence. During these years, too, newspapers began, again haltingly, to imagine a positive future for the Iztapalapan spectacle. Not only reporters, but the people who staged and supported the performances were now seriously examining the commercial possibilities for Iztapalapa and for Mexico at large.[2]

Only one chief organizer of the performances of Holy Week in the old days is known to us by name (Marcelino Buendía in 1914); beginning in 1934, however, this personage, first in the person of the local businessman Luis de la Rosa, assumes a definite profile. In that year, *El Universal* tells us, the tryouts and role assignments took place in de la Rosa's house on two successive nights; the actors left the clothes they would wear on the following days in that same house.[3] These clothes passed on from father to son over the years. Since de la Rosa was still head of the organization in 1938, it is perhaps right to think of this merchant and his house as the fulcrum for the preparation and execution of the yearly spectacle in the fifteen years under consideration.[4]

The absence of information regarding Holy Thursday and Holy Saturday events in the accounts before 1930 means only that reporters did not stay overnight. They came to the pueblo on Good Friday morning and returned to the center that same evening with their copy for the Holy Saturday editions. That journalistic habit would not change in the coming years, but in the meantime, two scholars, Frances Toor in 1930 and Higinio Vázquez ca. 1935 did stay overnight when they came to Iztapalapa and thus witnessed the whole event, writing substantial accounts of the activities of Holy Thursday and Holy Saturday as well as Good Friday. From these two narratives, as well as from occasional newspaper clips from these years, we know that here in Iztapalapa, as elsewhere, the dramatic events of Holy Thursday were the Last Supper of Jesus and his apostles, including his Washing of their Feet and his Prayers in the Garden of Gethsemane while the apostles slept. Overlapping these actions were Judas's Pact with the Pharisees and the subsequent Expedition of Spies and a Dog to discover the whereabouts of Jesus. Next came Judas's Kiss and the Arrest of Jesus on the Mount of Olives *(Prendimiento)*, followed by and concluding with his overnight Imprisonment *(Aposentillo)*.

Frances Toor begins her description of the 1930 events at Iztapalapa by stating that, after a nine-year pause, the events of that year continued a previously established tradition.[5] This assures us that the events of Holy Thursday in Iztapalapa, like those of Good Friday, were well established before this interruption, a fact we could not establish from the newspaper sources. According to Vázquez, the first action came early in the day, when the pharisees appeared, running through the streets and crying at the top of their voices that they were looking for Jesus of Nazareth, who was to be tried as a false prophet and deceiver of the people, "and as someone who did not want tribute to be paid to Caesar."[6] Incidentally, this idea of Jesus (or the Church?) as a tax dodger was an established one among the Iztapalapans. *Excelsior* in 1931 describes mounted *sayones* riding from place to place hoping that Jesus would be surrendered to them. Thus Holy Thursday began with various enemies of Jesus running or riding through the streets to seize a false prophet and give him over to popular justice.[7]

According to Toor, in 1930 the Last Supper, including the Washing of the Feet, took place in the Santuario, in the cave behind the main altar where the Cuevita was kept.[8] Apparently playing Jesus at table, the parish priest in that year was surrounded by "humble Indians" (Toor) playing the apostles. Vázquez describes in great detail the behavior, food, table decorations, and clothing of the apostles at that Supper.[9] Later that night, as both Vázquez and Toor note, a procession took form near the center of the town with many of the main actors dressed in fine rented clothing. They were bearded, Toor opines, to show more dignity. Included in the procession were the Nazarenes on foot, a group of old men. In effect, this was a procession from the Santuario to the parish church of San Lucas. At a certain point, Toor says, an image of Jesus seated on a litter and surrounded by a scenic garden of Gethsemane appeared and was borne into the parish church.[10] Perhaps this is where the story of Gethsemane was acted out in these years, for, though he does not specify the place, Vázquez seems to be referring to the area around San Lucas. More generally, it should be noted that both the Last Supper and Jesus's Prayers were enacted within the two main churches of the city.

After the figure or tableau of Jesus was ensconced in San Lucas, writes

Toor, a live Judas left the church with his spies and dogs and traversed the streets of the town looking for Jesus. Here is another scene of free-ranging individuals racing about in search of the intended divine victim. The traditional mad white dogs of the passion, described by Vázquez as wearing colored collars, would endure until 1976, when they were dropped from the performance.[11] But the spies or "multitude of phari-sees," in Vázquez' words, headed by Malco as mentioned in the gospel of John (18.10; *U*: 1941 and passim) seem much more significant, as we may intimate on reading Toor's description of the passion play at Tzintzuntzán (Michoacán) in 1925 and Foster's of the same site c. 1940. Toor identifies these "pharisees acting as spies" as young boys, so disre-spectful as to stop at every cross in their path and blow their whistles de-risively, a direct insult to Jesus and Christianity.[12] Foster notes that 96 boys, all about 18 years of age, took part in this rite in Tzintzuntzán. In the old days, he says, these spies began their activity not on Holy Thurs-day, but the previous day, Holy Wednesday, when they would first ride bareback and shoeless through parallel streets. They of course repre-sented the men who historically spied on Jesus and took him off to be sentenced, but, according to Foster, they also made sure then and later that no one was at work in the high holy days of this sacred week.[13] We cannot be sure that they ever exercised this latter role in Iztapalapa, to be sure, but it is worth keeping the connection in mind. The image is one of quasi-popular justice, the historical "populace" being, of course, the peo-ple of Jerusalem.

Soon after Judas and his spies and dogs left San Lucas, they encoun-tered Jesus praying in the Garden of Gethsemane, where he was placed under arrest by Malco. I earlier surmised that in Vázquez's time, c. 1935, Gethsemane was near or in San Lucas. But by 1941, according to *El Uni-versal*, it was on "a hill *(loma)* bordering on the church of the Calvary," that is, the Santuario. Judas then identified his victim with his kiss and Je-sus fell into the hands of the soldiers, who accused him before the au-thorities on the platform of the atrium of San Lucas. Toor specifies that the Jesus brought there for trial was "a *muchacho* representing Jesus." He was pulled by a rope tied around his neck and his head was already fitted out with a crown of thorns.[14] Holy Thursday then drew to an end with little Jesus being led to a prison where he would spend the night. Sig-nificantly, Toor in 1930 says that inside the church of San Lucas a (living)

Jesus was lashed to a tree,[15] while *Excelsior* the following year identified the *Aposentillo* or cell *(cárcel)* as located on the outskirts of the pueblo, "very near the trees planted originally by the Franciscan friars, who still harvest the olives."[16] Vázquez also found him there, being ridiculed by the "Jews, who yelled: "You say you are a king; where is your power," and "Where are those who would defend you? You are a madman, you are an impostor!"[17]

The scene at San Lucas that visitors saw when they arrived in Iztapalapa the morning of Good Friday was little changed, with only some new details emerging in the years 1930–1944. We learn in *El Universal* in 1933, for example, that that day's drama began with Pontius Pilate asking the Jews how they wanted Jesus to die. The Jesus who stood there to be sentenced was, throughout this period, a youngster, a native boy of such a young age that the *mayordomos* of the representation did not dare outfit him with a beard.[18] At this point, Pontius Pilate, saluted as the very "president of the republic" in these years (U: 1939), and in real life usually also the head of the organizing Comité, washed his hands of the affair, and then pitched the water that had fallen into the vase below his outstretched hands onto the audience, a moment of hilarity in the midst of tragedy that remained a standard feature of the judgment for some years after 1939 (U: 1940, 1941).[19] The sentence was then read aloud, while a herald rode about Iztapalapa announcing that Jesus was to be crucified.[20] The young Jesus was then led off to be whipped. In one reporter's words, Jesus's (feigned) flagellation in this period "occupied a signal place in the live commemoration that the natives staged." (E: 1933). In 1931 some 20,000 people stood "to one side and the other of a broad enclosure [which formed] the theater of the representation," the air filled with the ridicule and jokes that were directed against the boyish man/ God (also E: 1933). Nor were these whippings merely make-believe at that time or, often, thereafter (fig. 5). Indeed, an *Excelsior* reporter remarked in 1932 that the organizers "impeded the commission of the assassinations *(atentados)* of previous years, in which [while women wept] the native who played the Nazarene was cruelly whipped."[21]

Because of "special circumstances," as *Excelsior* mysteriously informs us in 1933, the Way of the Cross or *Tres Caídas* was not held in 1931 or 1932. Without the Three Falls, what was left were the quasi-ecclesiastical activities at the churches of San Lucas and the Santuario, and so we may suspect that these "circumstances" were related to lay-clerical tensions. But that great lay procession did in fact take place in 1933 and thereafter, forming an inextinguishable part of the total passion experience. It formed in the streets around San Lucas. Flags were unfurled to lead the way, and they might include not only that of Rome (S. P. Q. R.), but that of Mexico and even those of France and Belgium (U: 1941)! The young Jesus carried his cross through the streets, followed by the penitential Nazarenes, who (according to Vázquez, confirming Toor) were still elderly men between 50 and 60 years of age.[22] The two thieves as well marched to their death, and in El Universal of 1940 we see them alongside Jesus, wearing the broad sombreros of the Mexican peasantry (fig. 6).

Noteworthy in the Three Falls' processions of these years is the music, originally the Nazarenes' hymns (Vázquez transcribes a text of one such song).[23] But more distinctive are the sounds of traditional indigenous musical instruments, often commented on in these years. Easily the most often mentioned native instrument, "the chirimía sounds its lugubrious melody," remarks Vázquez, "and the Nazarenes [intone] their sad and melancholy songs."[24] Beyond the chirimía, which "cried out in [a mysterious] profound sadness" (U: 1933; Vázquez), there were the large drums (tambores), and Vázquez also mentions "the famous teponaxtles" and the fifes (pitos) as part of the native assemblage of music.[25] It is true that the sounds of these instruments had a profound effect on the capitalinos who heard them; it is just as certain, however, that several reporters also noted the "cacophony" of sound of which these indigenous instruments were a part (U: 1933). Not only did the military-style civic band that played the Marcha Dragón along with various overtures and arias (U: 1921; E: 1933) contribute to the "noise," but also the music from phonographs and radios, which the commune at one point tried to limit (E: 1946). And yet the native music survived elsewhere. Though nowhere near as popular in the more modern Iztapalapan passions—later reformers promised that this "grotesque music will be done away with" (E: 1957)—in the capital proper largely hispanicized citizens later revived the native music and instruments in a move to preserve the Mexican past.[26]

The second significant motif in reporting the procession of the Three Falls during these years is the presence of women. That certain women took on individual identities will not surprise those who know their Bible. There was Mary the mother of Jesus, then Mary Magdalene, and Mary the wife of Clopas, the traditional Three Marys. Veronica was also an important presence, since she would wipe the face of Jesus at her station in the Way of the Cross. But beyond these particular women there were those labeled by the gospel and our sources as the "virgins" or as the "pious women of Jerusalem," and in their numbers and despite the domination of the whole performance by men, this group together formed an important unit within the procession of the Three Falls.[27]

Before the earliest mention of women's function in the Iztapalapan sources (E: 1919), we know from earlier Mexican sources that the most important (if marginal) role of women in the passion processions was to wail at certain points (fig. 7). In describing the Tacubayan preparations for that town's 1840 passion, Guillermo Prieto documents the organizers' "raising a rigorous levy of pious old women, [and] timid and hypocritical girls for the famous procession of mourning," that is, for the Santo Entierrro or burial of Jesus after his Descent from the Cross.[28] Obviously, women came to specialize in such behavior much as did the *lamentatrices* of old and were praised for being able to cry spontaneously or doing so on command (E: 1946; U: 1970; E: 1987; E: 1999).

A second function of women, the ability to prophesy, was reserved to a particular thespian, Claudia, the wife of Pontius Pilate. She warns her husband now and ever more that she had been told in a dream that Jesus was the true lord (U: 1933, 1946).

The third and most fascinating function of women in the Iztapalapan passion was to represent Iztapalapan ideals of beauty. It is clear that the organizers of the Comité chose the girls destined to play roles through rudimentary beauty contests. Reporters repeatedly called the women, apparently all of native extraction, "pretty," "beautiful," or "comely" (*linda*).[29] That is why they were in the play in the first place. "For the roles of the virgin and of the Magdalene one chose the prettiest ladies of the pueblo," Vázquez recorded.[30] The *santas mujeres, El Universal* reported in 1940, were all indigenous women. These "prettiest local brown girls" had been "chosen" to represent the women of the gospels. "Note the Magdalene's beauty," read the caption under that woman's photograph in the same paper's 1944 story (fig. 8). That year's Veronica was a "very pretty" (*guapísima*) native, as she was again in 1945, when *El Universal* spoke of the wife of Caiaphas and other damsels being "selected from

among the pretty girls of the pueblo." Reporters emphasized both individual and group beauty. If Claudia, the wife of Pontius Pilate, was in *El
Universal*'s 1944 pages *una bella indígena;* so were her ladies in waiting, as
the same paper's 1945 story noted. They had, after all, been chosen from
among the pretty girls of the population.

Thus the male leaders of the community, perhaps in accord with its
older women, have historically used the annual passion play and other
occasions as well to display to the world those they considered the
town's most beautiful young girls and women. Each year, for example,
the pueblo sent one such girl to nearby Xochimilco to compete in a still-
functioning annual beauty contest for "the most beautiful flower of the
ejido" (U: 1965). The passion women too were so many Miss Iztapalapas:
biblical figures, yes, but also the objects of desire of the adult political
males of the population.[31]

At the same time, the distinction between the Christian and the non-
Christian women was clearly drawn. For all their beauty, the former
were simply clothed, as befit their religion. Hence the true female orna-
ments of the play were, rather, the ladies who formed the court around
the non-Christian and Jewish elite figures—Pilate, Herod, Caiaphas,
Annas, and the like. Just as important in this respect were the fantasti-
cally attired male enemies of Jesus, whose exoticism drew the regular attention of reporters. Complaining again of anachronism, *El Universal*'s
writer in 1944 said that while the actors looked vaguely like the ancients, their clothing smacked rather of the notorious spangles of the
huehuenches, with mirrors, colored glass, feathers and gaudy belts prominent in their outfits. These well-outfitted "pagan" male and female figures, together with the simply dressed Christian men and women of
natural beauty, formed two strands that were meant to ornament the
doomed savior about to be sacrificed.

It is interesting to observe how at so many levels "pagans" took the or-
namental and comedic lead. Certainly in earlier times richly dressed pagans were featured in passion plays controlled by the clergy because
the latter wanted to show how these lush pagans lost out in the end to
triumphant Christianity. For their part, the lay men and women who
played Romans and Jews in these plays may also have felt at times that by
playing enemies of Christianity they too contributed to the triumph of
the faith by coaxing out the religious sentiments of their thespian opposites.[32] At the same time, the joy at being able to glitter certainly moved

some of them. My idea is that as the laity of Iztapalapa developed their own play, whose *Tres Caídas* were being performed with less and less clerical input, the exotic pagan figures in these processions lost their homiletic meaning and came to seem to audiences a wondrous expression of the secular imagination.

To the prominence of music and of women must be added a third journalistic emphasis, which begins to get at the heart of what gives the Iztapalapan *Tres Caídas* its identity, at least in the first two-thirds of this century: that is, reports on the interaction between the actors and the still largely indigenous audience. One reporter says early on: "The most curious thing . . . is that the multitude takes part in the ceremony," with its role being an essential part of the total affect of the play (*U:* 1939). In the years before 1930, we found a strong dualism especially marked in the action *within* the performance, but after 1930, to some extent that dualism manifests itself especially in a strong polarity between the crowd and the actors. Together, in the words of *El Universal* in 1942, they "constitute a scene which is the purest manifestation of Mexican folkloric life." The details of these interactions deserve our attention.

On the surface, it might appear that the play alone continued to be the thing. In this spirit Vázquez records the still imposing presence of Barabbas, the epitome of the forces of evil. Dressed like an Apache and pulling along his enormous prisoner chains, he was followed by a multitude of natives also dressed as Apaches, the whole group hurling insults against the cross-bearing young Jesus. Yet a change is in the air. From now on, the emphasis lies as much on the spectators' punishment of Jesus's enemies as on that by other actors. In the words of *El Universal* in 1933, "each of the thousands of people present at this reconstruction desire[d] the same thing: to insult Herod, Pilate, the pharisees, the scribes, [in short] the whole malevolent and perverted rabble who wanted to lay violent hands on the Nazarene, nailing him to the cross." In a sense, then, a new type of play was taking form, in addition to that which pitted raucous actors—many still carrying their "vat full of Queen Xocitl's nectar" (*E:* 1931, that is, pulque)—against other actors: it was the play of the crowd against those finely dressed actors who persisted in torturing the "good rabbi." If not a "decent" representation of the triumph of the good, this at least marked a slight turn away from the merely thespian dualism so evident in the earlier plays.

Accompanying this increased emphasis on the interaction between au-

dience and actors came some modification of the framework of seriousness. As ever, reporters regularly railed against the irreverent actions of
those in the play, but in 1941 quite the contrary objection appears in *El
Universal*: the actors are serious, and it is the audience that is irreverent.
The latter spreads out on the ground around the place of crucifixion,
eating, singing, and drinking, in short, picnicking even while the crucifixion is carried out. Then in the following year, the same reporter spells
out his meaning: the players, whom the reporter calls *indios*, showed true
religious emotion, but the spectators were profane, as if they were at a
fair. Yet they were in fact two sides of that folkloric whole (*U*: 1942).

The first jarring encounter between the audience and the players in
the Iztapalapan passion of these years was recorded in 1933, when *El
Universal* noted that during the trial at San Lucas of Jesus before Herod,
the "gendarmes'" control of the situation crumbled before the impetus
of the crowd, "which did not want to miss a single detail." More often,
however, in these years the collision between the two camps happened
during the *Tres Caídas*. Thus that periodical's account of the following
year's via Crucis mentions for the first time "the accepted custom of
hurling *mueros* at the *sayones* who martyred the redeemer."[33] Though customary, such actions were taken as spontaneous. In 1939 women were
seen picking up dirt and hurling it at those *sayones*, an act the *El Universal*
reporter took as evidence of spontaneity: "It is curious to observe," he
wrote, "that the indignation of the crowd is authentic." Yet inversely, we
are told, "none of the native (*sayones*) took offense, because they knew
they were representing their roles" (*U*: 1934).

Such reports give us valuable insight into the psychological force of
the presentation in this era, as well as some sense of the borderline between theatrical and unplanned emotion. In many accounts from this
time forward, reporters will comment on the collision between those
who line the narrow streets of the via Crucis and the caped soldiers who
open up a path for Jesus to pass while at the same time goading the savior. The soldiers drive back the pueblo, which curses and insults the
armed men (fig. 9). Thus in a way these "armed" soldiers were actually
"victims," suffering as they did the outrages of the crowd. Indeed, such
forbearance is presented to us by *El Universal* in 1944 as the means by
which those playing *sayones* fulfilled their *mandas*, that is, the vows they
had taken on agreeing to participate in the representation: suffering such

insults was viewed by them as penance done for their sins, part of the contract these "soldiers" entered into when they joined the league of actors for the play.

The most interesting insight on the contacts between the crowd and the processors is that at times the Way of the Cross to Calvary was *purposely slowed* so as "to give the public time to insult the soldiers"! "They proceeded toward this place [of crucifixion] as slowly as possible ("con una gran lentitud"). They did this to give the public the time to insult 'the *sayones*' ("esto se hace para dar tiempo al público de que insulte a los sayones"). "Little children, men and old women uttered the worst possible things against the *sayones. Desgraciados!* Liars!, was the softest thing they called them. But they were content, precisely because they believed that suffering in this way is an obligatory penance" (*U:* 1944). Let us be clear. The pace of the Way of the Cross was timed to allow the enemies of Jesus to suffer, and give the crowd the chance to vent its rage at the impending fate of Jesus.

In discussing some of these important new elements and details of the procession of the *Tres Caídas* in these years, I have silently presumed that in this period, the Way of the Cross led from the church of San Lucas to that of the Santuario, where the crucifixion took place. However, this traditional trajectory leading to the Santuario only lasted through 1933. Almost certainly, after the performance of that year, the Santuario's position as the site of the crucifixion came to an end, perhaps because of enforcement of the already mentioned archepiscopal prohibition of representations at that site. A marked decline in newspaper coverage of the play, especially in *Excelsior,* does not help clarify the routing.[34] It is not until around 1944–45 that the route of the Iztapalapan passion reemerges in the sources, to remain more or less the same to this day.

An important change had obviously taken place in the itinerary, according to *El Universal*'s coverage of 1934. Referring first to days long past, when the Way of the Cross went from San Lucas "up to the top of the Hill of the Star (Cerro de la Estrella)," where Jesus and the thieves were crucified, the writer states that now the procession, still departing from San Lucas, went through the principal streets out to one end of the pueblo, whence it turned about and returned to the parish church.[35] This seems to imply that the actual crucifixion took place (in this year, at least) at the end-stop of San Lucas, a view that helps to date the report of

Vázquez Santa Ana, who states specifically that the crucifixion was effected within that church.

By 1939, however, the routing had shifted again, with *Excelsior* describing Jesus carrying his cross "to Mt. Calvary, that is (*o sea*) to the Hill (Cerro) of the Star." In that same year and again in 1941 *El Universal* does not refer to a mountain (Cerro de la Estrella) but to a small hillock (*loma, lomita*), so that we cannot be sure that the procession went all the way up the Cerro that towers over the town, the point that was, we are led to believe, the inspiration for bringing the *Tres Caídas* to Iztapalapa in the first place. Nonetheless, the historical memory of the Cerro de la Estrella as Golgotha was alive and well in Iztapalapa during the period when the crucifixion took place first on the facade of the Santuario, then perhaps within San Lucas, and finally on this otherwise unidentified hillock. Then in 1944, a decisive turning point seems to have been reached. *El Universal* announces that "the via Crucis was not carried out as was customary," by which the reporter meant a procession that went from "the front of the parish church to the plaza of Calvary," otherwise unidentified.[36] But now "for more realism," the organizers mounted three crosses "high up on (*en lo alto*) the Cerro de la Estrella," and from that day to this these three crosses tower over the town as a permanent monument. In the following year, the scholars Boggs and Mendoza furnish us with a map showing the location of the "Cerrito de la Muerte at the foot of Cerro de la Estrella." With that step, the organizing committee, probably with the agreement of the governmental Delegation, had restored the Cerro, since 1938 a national park, to its old place as the Iztapalapan Calvary.[37]

Fortunately for us, in 1930 the ethnographer Frances Toor stayed overnight, as reporters did not, and thus witnessed the actual culmination of events on Holy Saturday, or Glory Saturday, as Mexicans called the day. Hers is the earliest account of that day in Iztapalapa, and it provides more evidence of the ethnographic traditionalism that was so characteristic of these early years of the last century. After the thrilling singing of the Gloria! in the churches, the purple covers were pulled from the statues even as the bells pealed in and about the temples, announcing the end of Lent. The boy who had played Jesus the previous day was repulsed when he tried to enter the church, perhaps because, after all, Jesus was "dead."[38] After mass, many life-size papier-mâché Judases appeared, commemorating the apostle who had betrayed his lord. Already at this

date, at least in Mexico City proper (fig. 10), such Judases were used edu-
cationally. In addition to Judas himself, they represented devils, abstrac-
tions like alcoholism and vagrancy, and sometimes quite real enemies of
the people. Many were filled with firecrackers and attracted the children,
who delighted in their explosions, a rite whose vestiges can still be observed today in parts of Mexico (E: 1930). It was and is, of course, an un-
subtle example of the contemporary messages that often suffuse historical reenactments.[39]

With her ethnographer's eye, however, Toor saw that Holy Saturday
at Iztapalapa, much more clearly than the two previous days, was characterized by generational tensions. She describes how parents lifted up
their children by the ears on this day dominated by the punishment of
the traitor Judas, and whipped them on the buttocks with any switch
that came to hand. They did this to children who had disobeyed them,
"and as a penance so that they may be good and obey them and the Lord
during the coming year."[40] Elsewhere in Mexico at a somewhat earlier
juncture, the same generational heat was preserved, but in an inverse setting: in Sonora the "innocent" children beat their elders on Holy Saturday as punishment for the latters' sins.[41] At Iztapalapa in the 1930s,
though, elders admonished children and issued this conventional warning: "Just you wait, you'll get your Glory."[42] What emerges from this description is that, similar to traditional European and surely also native
American practices, parents brought their children out to witness this
popular justice as a warning not to violate communal norms. Nor was
that the end of it; through these very years, perhaps till mid-century, children playing Jesus on Good Friday were beaten by adults playing Roman
soldiers and executioners. It would be naive not to recognize that in the
so-called old and new worlds, the execution of Jesus was also viewed as a
visual admonition to those who did not obey their lords.

To conclude, one important thread of reportorial reflection bearing
on the future course of this spectacle is worth noting. No longer is the
talk only of doing away with the festival, as was common enough in earlier years. In these same years there evolves a new sense of the tourist
possibilities that this festival affords the town. Already in 1931 one meets
with a burgeoning sense of Iztapalapa's singularity, with *Excelsior* claiming that it "is the only pueblo that has revived the whole carnival that the
conquistadores planted in Mexico some 400 years ago." That had re-

sulted in a type of hybrid mix of "the fragrance of the fiesta and the taste of pulque (neutle), with Christian celebrations according to sixteen-century Spanish usages." Nor was the Iztapalapan passion an unremittingly disastrous doctrinal spectacle. El Universal would indeed claim in 1940 that such plays dated back to colonial times (before 1810), when the church made the fundamental decision that they were not irreverent, since they caused the natives to honor God and hate the Jews, his persecutors.[43] If the actors in these years seemed to visitors largely uncaring about what they said or did, that was of course what one might expect from such native actors, "who do nothing more than repeat the text of the Book of the Four Councils edited by Vanegas Arroyo" (U: 1941). Different from the denizens of Oberammergau, who come up with rich presentations and give the leading roles to the best available actors, "our natives, in their humility, only want to continue the traditions of their elders" in the teeth of opposition from the priests, who consider it "an actual profanation" (U: 1934, 1941). There it is. The play had been preserved across the centuries as a matter of customary right, to maintain the traditionalist organizers' efforts to defy church authority. This pedestrian goal, El Universal intuits in 1941, precisely explains why the Iztapalapan passion has the mark of a fiesta and not of a pious event about it.

Yet in the midst of such cultural musings there appeared a strong notion of cultural and fiscal possibilities. The first hint of this new attitude is found in an off-hand remark of Excelsior in 1933: although the Passion and Death of Jesus had not been as good this year as last, the writer opines, it did succeed in bringing in el turismo local. Evidently, the financial bottom line was an important consideration at this early point in time. Five years later we read that the fame of the Iztapalapan passion, done by natives, "is growing year by year" (U: 1938). In the following year, the dam bursts, and a qualitatively new note of optimism appears in El Universal. Under the headline "The Folkloric Passion of Jesus Christ. . . . Reproduced in Iztapalapa Just as It Is in Oberammergau, Germany," one reads that hundreds of people came to the play, including

a good number of tourists, who are especially attracted by our customs. The Passion of Iztapalapa is indeed far removed from the one done in Oberammergau, Germany, which year after year [it was in fact executed once every ten years] attracts thousands of tourists from every part of the world. None the less, each Good Friday the ingenious performers of the Drama of Calvary [in Iztapalapa] outdo themselves. We are certain that if these improvising actors were to receive help, suggestions, and a precise direction, their traditional fiesta could be converted into a tourist attraction of the first order, and its Delegación would be transformed into something like the Oberammergau of America. Clearly the folkloric stamp of the Iztapalapan passion, its unique ingenuity, must be retained, because its principal charm resides precisely in these characteristics. But when all is said and done, each and every impulse [helping to] orient [the activity] would be very useful.

Gone from this commentary is the dreary creole take on "our Indians" as only a problem to bemoan, replaced by a positive, realistic assessment of the native Iztapalapan population's ability to contribute to the larger commonweal.[44] And as the pueblo of Iztapalapa emerges onto the planning board of Mexican national tourist strategies, so are its actors finally individuated. No longer do we find the pueblo's Jesus regularly identified in photographs only as "the indigenous person who plays the Nazarene" (E: 1934, 1936; U: 1939, 1945). In 1941 and commonly thereafter, El Universal's reporter goes out of his way to ferret out and list the proper names of the Iztapalapans playing the major roles. Indeed, as El Universal easily states in 1945, "a [passion] play of this quality" ("esta clase de actos") could be found in only two places, Oberammergau and Iztapalapa.

Throughout the fifteen years covered in this chapter, the opposition of the local clergy to the performance of the outdoor processions and texts by the laity was unremitting but unsuccessful, largely because the Mexican government opposed church initiatives in this area, an antagonism that was anchored in the state constitution's prohibition of church statues or clergy being employed in the public streets. Yet toward the end of our period, a partial rapprochement between the two powers took place that was a portent of the future history of the Iztapalapan play. The newspapers reporting on Holy Week in

Iztapalapa give no sign of this rapprochement, but in covering a Good Friday service in 1976 in the section of La Candelaria, Coyoacán, to the north of Iztapalapa and within Mexico City, *El Universal* provides precious information on this change in course. According to this account, a certain Eusebio García Santamaría reminded the reporter that there had been passion plays in Coyoacán since 1586, until they were suspended in the 1870s. We have documented both these facts. As we know, that was precisely the time of the anticlerical enabling legislation for the Constitution of 1867. Now things had changed, García told the reporter, and he had been representing Pontius Pilate for thirty-five years since 1941, not four months, we might add, after President Ávila Camacho assumed office: "After [this] Catholic cult could again be freely practiced. For years before that, we could not do that because they would have lynched us. There were those [at the time] who thought that the Catholic church in Mexico would shut down permanently. And yet you see that quite the opposite has taken place. We have regained the free use of the streets!"

From a macrocosmic point of view, it is evident that this change of policy would have encouraged many a town and village to start their own passion play, not least to compete with that of Iztapalapa. From our microcosmic vantage point, however, it is just as clear that in Iztapalapa the clergy would try again in the coming decade and a half to reassert its control over the Passion and Death of Jesus.

1. Anonymous. "A Good Friday Procession of the Sixteenth Century." This shows Jesus's burial procession or Santo Entierro on the evening of Good Friday. In order are shown trumpeters; a wagon pulling the sarcophagus accompanied by Death; three (confraternal) banners; a group carrying the instruments of the passion; four secular and eight religious clergy; the Santo Entierro or wooden "corpse" with four litterbearers; a flagbearer; Our Lady of Sorrows with four litterbearers; eleven flagellants; St. Peter with four litterbearers; and Mary Magdalene. Drawing, location unknown; reproduced from González Obregón, *México viejo*, 472.

2. The atrium of the parish church of San Lucas. Before the 1960s this was the site with stands for the Jewish priests, Herod, and Pontius Pilate, who here sentenced Jesus and had him whipped. Beyond the portal of the atrium lies the modern esplanade (once ancient marketplace), where all this action now takes place. Photograph by the author.

3. The facade of Iztapalapa's Santuario. Photograph by the author.

4. Mount Calvary, elevated to the level of the second story of the facade of the Santuario, with brush covering the Way of the Cross. Until 1933, the person playing Jesus would step through the window into the upper interior of the church once he had been "crucified." Reproduced from Luna Parra, *150 años*, 37 (1931).

5. The Flagellation of Jesus, performed in the atrium of San Lucas in 1959. Archivo de *La Prensa*. Reproduced from Luna Parra, *150 años*, 49.

6. The two thieves, Gestas and Dimas, wearing "showy sombreros" and with hands bound, accompany Jesus to Calvary in 1940. Note that the thieves were taller than Jesus. Reproduced from *U*: 23 March.

7. The pious women wail at Jesus's third fall in 1992. Photograph by Eloy Valtierra. Reproduced from Luna Parra, *150 años*, 77.

8. Second from left, Santiago Guerra, the long-serving Pontius Pilate and head of the Comité Organizador. On the far right, "note the beauty of the Magdalene." Reproduced from *U*: 8 April 1944.

9. A *sayón* attacks the crowd in 1972. Photograph by Guillermo Aguilar Olivares. Reproduced from Luna Parra, *150 años*, 92.

10. The Burning of the Judases in central Mexico City, c. 1920. Archivo Casasola. Reproduced from *Los Judas de Diego Rivera*, 37.

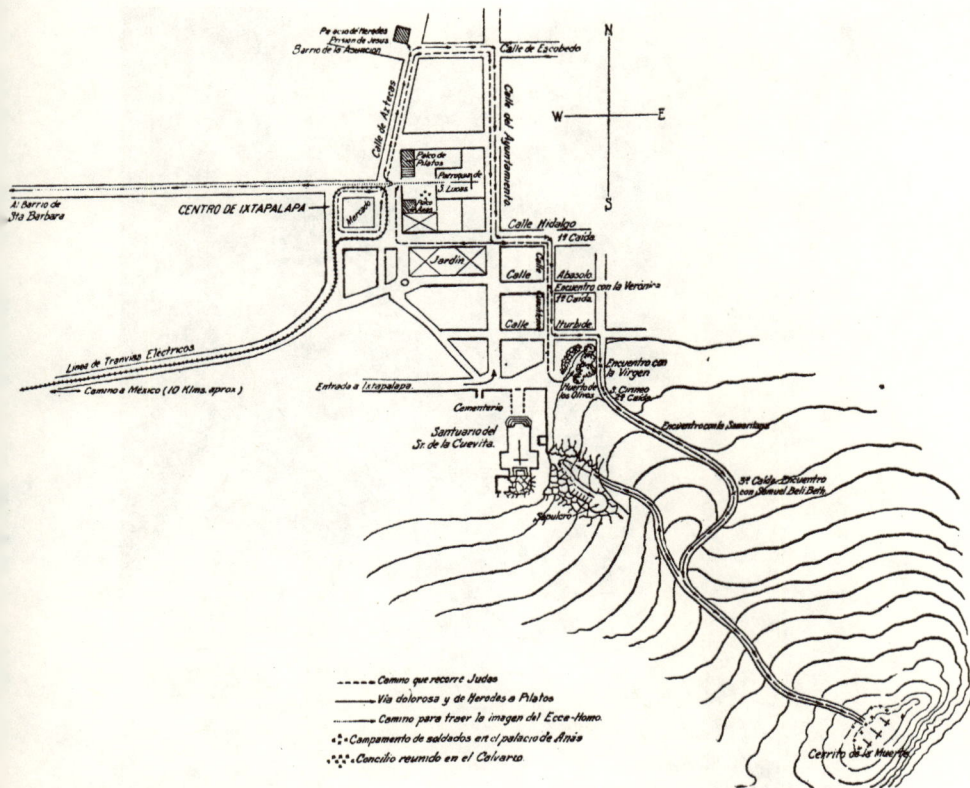

11. "Routes followed during the representation." Earliest itinerary or map of the Iztapalapan passion. Along with much else, it shows the fixed locations of Jesus's first, second, and third fall. Reproduced from Boggs and Mendoza, "Representación," 164.

12. Through a microphone, Mary mourns with Jesus. Reproduced from *U*: 2 April 1983.

13. Unusually, a priest directs activities at the crucifixion on the Cerro de la Estrella. Reproduced from *U:* 20 April 1957.

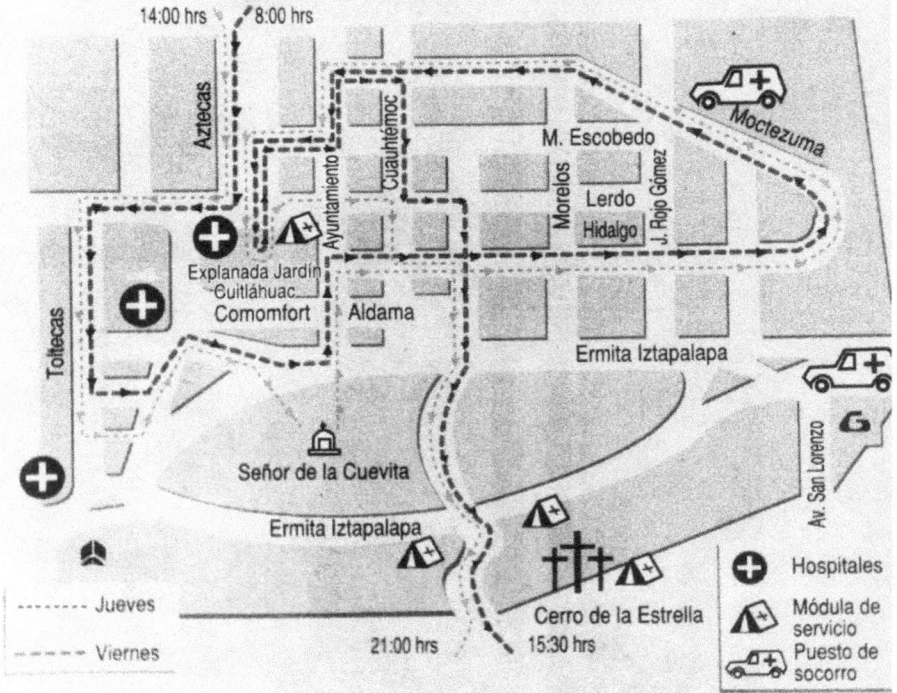

Procesión en Iztapalapa

14:00 hrs   8:00 hrs

Aztecas

Cuauhtémoc

Ayuntamiento

M. Escobedo

Moctezuma

Morelos

Lerdo

J. Rojo Gómez

Hidalgo

Explanada Jardín
Cuitláhuac
Comomfort   Aldama

Toltecas

Ermita Iztapalapa

Av. San Lorenzo

Señor de la Cuevita

Ermita Iztapalapa

Cerro de la Estrella

21:00 hrs   15:30 hrs

Jueves

Viernes

Hospitales

Módula de
servicio

Puesto de
socorro

14. Handout map of processions on Holy Thursday and Good Friday also showing locations of aid stations. (The misspellings of some streets are in the original.)

15. An advertisement for the film *Cristo 70*. Reproduced from *U*: 26 March 1970.

16. Jesus carries his cross. The figure on the right is St. John the Evangelist. Reproduced from *U*: 18 April 1981.

17. Photographers crowd Jesus in 1990. Photograph by José Luis Guzmán. Reproduced from Luna Parra, *150 años*, 97.

18. The modern esplanade, since the mid-1960s the scene of all events preceding the Way of the Cross. Photograph by the author, taken from the city park before all the sets had been erected, except for the palace of Pontius Pilate in the distance, to the left. The church of San Lucas is just out of sight to the right.

19. A forest of Nazarenes with their crosses, taken from the top of the Cerro de la Estrella. Reproduced from *E:* 15 April 1995.

20. The crucifixion scene in 1992, taken from the top of the Cerro de la Estrella and looking toward Mexico City in the distance. Note the rain clouds. Fernando Castillo. Reproduced from Luna Parra, *150 años,* 86.

21. "No, I'm not wearing a costume." (The unspoken subtext: "I really am poor.") Cartoon by Helioflores. Reproduced from *U:* 25 March 1989.

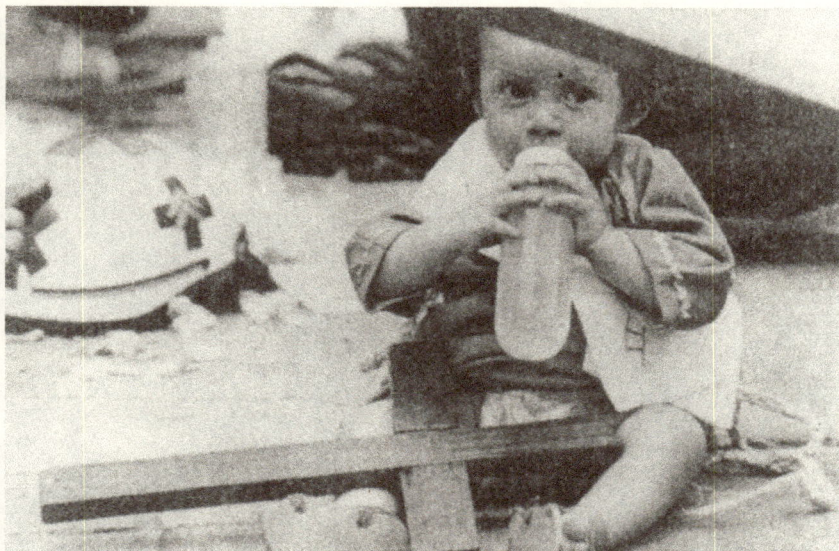

22. The one-year-old Nazarene, Mario Giovani, rests. Reproduced from *U:* 18 April 1987.

23. Armed with periscopes, the crowd watches events transpiring within the esplanade. Photograph by Imagen latina. Reproduced from Luna Parra, *Semana Santa*, 230.

6

TOWARD A "LESS GROTESQUE" TOURIST PASSION: CHURCH AND STATE EFFORTS

The decade and a half between 1945 and 1963 began with some evidence that the pageant of Iztapalapa, while remaining relatively modest in scope, had stabilized. In 1945 the first scientific paper dedicated to the spectacle came out, a work all the more impressive in that members of the Comité and some actors furnished the two authors (Ralph Boggs and Vicente Mendoza) with much of the information.[1] World War II was over, and things seemed poised to settle down in a period that is stamped by the personality of Miguel Alemán, the businessman president (1946–1952). Yet in fact events were conspiring to produce a crisis in the history of the Iztapalapan passion. As we saw in previous pages, sometime just before 1935 the Santuario and its atrium had ceased to be used for the finals of the *Tres Caídas* and the crucifixion, and the latter thereafter is said to be performed on the Cerro.[2] Confined mostly to the secular streets, the procession had less clerical participation than earlier, and the Way of the Cross, departing from the atrium of San Lucas, proceeded to that hilly point more or less without any clerical intervention.

Thus still without the commitment of police forces strong enough to subdue passions, so to speak, year by year the fiesta, its streets and air enveloped in clouds of dust, spiraled toward disorder. The account of 1952 warned of an impending explosion, which occurred in 1956, with aftershocks as late as 1962. The response of the state authority in 1956 was to direct the municipal officials to join with the clergy to insure a play that was "less irreverent" and "less grotesque." To put it simply, this was a period when the church attempted once again to superimpose itself upon the lay representation of the passion, and in this period, it came as close as it ever has to accomplishing that goal. At the same time, the aftermath of this explosion marks the political authority's irreversible entry into the guidance of the play. It could no longer ignore the staying power of this pageant or the annual danger it presented. It either had to be suppressed—and there were still those who desired that mightily—or it had to be fostered to exploit all its potential. This combination of reform forces occurred at a moment when Iztapalapa was ruled by a dynamic mayor, Ernesto Uruchurtu, head of the Federal District. In his two incumbencies (1952–1958, 1964–1966), this official would do much to make this now rapidly growing population center an attractive goal for visitors to the passion.

In 1945, a group of actors and scholars cooperated in assembling the materials for the first serious paper on the passion of Iztapalapa. Santiago Guerra, who had played the role of Pontius Pilate the previous year and would perform it for the generation to come, and Porfirio González, who acted as Captain of the Soldiers, dictated and orally reconstructed the text of the play for the authors of the study, Ralph Boggs and Vicente Mendoza. That text was drawn, as always, from the *Cuatro Concilios* of Francisco Ozácar and the *Mártir de Gólgota* of Pérez Escrich. Boggs and Mendoza then edited and published that text in 1947, appending to it an important analysis of both the narrative and the scenography of the play.[3] Just as important for the reader, the editors included a map in their publication, republished here, which shows all the routes of the action in 1945 (fig. 11).

This map furnishes an exact sense of the expanding spatiality of the Iztapalapan rites at that time. We read of a funeral procession proceeding to the western neighborhood around the church of Santa Barbara to fetch an Ecce Homo statue, one with its hands tied and covered by a purple mantle. The procession returned with it to the atrium of San Lucas, which remained the center of the trial, as it would for another generation to come. There it obviously served as the live Pontius Pilate's foil when he said to the crowd that he could find no fault with "this man here." Just as important, we find for the first time the place identified where Jesus will be kept prisoner overnight.[4] But perhaps most significantly, we find the route Jesus took marching toward his death, and it is *not* toward the Santuario.

Boggs and Mendoza inform us for the first time that certain players in this drama actually had to perform a type of purification before they played their roles. Specifically, it is said that Epitacio Ubaldo Granados, the person who was to play the role of Jesus[5]—thus a living person and a statue both still imitated the lord—was cloistered within San Lucas for the whole month before Holy Thursday. In that period he ate only sparingly, practiced spiritual exercises, and in this way sought to internalize his role so as to develop the necessary reverence. The two thieves, Dimas and Gestas, did the same, but only for a fortnight.[6] If an actor repeated the role of Jesus, as would Carlos Rivas, he also repeated this spiritual regimen in San Lucas. Indeed, the twenty-three-year-old Rivas told a reporter in 1979 that he had had no sexual experiences in the three years he had played the savior.[7]

Boggs and Mendoza's account makes clear that at least in 1945, after Pilate's usual judgment, sentence, and heraldic pronouncement in the atrium of San Lucas at about 3 P.M., the Way of the Cross, with a live Jesus up front, proceeded through the various streets of Iztapalapa, past different corners where he performed the Three Falls and met Veronica and Mary, to a spot about one kilometer from San Lucas. This spot, at the foot of the famous Cerro de la Estrella, was called, perhaps significantly, the Cerrito de La Muerte, and it was there that the crucifixion of the three was carried out, just as it had certainly been in the immediately preceding years.[8] Unfortunately, our authors do not describe the minutiae of the crucifixion itself, but the accounts of subsequent years will show that the procedure in these years as thereafter was to switch from a live to a figured Jesus at the moment of crucifixion.[9] Then, again as had already been the case back in 1867, live thieves were tied to their crosses to either side of the figured Jesus. For our sources describe how "the body of Jesus" was taken down, and, obviously after the normal procession of the Santo Entierro,[10] was deposited by Joseph of Arimathea at the bottom of a cave among the rocks east of the

Santuario. This presumably could only have been done with a carved statue.[11]

Thus for reasons that are not totally clear, the Santuario was no longer being used for any part of the crucifixion, as it had been for years before. Instead, after the atrium of San Lucas had served as usual for the trial, the Iztapalapans now fanned out and used the whole fabric of the city for the great procession of the *Tres Caídas* and the crucifixion itself. Just as significant a departure from what had become customary in the 1920s and 1930s, however, were the facts surrounding the figure of Jesus. Boggs and Mendoza's reference to an Ecce Homo statue being used, presumably as part of the trial of Jesus, is the last such evidence of a figure in the Comité's execution of the trial and the Way of the Cross, if not yet the crucifixion. From now on there is no mention of an image of Jesus in his trial, and further, there is no longer a boy Jesus either at the trial or during the Way of the Cross. Now only one, live, adult Jesus functioned as such from the beginning of the play up to, if not including, the moment of crucifixion.

In 1945, that Jesus was Epitacio Ubaldo Granados, who was 36 years old,[12] obviously older than the *niños* who had earlier played that role. Thus as the festival turned slowly from imaged to live Jesuses, it also moved from child Jesuses to adults, who could better bear a heavy cross through the streets of Iztapalapa in the wholly lay *Tres Caídas* that was now central to the total theatrical impression. Granados, the Jesus of 1945, helps explain how that change came about. In an interview for a 1992 publication, this man, who had gone on to become perhaps the most famous make-up artist of both the passion play and local carnivals, told how in the old days the play had crucified an image, to be sure, but on the Way of the Cross the organizers had regularly employed a "minor who stood on a litter carrying a cross, while a group of persons carried him." "I did not like this," don Epitacio told the interviewer, "because the Jesus Christs of the images [in the churches] are tall and handsome and not some child." By now social and cultural historians are well aware how church images form people's notions of the actual appearance of the divinities to whom they pray. Here is that influence in recent Iztapalapan memory.[13]

Don Epitacio goes on with his story. He addressed the Council, "suggesting to it that the Christ be more real, and that he be of a more similar age and size." They in turn told him to search out such a person. "And so," Epitacio continues, "when I returned to the street, I dedicated my-self to studying the comportment, color, and character of the *muchachos*. This was how I encountered Marcos Hernández, a boy of 18 years." Epitacio tells how he got the family's permission to have Marcos play Je-sus, then how on the following Palm Sunday the boy mounted a live ass and played Jesus entering Jerusalem in triumph.[14] Holy Thursday found the boy "handsome like Christ," while on Good Friday, don Epitacio himself made up Hernández's whole body so that "when they beat him, all the wounds and blood would show."[15] It was Lent 1946, as *Excelsior* confirms by naming Hernández as the Jesus of that year.

Though a slight failure of memory may be at work in this account (Granados does not mention that he himself had ever played Jesus in the pageant), the central fact is clear. In the 1946 and subsequent perfor-mances, a strapping young adult, if still not a Jesus of the master's conventional thirty-three years of age, was made up to look the role of Jesus and played him all the way through the passion until the mo-ment before the crucifixion, at which point an image was substituted. Je-sus, and perhaps other actors as well, now had to look like the figures they played, rather than follow the noncanonical traditions of an earlier time.[16] Clearly, in his thirst for "realism," Granados did not consider that sinful adult Jesuses might be less "realistic" than the innocent child-Jesuses they here replaced.

The Boggs-Mendoza account has one further surprise for us. On the morning of Holy Saturday, by means of some mechanism at the bottom and ropes at the top, the image of Jesus rose up to heaven over some white and gilded cardboard clouds.[17] Pedro Guillén identifies this repre-sentation as that of the resurrection: Jesus was tied around the waist with a rope bound to a tree. At the moment of resurrection he was pulled up ten or twelve meters.[18] One may doubt that this was truly an image of the resurrection, for the description rather matches what one might expect of an Ascension representation, though that feast day was still weeks away. Either way, it is clear that an event was being reenacted, in church, that did not occur on Holy Saturday. Again, one may suspect that a type of Corpus Christi encyclopedic representation lingered in the minds of these stage masters, where all manner of sacred stories might be thrown in by priests not eager to be left out of the whole passion rep-resentation.[19]

It can be no accident that no clergyman is mentioned in the Boggs-

Mendoza account of 1945. Indeed, even in the 1980s a member of the organizational Comité remembered the years between 1947 and 1952 as a particularly strife-ridden period in local church-communal relations, just as did the parish priest, who labeled it "difficult."[20] Note that this was also the period when the newspaper *Excelsior*, whose reporting over the years has been distinctly more clerical in cast than *El Universal's*, often did not cover the Iztapalapan procedures. Although the paucity of the newspaper sources in these years inhibits our search for details, the church appears to have continued its war against the whole celebration, circulating fliers and denouncing the organizers verbally. One of the signal reasons for its opposition, according to this Comité member, was that while the Iztapalapans were perfectly ready to follow the actors into church, they would not follow the curates into the same churches.[21] The age-old opposition between clergy and *histriones* was alive and well. Inversely, the Comité resented the curate's insistence on pre-reading or censoring the *parlamentos* or counsels that were enunciated by the Jews and the Romans during the trial. Finally, and strategically perhaps most important at all, there was the story that once, when the curate demanded that a member of the Comité leave the church, the man protested mightily that "he would not leave, because the atrium belonged to the pueblo."[22] There was more than a grain of truth in this remark: the atriums or (originally) Open-Air Churches before the entrance to churches had indeed been the sacred place of the native Americans in the first centuries of the Spanish regime. This small event makes clear that claims to certain spaces, themselves contested by state and archepiscopal authorities, formed a node of contention between the laity and the churchmen at the local level as well.

In the immediate years to come, a dramatic series of events mark a decisive turn in the history of the Iztapalapan pageant. They were thenceforward characterized by an important, if temporary, shift back toward clerical participation combined, unexpectedly, with an innovative exploitation of the city streets by the lay organizers, who still struggled to retain some of the celebration's traditional features.[23] The first signs of an impending crisis came in 1952. The Delegación of Iztapalapa was growing quickly, by 1960 having a population of a quarter of a million.[24] As a concomitant of that general increase, the estimated numbers of visitors to the passion play began to rise as well. In Holy Week 1952, some

100,000 people—from the city, from the surrounding villages, and "an infinity of foreign tourists" (E: 1952)—descended on the host town. According to the same report, taxis charged the exorbitant fare of 20 pesos instead of the normal 3 to get to Iztapalapa, while on the Calzada de la Viga south of Jamaica, on the road to Iztapalapa, travel facilitators also enriched themselves at the expense of tourists by charging them top peso.

What did they find when they arrived? The same reporter from *Excelsior* was not pleased. Under a headline reading "The Fiestas of Ixtapalapa Characterized by Disorder, Theft, and Libertinage," he painted a picture of dusty streets full of prostitutes and beggars, hard liquor for sale, and numerous traffic accidents. The reporter found little to praise. He did notice that Caiaphas, "muy a la moderna," spoke through a microphone. This is the first mention of this device in Iztapalapa, and it indicates that the play now was being performed before a mass of people who could otherwise not hear what was transpiring.[25] But overall, his tone was one of outrage at this badly organized display, an impious mockery of the Bible by indigenous people who, in that reporter's words, could not do anything right. Certainly tourists had come, but the photographs they would take back to their homelands would prove "that Mexico is an uncivilized country and a profaner of such a sacred day as Good Friday."[26]

El Universal in that year was only slightly more sparing. Its writer described some 200,000 people trying to reach Iztapalapa on trams so full that many held on only by a thread, while many others deserted the trolleys for buses, even though the latter took much longer to reach the site of the play. The reporter did speak warmly of the humble citizens of the town who put on the pageant, but then turned his attention to the crowd on the Cerro de la Estrella, where Jesus was to be crucified. Implicitly contrasting the "humble" locals with the rowdy tourists, and the *Tres Caídas* in town with the goings on up on the Cerro, the reporter regretted that the crowd showed "no pious spirit, but rather a pagan attitude," and the visitors "had with them all types of drinks." By now, it was not uncommon for tourists to ignore the passion events down in town and upon arriving in Iztapalapa climb right up the Cerro, laden with food and drinks, and settle down for the day, thereby guaranteeing themselves a prime view of the great event on the Cerro in mid-afternoon, the crucifixion. *El Universal* here furnishes an image of the pageant as it would increasingly unfold in the age of mass audiences. The finger of blame for disorders would be pointed at those who watched the events as well as those who performed the passion.

What seemed like a ship destined for wreckage continued to provoke journalistic outrage. In 1954, El Universal reported that this pageant, which sometimes turned into a bloody joke (burla sangrienta), had been condemned not just by the Catholic church, "but by other Christian denominations," certainly a cry of pain in a country still overwhelmingly Catholic! Thus it can hardly have been surprising to capitalinos when on the last day of March, 1956, they picked up their El Universal and read the headline "Many Hurt in the Denigrating Burlesque Masque (Mojiganga) of Iztapalapa!" The story, by Mario Quintero Becerra, described a "bloody bacchanal" before some 300,000 visitors (note the geometric increase in the reported number of visitors) that had been dedicated not to the passion, "the most significant event in history," but rather to drink. The immediate provocation for the fighting seems to have been blockage of the route of the Three Falls procession by an Iztapalapan audience desperate to be next to Jesus.[27] The mounted police had to intervene, charging witnesses to the play, and they just as surely fought back against the forces of order, this lucha en toda forma leaving about 20 people seriously injured. Again, the irreverence was not attributed to the players but the bystanders. Another group in the crowd drank themselves silly, producing scenes, the reporter assures us, "unworthy of a civilized people and all the more damnable because this was Good Friday." With a clear reference to Oberammergau, Quintero rasped that the play at Iztapalapa did not even have the excuse of being artistic, as it is in other places of the world, "where similar ceremonies unfold within an ambience of culture, where there is respect for religious questions." Once again, if anachronistically, the everlasting racism at the heart of so much Mexican assessment of "our Indians" raised its ugly head.

The memory of this ruckus did not quickly fade away to be dismissed as just one more drunken Indian brawl. The violence of this episode was not only significant; it obviously was emanating from the ever-increasing audiences, presumably as yet still more mestizo than the Iztapalapans, more than from the players. Patently, something had to be done, and in its long report of the following year, 1957, El Universal made clear that a campaign led by the press, combined with alarm calls from the archbishop and assistance from Mayor Emilio Uruchurtu (then in his first term), resulted in serious steps "to try to dignify the staging of Iztapalapa." Of the many reforms, some lasted, but others did not. We begin with the successes, which are best seen in retrospect when, five years after the riot, the *Excelsior* reporter in 1961 gave credit where credit was due. They were the work, he said, of "a cataclysm named Uruchurtu."

In terms of lived experience, the Iztapalapans surely regarded the first step as more a revolution than a reform. Uruchurtu started laying pavement in the town, including along much of the route of the *Tres Caídas*. No less important, he radically improved the approaches to it, broadening the Calzada de la Viga, for example, to double the traffic it could move to Iztapalapa, which probably explains the exploding number of visitors claimed for the fiesta. In a few years, the yearly reportorial denunciation of the dust raised by the masses who trod the borough on Good Friday, including that stirred up by Jesus's march to Calvary, would be only a memory.

Still more sensational because introduced all at once was the mayor's enactment of a dry law *(ley seca)* that forbade the sale of beer, pulque, and all other alcoholic drinks during the second part of Holy Week. Drinking was customary not just for the audience, but was also part of the actors' Good Friday experience. At best, this meant that the moment the religious event ended, the fiesta began, with drink aplenty for everyone. But as *Excelsior* reports in 1961, in the old days (before 1956) all the actors, including Jesus, drank pulque, beer, and tequila throughout the whole ceremony. To be sure, this reporter continued, closing the *pulquerías* did not please the Iztapalapans, but it was a great relief to the tourists. Now they could bring their wives and children from the nearby settlements *(colonias)* without fear of having some Roman, centurion, or Jew thrust a knife in their faces.[28] In this way the dry law would increase the Holy Week tourist traffic to Iztapalapa, including that from nearby native American and mestizo communities. It was indeed an epochal move, a true cataclysm in the festive life of Mexico, and despite some cheating, the prohibition has been maintained to this day. As *Excelsior* wrote in 1961, the fiesta would still follow upon the religious pageant, "but without drink."

With this type of support at the political top, churchmen had every

reason to believe that their future was promising as well. Through reform, the rector of San Lucas, Luis Victoria, told the *El Universal* reporter
on his visit to the pageant in 1957, the panoply of Iztapalapa can be
made to render honor and profit *(provecho)* to everyone, "just as in
Oberammergau." The priest and reporter both saw the profit potential
of this tourist event if only the theater could be regulated. Everyone, including the local church, now recognized that material gain was a primary goal of the pageant activity. Indeed, Victoria asserts that the actors
had to learn to act, while of course preserving their (native) spontaneity,
a breathtaking departure from the age-old clerical antagonism toward
their thespian opposites. This radical turnabout, in which the thespian
impulse came to the center of the liturgical undertaking, was in itself inspired by the distant Roman pontiff, who was at this very time making
the acting-out of Jesus's trail to martyrdom his very own. The phenomenon of historical reenactment, so persistent and evident a mark of modern cultures, had now reached all the way to the tiara.

A second consensus point right after 1957 was that in the view of the
lay (as well as the church) authorities, the local church was the only body
that could produce both profit and honor for the town's spectacle. For its
part, the clergy would attempt to reach that goal while pursuing a higher
one: to reliturgize a pageant that was already more or less under total lay
control. Given the ingrained opposition of the Comité and its supporters
to any attempt of the priests to run their spectacle, that would ultimately
fail. Its failure, in many ways, is a metaphor of the failure to date of the
official Mexican church to regain its liturgical authority in modern secular society.

Maintenance of order was the most immediate problem addressed by
the clergy, a task the more incumbent on them because there is no indication in the years immediately after the riot of an increase in police
presence. According to *El Universal* in 1957, the priests had enlisted the
San Lucas branch of the Catholic Youth Action Order (Acción Católica
Juvenil Mexicana), which helped maintain order that year. This may be
the local branch of the Asociación Católica de la Juventud Mexicana,
which in the War of the Cristeros of the late 1920s had opposed the
Mexican state. But the newspapers do not mention this group in subsequent years. Even more successful was Victoria's determination to
change the event's internal format, a step which could only indirectly

help to maintain order, but would directly make the spectacle appear much more liturgical in nature. The form this offensive took was to eliminate the "grotesque" from the performances. This suppression again demonstrates that, for the church, a portrayal of the passion of Jesus could only be achieved by destroying the imitation of that historical event.

The parish vicar, Luis de Uriarte, told *El Universal* in 1957 that the priests were determined to produce "a less grotesque representation, [with] more respectable gestures." He told the reporter that the "grotesque music," by which he certainly referred to that produced by native instruments, was to be done away with.[29] Uriarte continued enthusiastically with the clerical plans. Holy Saturday, he said, would be "a day of mourning, not of Gloria," while Easter itself would become glorious. While Uriarte had authority on his side, Rome having in 1955 implemented the suppression of the hilarity that was customary in Catholic churches on Holy Saturday,[30] Uriarte's obvious belief that by a parochial order one could shut down traditional ceremonies on that day was almost the height of naiveté. The absolute peak of such naiveté, however, was the notion that clergy could convert Easter Sunday into a significant feast at Iztapalapa. That day had never figured prominently in the pueblo's festive calendar. Killing the man-God on Good Friday had, after all, simultaneously brought Jesus back to life. Anyway, historically Easter was a feast for the middle and upper classes, which had indeed risen, and not for the poor inhabitants of towns like Iztapalapa, who in Jesus's and Mary's agony discovered their own determination to go on living. To this day Easter is still not important in the town's festive calendar.

Perhaps the pinnacle of the priests' attempt to render the spectacle of Good Friday "less grotesque and more respectable" was Uriarte's plan for what was henceforth to transpire at the crucifixion on the Cerro de la Estrella. First, Jesus, in the person of Fidel Hernández since 1956 (and until 1964), was no longer to be "attached" (*atar*) to the cross, the priest told the same reporter of *El Universal* in 1957. Clearly, at this date a live actor climbed onto the cross in Iztapalapa, but we must wrestle for a moment with our sparse sources to background this important development. So much is clear: while there are many photographs of live Jesuses carrying their crosses in our period, the first actual pictures of the crucifixion itself in either newspaper or in the printed collections of

Iztapalapan passion photographs date to 1951 and then 1952, when *El Universal* below its photograph specifically states that the living Jesus of the *Tres Caídas* mounted the cross and hung from it. Until more evidence is available, we are left with little choice but to assume that it was not long before mid-century that for the first time a live Jesus hung from the Iztapalapan cross on the Cerro de la Estrella rather than an image, and to suspect that the reason for this change stood in some relation to the old laws against religious images being employed in public and to the historic tension between the local church and pueblo.

Now in 1957, the rector of San Lucas, padre Victoria, told *El Universal* that this was done "so as to cut down where possible on the grotesque aspect and also to try to avoid [Hernández] suffering unnecessary physical pain." Victoria obviously considered the living recreation of Jesus's agony, *and thus also Jesus's own,* as "grotesque," even though no actual crucifixion took place. Thus the plan was for Hernández to slip away and rest in the moment he reached the Cerro, to be replaced by a "giant" wooden crucifix that would be hoisted into place between the two living thieves. In short, the priests wanted to return to a previous era when through control of a religious image they could control the passion as a whole.

And so, it seemed, would be the case. During the passion play of 1957, different preachers again addressed the crowd on the meanings of the passion events. The priests were outside, in force, performing para-liturgical rites, which can only mean that the laws of 1874 directed against public religious services had been waived or repealed. We will return to this phenomenon later. But in the meantime, it is clear that padre Uriarte indeed preached at each of the Three Falls in Iztapalapa itself, then ascended to the Cerro de la Estrella beneath the image of the crucified Jesus, "with a microphone preaching the eternal theme of the passion," even as he directed all the acting, according to *El Universal.* A photograph published in the same *El Universal* shows the priest present at the crucifixion (fig. 13). For his part, father Victoria, presumably from the same bluff, preached each of the Seven Last Words of Jesus as the hour of Jesus's death approached. Once that passed, the wooden figure of Jesus was lowered from the cross. At this point Uriarte cried: "Long Live Christ the King!" "Long Live the Christian Spirit of Mexico!", and "Long Live Fraternity Between the Peoples!" It was an implausibly artistic, daring synthesis of what might appeal to both the laity and the clergy. Clearly plugging into the antistate history of the Mexican church, which had adopted *Viva Cristo Rey!* as its war cry in the War of the Cristeros of the 1920s, the good father also knew how to ingratiate himself with the people by uttering the revolutionary slogan of fraternity.[31] It seemed clear by now that the clergy had truly seized control of the representation of the passion of Jesus in Iztapalapa.

But the clerical retro-imagination had still to run its course in 1957. Immediately following the Descent from the Cross, the priests sought to reinvigorate the increasingly moribund procession of the Santo Entierro, which had been in decline once the Santuario had ceased after 1933 to house the crucifixion, which had moved definitively to the Cerro. Originally Spanish or Italian, the para-liturgical rite of the Santo Entierro was a funeral procession that bore the statue of Christ, just taken from the cross, to its sepulcher. In many parts of Europe and Mexico, it was the terminal Good Friday rite. Yet though mentioned in the very first Iztapalapan Good Friday report in 1867, the Santo Entierro in this town gained only infrequent attention. Surely this happened in part because the newspaper reporters left after the crucifixion to return to their downtown offices, but no doubt the decline of the Santo Entierro was hastened once a living person began to play Jesus at the crucifixion, so that the play ended in effect upon the deposition of that actor from the cross. Once the *Tres Caídas* had all live actors acting out Jesus's passion until his death, it was inevitable that the reverse procession back into town of the Santo Entierro, though still popular elsewhere, was simply not going to get much attention in Iztapalapa.

True . . . unless, of course, the play were to readopt an image of Jesus to place on the cross, around which a (clerically controlled) liturgy could be developed. Just such a takeover was now planned by the clergy. As reported in *El Universal* in 1957, once the image of Jesus was taken down from the cross, it was placed on the hilly soil of the Cerro. The people then passed by the image in good order, kissing the wounds on the figure. After that, a priest having presumably had the image placed into a funeral casket, devotees followed the savior "in pious pilgrimage" *(romería)* to the Santuario, where it remained exposed to public veneration until 11 o'clock at night.[32] The Santuario was back.

Thus having departed on Good Friday from a place of crucifixion that was back under the control of the clerical authorities, the image of Jesus ended back in the clergy's house. Just as in the good old days, the priests must have thought. In 1958, *El Universal* again praised the new pageant for its "sobriety," and in 1959, the same paper turned effusive in its praise. Thanks to a padre Sánchez, the festival, this reporter effused, had unfolded "under the sign of more dignity and decorum. For the excesses of the pueblo, the disorders of the crowd in all its many colors, are disappearing." Now there was more law enforcement personnel. The police, members of Catholic Action, the youth of the Franciscan Third Order, confraternities and other parochial organizations created a fiesta that was free of the "previous depressing spectacles provoked by alcohol, disorder, and the absence of vigilance." Why, the representation of this year, he said, was even more ordered than the one last year! By 1961, *Excelsior* could report that that year was "the first time in many years that no significant incidents or wounds occurred."

Alas, by 1962, the halcyon processions and tableaux of the preceding years had passed. While insisting "that there were not many irreverent scenes," *El Universal* did note that there were some drunken gangs of tramps *(pandilla de vagos)* "dedicated to scandalizing and molesting the women." Signs of regression were evident, though the sources of the new disorders were now thought to lay elsewhere. Under a headline "Heat, Dust, Tumults and Lost Children During the Crucifixion in Iztapalapa," the *Excelsior* reporter in this year protested against being "in the presence of a disordered multitude of the faithful who were in a very emotional state, yelling and showing their indignation at the tortures to which the Nazarene was submitted." Though this reporter described what he saw as an emblem of a more general disorder, one which the 20 penitents who were present could not efface, it in fact appears that as the pageant evolved, *Excelsior* was shifting its historic displeasure with the spectacle to another level: from complaints of drunkenness to outrage at the locals' inability to distinguish a passion play from reality. In fact, it is only in these years that we gain our first real insight into the psychology of those among the crowd who were near the action of the *Tres Caídas*. Let us hope it will help us grasp the relation between religious sentiment and festive disorder.

We first encounter audience protest in 1946, directed at the treatment of Marcos Hernández playing Jesus. The *sayones* or soldiers, *El Universal* reported, "whipped [Jesus] brutally. This scene," the reporter continued, "profoundly impressed the people. Absorbed in the representation, they actually experienced the real Calvary of Christ." Here is a stunning recognition of the successful imitation the Iztapalapan passion could afford. But was it good to actually experience Calvary, as this reporter obviously felt, or was it problematic when, looking at the faces of the Iztapalapan audience, it became clear to the El Universal reporter in 1959 that though the whole was not real *(una ficción)*, the audience could not tell "that that which was happening was not real"? The organizers encouraged this confusion, especially when they began the process of locating the places for particular moments in the passion story at different points in the city outside the churches. Nothing set the tone for what was to come better than the flagellation of Jesus, which occurred right after he was sentenced to death. In 1961 *Excelsior* reported women and children crying, and even the men being "sincerely moved." But in the following year the same periodical spoke of an outraged audience "who were very emotional, yelling and showing their indignation at the tortures to which the Nazarene was submitted." It tells us that Jesus was raised up on a small platform in the town plaza—the first reference to a passion ever executed in a new central esplanade—so that, played by Fidel Hernández, he could be whipped for all to see. That quickly brought on protests, witnesses yelling: "No! Stop it! You wicked men! God will punish them!" As had long been intimated in Iztapalapa, the Flagellation of Jesus was one of the highlights of the Iztapalapan passion. The reports of these and later years are filled with great emotiveness all along the route of the subsequent via Crucis. But the flagellation set the stage.

It is in this period as well that the route leading to the Cerro de la Estrella became fixed, including the points at which Jesus would suffer each of his three biblical falls, and be whipped as he struggled to rise up again. This itinerary was first spelled out in El Universal in 1961, and then fixed in a map that still is afforded visitors to Iztapalapa for Holy Week (fig. 14). The first fall was to take place at the corner of Aztecas and Manuel Escobedo streets, the second at the corner of Lerdo and Cuauhtémoc Avenue, and the third where Estrella St. crosses the highway Calzada Ermita-Iztapalapa, in other words, at the beginning of the steep ascent to the Cerro de la Estrella. Routings with only slight variations are given in some later years as well.[33]

How to account for these outbursts of emotion, when it was universally known that (usually) the punches were pulled on all these punishments, real though they might seem to witnesses? It is not necessary to credit the notion that the inhabitants of Iztapalapa could not distinguish the real from the imaginary any more than the most modern of audiences, which may become just as emotionally identified with theatrical situations. Whatever their comportment during the procession, citizens of that town would, of course, have assured anyone on the eve of the passion representation (or after it) that they witnessed a historical reenactment, if one with sacred subject matter. To be sure, perhaps some of the protests were in defense of the local young man who was playing Jesus, rather than in defense of Jesus himself. But what is important is that in mid-century the Comité organizing this performance did succeed in involving spectators in com-passion, the core element of the *imitatio Christi*. And they had done so by means of disorder, involving an "undisciplined" crowd in the merely theatrical pain of a latter-day savior. Of course, the encouragement bystanders offered Jesus never did postpone the inevitable, for, after all, Jesus did have to die for our sins. According to *El Universal* in 1962, Jesus, accompanied by his guardian angel, was indeed crucified between the two thieves, while in 1946 *Excelsior* reported, surely from the Cerrito de la Muerte, that when the image of Jesus died on the cross, "some women wailed in high voices, and the children did the same when they saw their mothers crying."

7

THE WORLD PRESSES IN: PASSION COMPETITION IN THE NEW MEDIA AGE

The seven-year period, 1963 through 1970, is memorable in the history of Mexico. In 1968 the country at large watched the Summer Olympics in the capital, just after an uprising of students, of incomparably greater import, had been crushed by President Gustavo Díaz Ordaz at Tlatelolco. Even tiny Iztapalapa saw major changes within its limited horizon, in the superstructures hovering above the town's passion play. In these years of Vatican II, during Holy Week the Roman pontiffs themselves stepped onto the world stage as actors miming the behavior of the Christian savior, perforce legitimizing the humble performers of Mexican passion plays who had for so long been derided by the prelacy. Indeed, the pope's actions also converted local prelates, now themselves partisans of the Institutionalized Revolution the national president saw threatened by the "communist" students, into a thespian troupe whose sacrificial and liturgical functions the contemporary press viewed as less and less interesting. One may speak of the slow victory of religious narrative drama over ecclesiastical services in the city and beyond.

A second superstructural shift occurred at about the same time not only in central Mexico, but across much of the Catholic, nay Christian world at large. From Colombia to the Philippine Islands, the world now appeared full of passion reenactments. At the local level, Iztapalapa re-

sponded to the Mexican challenges to its supremacy by essentially changing the town into a series of stages for the passion season. The most
breathtaking step on this path was to move the ancient market away
from the center and replace it with a huge esplanade or square of mac-
adam that for most of the year goes unused, a constant reminder that
the town was now essentially identified by its representational self.[1]

On top of this validation of the passion play by traditional authority
came the invasion of outside media. This made for serious competition, but it also gave the Comité the chance for endless propaganda.
Iztapalapans had long known that films showing Jesus's passion, and now
even great enclosed theatrical productions, some in sports stadiums,
were a threat to their play's endurance. Yet the very archaic nature of the
Iztapalapan show, its decisively folkloric tone with a minimum of modern technology, boded well for continued popularity. This was confirmed
when the Iztapalapans in these years hosted some of the largest world
television networks for the filming and selling of this bit of their past to
all corners of the world.

Our attention in this chapter is particularly drawn to the major superstructural changes which have given us the modern Jesus passion. Yet we
cannot ignore some remarkable internal developments that affected the
passion, if only because they too reflected the world outside. Most striking, in these years the *Tres Caídas* became a type of athletic contest
whose purpose was to determine the macho qualities of each year's Jesus. This emphasis on adult individualism is also reflected in the reportage, which makes a point to list the names of all the major players.
Finally, all these secularizing trends did not bode well for the priests, who
tried in these years to maintain the influence they had just recently won
over the pageant, only to lose it in the last years of this decade. By 1970,
the play of Iztapalapa had become a spectacle that no longer needed the
church to make it run.

The crucial decision of the modern papacy to represent its
long denied theatrical inheritance would be quickly recognized by Mexican observers. The popes began to take part in
passion plays and to play Jesus. In 1959, *Excelsior* in its report of Good
Friday activities shows a bare-footed pope John XXIII kneeling to pay

homage to a religious image. According to *El Universal* of 1960, the same pope had also taken to washing feet in public as part of Holy Thursday ceremonies. This practice dated back to Gregory the Great, the writer noted, but had fallen into disuse until John revived it in 1959. Clearly, in that year this reform pontiff had chosen a path emphasizing his public *imitatio Christi* as a part of Holy Week. Then in 1964, in the midst of the ecumenical council Vatican II, Paul VI began to carry a cross annually along a Way of the Cross in Rome each Good Friday, just as practicing Christians had in Jerusalem almost since the beginning of that religion, and *Excelsior* front-paged this image during Holy Week of 1971.[2] Back in 1964, *El Universal* reacted to the pope's act as to a world-historical event: "For the first time in this century [the pope] took part in the Roman procession of Good Friday. He took up the cross on his shoulders at the thirteenth station." Mexicans now saw in their newspapers and on television the head of this universal church, the *vicarius Christi*, doing the very thing—"self-punishment *(autocensura),*" a later paper called it (*Novedades,* 1999)—which the humble, despised *indios* of various Mexican pueblos did every year to commemorate their lord, but which they could not imagine their own prelates doing even with the greatest of difficulty.

Simply put, the events taking place in Rome had the effect of validating the thespian aspect of the clerical way of life over and against that clergy's ecclesiological emphasis. And that shift could not have come at a more crucial moment in the history of the conservative Mexican church. This was, after all, still officially an anticlerical country, and in most parts of the Valley of Mexico, at least, that meant that throughout the decades of the Revolution and the Cristeros most communities had not been able to carry out religious events in public, because a "religious event" meant the involvement of clergy. Iztapalapa's play, as we have seen, had survived largely without clerical involvement into the scandals of the 1950s, but it was an exception.

Then in the 1940s, the conciliatory regimes of presidents Manuel Ávila Camacho and Miguel Alemán determined that the neighborhoods of the capital and the pueblos could again perform their outside Holy Week ceremonies without running the risk that through its involvement in those rites, the church might again subvert the state. In 1949, said a gratified source in Taxco, the state "again authorized [Holy Week processions]" (*U:* 1991).[3] Not surprisingly, the local clergy in Taxco as elsewhere soon became the masters of the new representations, and it is certain that the government of this one-party state saw in the clergy an ally in the preservation of social peace. What this meant for Iztapalapa, which had avoided definitive closure of its passion, was that the clergy could reinsert itself into the ongoing lay spectacle if the opportunity arose, as it did in the 1950s. But what it meant for literally hundreds of neighborhoods and pueblos across Mexico is that they could make new passion plays with the help of their rectors, or even, as in Puebla, redeploy clerically dominated plays that had been suppressed at the time of the anticlerical laws of the later nineteenth and early twentieth centuries. These plays had been suspended in Puebla since 1856, one source informs us, but now resumed "as [they were] before the Reform Laws" (U: 1992).

The first indications of this new activity appear exactly in this midcentury time frame. In the third and fourth decades of the century, neither El Universal nor Excelsior carried any stories of extra-liturgical ceremonies other than those in Iztapalapa. Now El Universal in its Good Friday edition of 1948 has a substantial report describing a fascinating procession that took place that year in the city of San Miguel Allende on the Friday before Good Friday (Viernes de Dolores), complete with representations from the Old and New Testaments. We then learn from Excelsior's Easter edition of 1953 that on Good Friday evening of the previous year, the town of Tepeji del Río (Hgo.) had held the first of what were to be many subsequent Processions of Silence, that is, of the Santo Sepulcro or Santo Entierro. Obviously, a new age of passion representations had just started across Mexico.

The richest document I have found describing this governmental turnabout is an already mentioned Good Friday interview given by Eusebio García Santamaría and printed in El Universal, 1976. García was the subdelegate for the neighborhood of La Candelaria in the Delegación of Coyoacán (Mexico City), and for the previous 35 years, he said, he had also played the role of Pontius Pilate in that neighborhood's passion play.[4] The year 1941, he said dramatically, was when Catholic cult regained its liberty. He pointed out proudly and rightly that the passion had been performed in Coyoacán as early as 1586, and implied that these representations had continued to be performed right up "to the 70s of the previous [nineteenth] century, when they were suspended, until he and other neighbors revived them 36 years ago."[5] From the Taxco report, we can fill in what García did not say: there can be no doubt that this action of the subdelegate was taken only with the approval of the proper national authorities. It would seem that at this or at a date slightly closer to mid-century and to the rule of Alemán, the long, long legacy of official anticlerical policy in Mexico had begun to soften. The people of Mexico were able to start again their representations of the death of Jesus.

Needless to say, whatever they said, the pueblos that did put on the plays could not simply resume an established set of practices and staging from ancient times, but rather tailored their plays now and later to contemporary conditions. Perhaps the greatest theatrical evidence for that flexibility was what proved to be an often irresistible urge of towns to convert wood Jesuses into human ones, an urge we have already documented in Iztapalapa. Quite various forms of passion emulation soon emerged on the streets and roads of the country. They stretch from plays performed *in situ* to those that were really only processions of one or more aspects of the passion— like the ecclesiologically favored Procession of Silence or Santo Entierro that only buried Jesus—through various mutations of the *Tres Caídas* up to plays that were similar to the living theater of Iztapalapa. The material objects employed also had a broad range, from clothes meant to identify passion figures worn by persons with no other theatrical duties, through litters bearing papier-mâché figures of particular passion scenes, to a fascinating passion integrally reenacted by an articulated wood statue in Papalotla (Edo. de Mex.), and so on.[6] Several of the passions were allegedly copied from famous old-world models (San Luis Potosi from Seville [U: 1966], Taxco from Cadiz [U: 1991]), while others, for example in Nayarit, Sinaloa, and Sonora, preserve such a powerful overlay of native religion that their European roots can almost escape notice.

The two newspapers utilized in my research provide an almost crushing amount of often in-depth documentation on perhaps a score of these spectacles. The task of exploiting this documentation must fall on my successors, presumably working on individual passions or at most on regional groupings. All the same, I do want to make certain observations about these mushrooming "traditions," most of which got off the ground in the 1950s and 1960s.

The first observation is that those spectacles that included an acted Way of the Cross commonly used the text of Pérez Escrich. Indeed, it was not uncommon for a former Iztapalapan who had moved away to become director of a play in his new residence, despite the attempt of the Comité to forbid that practice.[7] Secondly, the directors of these many plays always sought to add something unique to their productions. We know this because they repeatedly pointed out how their play was different from that in Iztapalapa, which throughout the last third of the past century remained the great measuring stick for all such plays. The comparisons to Iztapalapa were predictable. There were several protests against the Iztapalapan use of a live Jesus, usually because a wood statue got more "respect" (E: 1 April 1994), whereas a living Jesus ran the risk of attracting laughs from his friends. Needless to say, the clergy had an interest in such an argument, because the churches usually owned the statues. One reporter ventured the thought that a live Jesus had pre-Hispanic roots—thereby suggesting a relation between Aztec and Christian human sacrifice—but that idea does not recur (U: 1995). Another recurrent theme among Iztapalapa's competitors was that their productions aimed not at "a folkloric production" but rather at "an up-to-date message from the church";[8] Iztapalapa's play, on the contrary, was "just theater" (E: 1976; U: 1979, 1990).

Another way to assert a valuable difference was to point out, as did the pueblo of Cuajimalpa, that it was still in the countryside, while Iztapalapa (which had just recently opened its subway stop) was city (E: 1990). In other words, visitors to outlying places could still relive time-honored pilgrimages. This archaic dream was, of course, one of the motives that had for decades led people to visit the towns in the wetlands south of the capital, but nostalgia was particularly strong at this juncture. In the city, and perhaps especially in the parishes of San Angel and the new bourgeois enclave of Sagrada Familia, unmistakable evidence exists of a revival of the ancient native musical tradition in the Good Friday processions of their mestizo parishioners (U: 1963, 1966).

Finally, the matter of the antiquity of one's local passion in comparison to that of Iztapalapa was of no little importance, as the records regarding those of Cuajimalpa, on the west side of the Federal District, demonstrate. Its promoters start out modestly enough, with El Universal in 1971 and again in 1973 informing its readers that this fascinating spectacle, which featured different passion groups beating up each other "to cure their mutual guilt," had begun as early as 1928 or 1929. Yet even that date appears fudged, for the organizers said that little was known of these early years because the original organizer of the play was opposed to photographs. Besides, he "wanted still less that something would develop here comparable to what Iztapalapa offers to the public"! The early passion there was, in short, just meant to attract outsiders.

Yet soon enough, the rage for antiquity and folkloric authenticity, which the Iztapalapans themselves were not immune from, proved too much for the Cuajimalpans; they had to outdo their neighbors. In the very next year, 1974, the same journal passed on the claim of local organizers that Cuajimalpa's performance was "more than 100 years old," conducted since 1874 at the latest. What could have stimulated such a reckless claim, we ask, and are answered almost immediately with a still greater claim. *El Universal* of 1986 reports that the passion had been performed for more than 130 years (=1856), "and thus it is older than Iztapalapa's." As if to be sure that no one would ignore that challenge, a separate story in the same day's *El Universal* repeated this claim.

However amazing, these wild historical claims at Cuajimalpa and elsewhere certainly put into context the Iztapalapan Comité's own distortions. But a marvelous conjuncture results from these stories that deserves mention, for this Cuajimalpa information provides important information about Iztapalapa. Clearly, the Cuajimalpans in 1986 claimed their play began in 1856 to prove that it was older than Iztapalapa's, presuming that their competitor's origins lay in the 1880s, which, until 1976, was the Iztapalapans' understanding. But Iztapalapa, we have seen, was engaged in a comparable manipulation of the evidence, and the Cuajimalpa data add to this picture. Why else would Iztapalapa's Comité take a jump from the actual founding date in the 1880s back a half century to 1833 (in 1976) or 1843 (1979)? Can there be any doubt that competition for antiquity was the cause? Certainly the answer must be "no," when we see that after Cuajimalpa in 1974 had catapulted the origins of its performance at least back to 1874, the story just two years later in Iztapalapa was that its great play had not in fact originated in the 1880s, but rather in 1833. It appears, in short, that Iztapalapa's claim that its spectacle went back to the cholera epidemic may have been directly inspired by Cuajimalpa's competition!

Doubtless, the antiquity of a person's hometown play seemed the ultimate weapon that one could wield against the Iztapalapan gorilla. Yet if that failed, towns and villages in the hustings might attempt to outdo Iztapalapa at its own game, imitating the model but just doing it better. Especially in the realm of violence, there is some evidence that as the level of brutality evidenced in the passion of Iztapalapa grew, as we shall later document, so did other towns attempt to outdo the master in this realm. Cuajimalpa again provides perhaps the prime example of the use of violence to attract audience or, as the organizers explained, "so that [the play is] as realistic as possible" (U: 1971).

On Good Friday 1974, the zealous young man who was to play Jesus in the Cuajimalpan passion gave a fascinating interview to El Universal's reporter; as usual, this was then reported in the paper's Holy Saturday edition. "Jesus" insisted repeatedly to this journalist that he wanted to bear a heavier cross than had previously been done, perhaps about 35 kilos in weight, "so that my representation will be more satisfactory to Our Lord." He also insisted on being "really scourged." "Write down," he admonished the writer, "that I want this!" Well to the south, the famous processions of the flagellants of Taxco had by now become famous for the imaginative brutalities they visited upon themselves, even if their processional order varied significantly from that of Iztapalapa. These examples could be multiplied. Several towns attempted to attract attention from Iztapalapa by ever more drastic mutilation.

Competition explains in part why in the second half of the twentieth century scores of towns would take on the substantial task of presenting a Holy Week spectacle. Occasional references to "paying back" debts to supernaturals are encountered, but we may rule out spiritual excitement as a driving force, because local miracles, relics, visions, and the like never assumed any notoriety. What about secular explanations? Doubtless many a village or town father, like don García of Coyoacán above, recognized that the labor involved in and the production of a passion theater could give the citizens of that village a sense of coherence and integrity otherwise threatened in the modern world of mass media dominated by Mexico City. For instance, at Castillo Chico, Cucuitepec, residents had developed a living passion to encourage a citizenry depressed by a wave of drug addiction (E: 26 March 1978). But while individuals may have been motivated in this fashion, this answer cannot explain the planned explosion of passion plays in this period—in the state of Mexico alone there were 214 Good Friday performances in 1992 (U: 18 April).

While not wholly conclusive, tourism certainly provides a forceful one-word explanation. We have seen it regularly cited as a reason for favoring the Iztapalapan passion, so the communities that envied Iztapalapa for its large crowds would also be likely to put tourism up front as a motivation. On the one hand, substantial towns well outside the metropolis, Taxco among several others, emulated Iztapalapa as a regional center. On the other hand, there was intraregional traffic. One of the recurrent themes in our journal reports is the number of tourists who came to Iztapalapa each year not just from the capital, but from the surrounding towns and villages. If any one of these towns developed a passion play that could even begin to compete with that booming center-for-a-day, at least their inhabitants might be persuaded to stay at home in Holy Week, to the profit of local businesses. Thus in the *colonia* (district) of Santa Fe, Mexico City, the Holy Week representations are said to have "served to stop the colony's residents from going to other places to see something we could do here" (U: 1977). Indeed, perhaps residents of the metropole itself, so notoriously empty during Holy Week, might be induced to visit such *colonias* rather than go to Iztapalapa or to the beaches. Iztapalapa was showing that a town could prosper through an annual thespo-religious spectacle. Why not ours?[9]

Again, the sources speak volumes in this regard. The head of the Taxco Comité in 1991 told *El Universal* that if the Holy Week processions were stopped, Taxco would crumble. That was how important the tourism associated with this religious event was in that Guerrero town. This was what towns dreamed of when they originally determined to compete with Iztapalapa, and by this late in the century sought out governmental aid to do so. Thus the tiny town of Santa Rosa Xochiac near the Desierto de los Leones outside the metropolis had, with the assistance of its parish priest, struggled to perform the passion for five years straight without any governmental support, in 1986 attracting 80,000 visitors. Now they went to their Delegación of Álvaro Obregón, bravely demanding that it carry out "promotional activities that would allow them to compete with what Iztapalapa achieves." Such promotional efforts, they continued, "could help attract more tourism, just as does the event that has been performed in Iztapalapa for years" (U: 1986).

After mid-century Mexico experienced an explosion of passion plays, all intended to benefit from the evident success that Iztapalapa was enjoying. Nor was the popularity of these plays limited to Mexico. One factor that unites them all to some extent is the violence they portrayed in the *imitatio Christi*. It is as if worldwide, the increasing availability of the visual was having an impact on the reenactment of history, making it ever more "realistic." Long since the cinema had penetrated down to the village and small-town level, but now with the dawn of television one could rerun the movies and also witness the violence of the past and of the present.

The violence directed against Jesus and his followers is journalistically particularly well documented in three foreign passions of this period, which are significant to our context because the Mexico City papers thought them relevant to the celebration of their own Good Fridays. The first performances were the famous Penitente Ways of the Cross and crucifixions performed by Hispanics in northern New Mexico and southern Colorado, essentially the only non-Iztapalapan passion plays reported by the Mexican press before mid-century.[10] The Mexican press was not interested in the indoor passion plays that had caught on in the United States some time earlier.[11] What did draw their attention was, rather, the penitents' flagellation and their (perhaps undeserved) reputation for actually nailing one of their brothers to the cross each Good Friday, a practice not completely unknown in Mexico itself.[12] In 1937, *El Universal* ran a United Press story referring to the flagellations of these brothers. Ten years later, *Excelsior* carried an Associated Press story saying that the *penitentes* were now silent and no longer bled while carrying their huge crosses. And in 1949, *El Universal* reported that the processions continued in some 20 small towns "in the distant colonies of New Mexico." However, the journalist continued, there have been few documented cases in recent years in which flagellating brothers have been permitted to have themselves crucified, instead remaining bound (*atado*) to a cross until they lost consciousness. The last documented case of this type, our reporter concludes, "occurred in 1939." With that notice of the end of self-mutilation in New Mexico, the Mexico City press stopped reporting on the events in this "distant colony," yet a generation later returned to feature such gruesome events elsewhere. In extensive stories that began in 1970 (*U*) and lasted through 1978 (*E*), both our sources regularly passed on wire stories describing the bloody practices at Santo Tomás, south of Barranquilla, Colombia. Despite a formal episcopal statement of disapproval in 1969, somewhere between 12 and 50 flagellants followed a Way of the Cross that involved incising their backs so as to draw blood from their mutual flagellations. This "barbarous" practice, as it was labeled in the Mexican press, was conceived as an exchange, perhaps a payback to God for a *milagro* received (as distinct from reparation for one's own sins). But the flagellants too were paid once they finished. As revealed in a 1975 report by Agence France Presse picked up by *El Universal,* at least three of the flagellators were supported *(apoyo)* by one or more patrons, from whom they received rum and money. The purpose of this backing was "to promote the brand of a liquor or other product" *(para anunciar la marca de un licor o de otro producto);* scourging itself becoming in this way not only a guarantee of the advertised product but an object of consumption. And the newspapers display obvious eagerness to narrate the brutality of the behavior engaged in by these foreign flagellators.

Besides the general similarity between many of the passions enacted from Iberia through the Americas to the Philippines, the reader experienced in the comparative elements of such behavior cannot help but be particularly struck by the strong similarities between the Colombian passions and those in the Philippine Islands. The latter began to be reported in the Mexican papers in 1971, nine years after live crucifixions were inaugurated in the Philippines, and they continue to command reportorial space into the new millennium. Mexico is not alone: almost every Good Friday, the American television chain CNN carries reports on passion plays not just in the United States of America but in the Philippines, not uncommonly featuring such mutilations.

As Nicholas Barker has shown, the passion of San Pedro de Cutud, dating back to our era, has by now been patronized by the Philippine government for many years, and for straightforward reasons of tourism. Two particularly striking practices draw crowds. The first is the extremely vivid mutual and self-flagellation performed in the village of San Pedro and in the city of San Fernando itself, involving hundreds of young men and recently some women. It is, to be sure, formally opposed by the clergy, but vividly experienced by the participants and by the audience. Here one has since 1962 seen collective devotions that today are rarely to be found elsewhere: boards embedded with glass slammed against different parts of the body to provoke bleeding, and the like. Doubtless most of this vocabulary must ultimately be traced back to Spain and thence to Italy, where traces of it can still be encountered.[13] The second unforgettable aspect of the Philippine passions are the crucifixions. In the village of San Pedro Cutud outside the city of San Fernando (Pampango) north of Manila, a group of men and women, commonly faith healers promoting their services, upon request are actually *nailed* to the cross on Good Friday afternoon for some 20 to 30 seconds, until, that is, they can no longer stand the pain; such practices again date back to the early 1960s.[14] Accounts of such self-mutilation, especially when they come complete with photographs showing the crucified's hands nailed to the cross, have proven irresistible to the Mexican press, and almost every year from 1971 till the present there is such a story in the newspapers. Again, the element of this story featured in the newspapers is its "brutality," as the reports often characterize the activity.

This rapid survey could be further extended to include, for instance, the six-column wide, half-page deep front-page picture of a "crucified" American grade school student "portraying Jesus" while his classmates "keep a solid watch."[15] Such vivid passion plays in different parts of the Christian world suggests that the later twentieth century has been increasingly saturated in social violence—an ever-more-real *imitatio Christi.* By way of placing Iztapalapa in that context of vivacious violence, I want to describe the competition it faced from three major players in its media environs: first, conventional enclosed theater in Mexico City; second, the cinema; and last but ultimately most important, television after mid-century. As a result of these competitive media, newspaper formatting itself was modified, curiously to the advantage of Iztapalapa.

Of the three media, indoor theater is certainly the oldest, even if as late as 1972 an editorial writer in *Excelsior* had to remind those opposed to any theatricalization of Jesus's life that missionary theater stands as the very root of the Mexicas' conversion to Christianity.[16] Still, by the early twentieth century, critics saw theater and film together as one common image producer leading the faithful astray. In *El Universal* (15 April 1927) I encountered a favorable Mexico City review of the New York opening of Cecil B. De Mille's *King of Kings,* and so it is not surprising to find in the same paper as early as 1923 a general condemnation of these

media, which were both inimical, we are told, to the correct celebration
of Holy Week. The unnamed reference is certainly to Iztapalapa:

> The movie houses announce biblical films, while others serve up to
> popular curiosity the passion and death of Jesus. An anonymous au-
> thor has the sweet figure of the Rabbi [Jesus][17] appear on the stage
> of a neighborhood theater. This is something Maeterlinck himself
> would not have dared. In another place . . . for variety, one again
> displays the passion, this time on panels *(cuadros plásticos)* autho-
> rized by the ecclesiastical authority, say the programs. One does not
> have to be a model believer to scorn such an audacious speculation
> for gain.[18]

The arrival of television soon trumped theater and films as competition for the attention of potential passion visitors. Now people did not
even need to leave their homes to watch these services, while television
offered a wealth of other diversions as near as the switch on the set. All
these media were powerfully represented in the newspapers themselves.
If by the seventh decade of the century it had long been true that Holy
Week stories covering Acapulco and other beaches were taking up more
and more space in the newspapers, what appears now is an ever enlarged
advertising and entertainment section prominently figuring films, theatrical productions, and now television shows regarding the passion of Jesus. It might be a pitch for the film *Constantine and the Cross* (U: 1964) or
for the live theater held in the Ciudad de los Deportes in 1968 (*U*), entitled *El Mártir del Calvario* and approved by the church.[19] But the goal was
the same, to compete for the tourist peso with the towns on the southern border of the metropolis. As the *Excelsior* headline had it in 1963,
"The Heart of the City Empty. The Woods, Xochimilco and Iztapalapa,
Overflowing" (*U*).[20] "What does the eternal example of the life of Christ
mean for the youth who rebel, accuse and protest," asked an advertisement for *Cristo 70* in 1970 (fig. 15). "See it!", the ad for the new film, *Jesus
Nuestro Señor,* screamed four times in the Good Friday edition of *El Universal* in 1971, "whether you're a Catholic, Protestant, Christian or an
Atheist." Looking back on Good Friday 1999, *El Sol de México* reflected
on "how important Jesus had been in the movies, but also to theater
and television." Many actors had wanted to play Jesus in Javier García

Mendoza's story *El Cristo de Iztapalapa es de Carne y Hueso,* and many had done so in a number of films the writer proceeds to list. Not the least of these is a Mexican film of 1970, today rare, entitled *El Elegido,* starring Katy Jurado and Manuel Ojeda, which tells the story of a young man who was elected to play the role of Jesus in the Iztapalapan passion.[21]

The newspapers were actually being reshaped as the combined weight of all the various films and indoor theatrical works sank in. The new papal *imitatio Christi* in the different passions of these years was also newsworthy. Until about mid-century, the religious content of our two periodicals was dominated by a substantial ecclesiastico-liturgical section which printed the schedules of upcoming Holy Week events in the various churches of the city and then reported on the events themselves, usually complete with solemn pictures of the archbishop performing various rites. Reports on the Iztapalapan passion were secondary, clearly distinct and separate from the official ecclesiastical, religious, information. This whole section of the newspaper is now in decline, by the last third of the last century at times almost to the point of total neglect, while reporting on the theatrical passions in the Valley and around the world increases apace. A second and equally important trend is visual in nature. As photographs of the popes performing theatrical imitations of Jesus increased, so did those of the archbishop of Mexico and other local prelates start to appear washing feet, carrying the cross, and the like. But not surprisingly, representations of this type obviously enticed editorial layout at these journals to place alongside these photographs other pictures of the laity of Iztapalapa and occasionally those of other towns performing their own theatrical representations. The result is that in year after year in the second half of the past century, as interest in ecclesiastical doings declined, the visual imagination of the reader was sated with front-page photographs that focused completely on the lay passions (see fig. 16). In a world of competition, passion theater ruled.[22]

Like most "Indian" villages, *Excelsior* states in 1964, "Iztapalapa is a silent and sad pueblo" for most of the year. Yet today, despite "the dust, the scarce public transport, the pushing and shoving, and the 'Roman' cavalcades," Iztapalapa, one of the poorest sectors of the Federal District, awakens to find itself the center of international attention, according to the same paper's 1968 story. Jesus was captured, one reporter wrote by way of commenting on the ubiquity of the photographers, not by the soldiers but by the cameramen (E: 1967). Having surveyed the competitive passions outside town in this period, and now being in a better position to gauge the pressures of context upon it, we reenter Iztapalapa with the goal of observing the major changes in its passion during the period 1963–1970. In this we make use of these photographers, who in this period truly determined to make Iztapalapa their own. They were everywhere, searching out their pictures and demanding their place in the sun, a solicitation the organizers would ignore at the peril of lost publicity (fig. 17). They so regularly complained that they could not see the judgment and sentencing of Jesus in the atrium of San Lucas (E: 1968) that a platform had been erected there for them. It had collapsed in 1963, wounding two (U). The cameramen were even more determined to catch their shots during the subsequent Way of the Cross, and they doggedly pursued Jesus and all the action the soldiers directed against both the savior and the audience till the bitter end on the Cerro de la Estrella. As a result they were sometimes attacked by the *sayones,* who claimed they did not realize that their victims were not actors in the spectacle proper (E: 1970). The welfare of these cameramen would always remain a concern of the organizers, because it was they who showed Iztapalapa to the world.

As the 1960s progressed, it became clear to the organizers that the photographers of the new medium of television were twice as important as the others. If television might keep some potential visitors at home before their sets, it could also broadcast images of Iztapalapa. The speed of communications almost outpaced the events. While tourists normally came by tour buses as late as 1968 (E), one great television chain after the other descended on the town in these years, sending these events, even live at times, to the furthest parts of the world at lightning speed. In 1963 came the television cameras of the American and British broadcasting companies (ABC and BBC) (E), and then in 1973 French TV appeared (E), ready to beam parts of the spectacle beyond Mexico to the rest of America and to Europe. It was not long before diplomats made their presence felt: in 1967 the Danish and in 1968 the Japanese ambassador to Mexico witnessed what had become a world event (E). Perhaps the reader can now more readily assess the powerful forces that were acting not only upon the Iztapalapa organizers, but on the Delegación government of the area, and, just as surely, upon the federal government, which by now recognized the tourist magnet that the once modest play represented.

Looking back in 1992 to the divide that marked off the traditional from the modern play, the 72-year-old merchant Hugo Calderón reminded us how things were in earlier times.[23] The Calzada de la Viga was one lane at times, so it was difficult to motor into the borough. Most people who came to see the play were from the communities around Iztapalapa. The capitalinos who came to the town usually continued their way up onto the Cerro de la Estrella, where they opened up picnic baskets and enjoyed the cooler air while awaiting the crucifixion.

Then things had changed radically, Calderón continued. During Ernesto Uruchurtu's two terms as regent of the Federal District (1952–1958, 1964–1966), the Calzada de la Viga had been upgraded into a major thoroughfare; already in 1961, we remember, El Universal referred to this construction as part of the regent's "cataclysm." It was then, Calderón says, that the celebration became famous and the masses began to flow into the crowded market in the center of town. But this bottleneck as well was quickly set aside by the enormous esplanade first mentioned in 1963 (E). Another, younger Iztapalapan gave a different, more domestic, reason for the growth of the festival. Her family told Berenice Baltazar Roldán, who in 1988 played in one of the groups in the play called "the virgins of the pueblo," that the spectacle had grown once the organizers had stopped using images to represent the ancient figures, and started to use live actors.[24] This is of course misleading, for we know that living actors had held almost all the roles since early in the twentieth century. What had happened recently was that the press had taken to identifying by name the strapping young man who played Jesus, and in time most of the other main actors as well came to be named in the press.

Not surprisingly, contemporaries were rarely cognizant of the outside forces described earlier that were propelling their spectacle to an almost baroque size; they were more cognizant of the inside forces at work. We shall examine both these new inside phenomena that go to make up the modern performance: the creation of the esplanade and the emergence of the individual personage in the press coverage of the time. Finally, we shall show how after a period already described in which the local church had regained some role in the spectacle, the early 1970s again saw the dissolution of the church's influence.

But first, let us note just how confident the Comité showed itself in these years in building up the myth of Iztapalapa. Seduced as it was by world attention, it began fabricating legends that were quickly consumed by uncritical journalists. The play is 150 years old, *Excelsior* says for the first time in 1968, and in this same account we hear for the first time that Zapata himself had assured its performance in 1914 and thus uninterruptedly thereafter, a claim linking the play in this way to a Mexican folk hero. The people of Iztapalapa responded to their fame by joining the play in ever greater numbers, and before long the organizers would inflate the number of those attending to enormous numbers.

As the spokespersons pumped information to the media and honored guests, a look around town by journalists revealed a radically redefined center. The church of San Lucas, which for so long had staged the judgment and sentence of Jesus in its atrium, was now "in ruins," and its rector, Antonio Herrera, had "abandoned" it in 1957 (*E: 1967; U: 1969*) because of its decrepitude, moving most divine services to the Santuario while substantial repairs were made. Pánfilo Cruz Martínez, member of the newly constituted Committee for the Reconstruction of the Parish of San Lucas, assured the *El Universal* reporter in the latter year that San Lucas was the third oldest Catholic church in Mexican Christendom, having been built in 1534–1539.[25] Now this committee, funded in part by money earned from the Holy Weeks and thus working with the Comité organizing the performance, was in charge of reconstruction, with the approval of the Secretary of the National Patrimony. Needless to say, the atrium of the same church was itself not long able to fulfill its ancient duties of staging the judgment and sentencing of Jesus. Certainly the platforms built in that narrow space were insufficient, even "badly constructed" (*E: 1967*), and in fact the last record of the atrium being used for this theater was in 1965 (*U*), just one year after the first and only colored photographs of those acts appeared in the periodical press.[26]

It was perhaps as a direct result of this near collapse of San Lucas that the new paved esplanade just in front of that church's atrium replaced the old marketplace in the town's center, with profound implications for pueblo and festival. Its singular function was to hold two, and later three large stages on which were to be performed most of the events of Holy

Thursday and all those of Good Friday preceding the Way of the Cross.[27] It looks like an empty outdoor parking lot in the middle of town during most of the year (fig. 18), but on Holy Thursday and Good Friday this space outside church grounds and beyond ecclesiastical associations became the focus of civic life. Temporary stands were and are erected to host visiting guests and, at the center of the vast esplanadal space, a raised platform ultimately came to hold photographers of all kinds, who with relative comfort could record the action that swirled around them. In the classical format of the event in the latter part of the twentieth century, these photographers first aimed their cameras toward a large platform or stage at one end of the esplanade that served as a stage for the Last Supper and Washing of Feet on Holy Thursday, and the Palace of Herod on Good Friday. Then on Good Friday from the same perch they made photographs of another great platform which served as the Palace of Pontius Pilate. Finally they aimed at a third, smaller platform within the esplanade where Jesus was whipped after being sentenced. Throughout all this, outside that huge charmed rectangle, after 1965 and to this day the old atrium of San Lucas has usually stood off empty and silent.

The Delegación's decision to build the esplanade certainly resulted in large part from the woeful condition of San Lucas and the increasing popularity of the spectacle. There is, however, one further motivation. In 1965, the *El Universal* reporter observed that most of the crowd at the spectacle was on the Cerro de la Estrella, not down in the center of town to witness the action before the crucifixion. As we have seen, the Cerro had for decades been a favorite picnic area for visitors to the city. But for at least the last three decades it had been the site of the crucifixion and thus the culmination of the show. Indeed, this is the sight that brought many of the tourists to town in the first place. Clearly, Delegación and Comité both hoped that a huge new esplanade would draw large numbers to witness the earlier parts of the passion.

The major change in the spatial structure of the center meant that the nature of the reporting of this spectacle would itself change. Thus increasingly in subsequent years, journalists and photographers arrived in Iztapalapa on Holy Thursday, not Good Friday. As a result, newspaper readers in the metropole now received live reports of Holy Thursday activities, for after reporters witnessed that evening's events, they might send that copy on for the Good Friday edition of their paper. Just as important, the presence of reporters and photographers in Iztapalapa on Holy Thursday meant that readers would receive much more information on the preparations for the spectacle, not merely on the performances themselves. A shift to human interest, a concentration on the experiences of individual participants gearing up for their day in the sun, now became an important element in the reporter's arsenal. Moreover, journalists now began to provide their readers with occasional lists of all the major actors in the play, a practice that brought with it the individuation of those thespians in their own and in the public eye. Thus space, time, and, as we see, characters had all been remolded to make possible the modern delivery of the journalistic product.

As the journalists who had arrived around noon on Holy Thursday awaited the beginning of the events later that afternoon, they spread out to pick up pieces of local color for their stories. They might encounter "Jesus," "Herod," "the Wandering Jew,"[28] even six of the "Twelve Apostles" busy erecting the platform on which they themselves would reenact the Last Supper that very evening (E: 24 Mar. 1967). The same reporter found the Comité still hard at work on the text of the performance so as to eliminate repetition. The rector of San Lucas, whom *Excelsior* identified in 1964 as part of the organizing Comité and indeed as the "principal inspiration of that year's performance," is seen on Holy Thursday 1967 (E) instructing the players in the Bible story. But along with these human interest appeals to the traditional reader, our reporters also observed something else that was fairly recent, an attempt to raise the caliber of the acting by the use of professionals. In 1957 the parish rector saw training in acting as one means to end the chaos of the previous years, of course "without losing their qualities of spontaneity" (U). In the sixties we now find repeated references to this matter. In 1964 "famous actors" stepped in to help out (U), and by 1969 *Excelsior* could assert that (drama) students were slowly replacing even some of the old Iztapalapan actors. The increasing emphasis on professionalism, with each actor now providing his or her own costume,[29] especially touched the person playing Jesus, who was of course the most important of all the actors, and the need for a Jesus polished in both appearance and gestures was already recognized in 1956, when a young drama student, Fidel Hernández, was elected to play Jesus, the first of nine consecutive times that this fledgling thespian would do the role, and a record for Iztapalapan Jesuses.

The character individuation to which the reporters increasingly drew attention cannot be grasped without a recognition of the role that reportorial collectivism played in isolating this individual. I mean to say that the reporter's singling out of the individual in these years was accomplished in part by encasing that single person within a set of collectivistic images. As we set out again to make our way up the streets toward the Cerro, the Nazarenes provide a good example of what I mean. Recall that originally these Nazarenes or penitents were seniors, in their procession less doing penance for their sins than fulfilling *mandas* or vows that they had made to various supernaturals in exchange for expected favors.[30] In these years, however, we see clear signs of a movement from adult to child Nazarenes, as the rows of these penitents became longer and longer (fig. 19). In 1964 one hundred (*E*) but in 1976 five hundred (*U*) Nazarenes processed, each with a cross of his own, but in 1968 *Excelsior* specified that thirty among the Nazarenes were *niños*. This is the first indication of the trend that the Nazarenes were being transformed from a body of adults to one that is today overwhelmingly made up of children and young teenagers, as we shall see. These juvenile Nazarenes would of course continue to state that their "penance" on Good Fridays issued from promises they had made, but the irony and the anachronism were clear. In fact, these youngsters were *acting like adults,* rather than expiating sins their young hearts had not committed. Carrying his own cross, each one of them amongst his massed fellows was a reflection of the (young adult) superstar at the center of everyone's attention. Their collective, sinful innocence threw a stark light on the individual Jesus now taking up his cross to Golgotha.

Both by design and fortuitously, Jesus's painful procession through the streets of Iztapalapa and then his ascent to the high Cerro in these years tell a romantic, tragic story of the challenges facing mature males. Each individual Jesus worked to achieve this appointment with crucifixion, just as the town itself struggled to bring off this spectacular with honor and profit. The mental world of the Iztapalapans from now on in these years will in fact be dominated on each Good Friday by two central questions: will Jesus "carry the heaviest cross of all time . . . as if it were a weightlifting championship?" (*E*: 13 April 1979); and, loaded down with that cross, would our Jesus be able to survive the three- to four-kilometer march up the Cerro, to then be mounted on the cross, all, as the same reporter noted, "without the help of any Cyrene?"[31]

In 1964, *Excelsior* for the first time specified the weight of the cross (78 kilograms) borne by Jesus—whose identity was by now regularly revealed. Thereafter, each newspaper gave that weight each year, and it increased annually. After achieving what a reporter significantly called a "nuevo récord" of 80 kilos in 1979 (*E:* 6 April), the figure rose in the following decade up to 100 kilos, where it remained for several years.[32] One reason for this recordkeeping might be religious in nature: the greater the weight of the cross, it was said, the greater the remission of the temporal punishment due to sin.[33] Nor is this emphasis on athletic performance in public religious mortification new; for centuries the ability of Southern Europeans to bear the weight of a cross and absorb floggings might at the same time be a sign of religious blessing and witness of one's chivalric love for some young girl.[34] Still, the explanation offered by our sources is much simpler. From the mid-1960s, the macho image of the Iztapalapan man was in play when the individual Jesus set out to prove himself, and his community, foremost by shouldering these enormous crosses.

But it was one thing to take up one's cross, and quite another to survive the ordeal that took Jesus up the four-kilometer path and onto his cross. As noted earlier, the clerical attempt after 1956 to regularly nail an image of Jesus onto the Cerro cross had failed, and the live Jesus of the Way of the Cross again attempted to fulfill his crucifixional destiny. The years 1963 and after, however, now witnessed a series of human failures, as one Iztapalapan after another collapsed in the attempt.[35] When Fidel Hernández failed that year, he was replaced with a corn-pith Jesus on the cross (*U*).[36] In 1964, the same Hernández, playing Jesus for the ninth and last consecutive time, could not make it up onto the cross, and the reporter noted with irony that while he lay stretched out on a Red Cross litter, a wax image of Jesus arrived on another litter, to be raised up onto the cross between Dimas and Gestas, the two (live) thieves.[37] The same thing happened in 1965 (*U*), and again in 1966, when the new Jesus, Manuel Nerio, variously described as rental car entrepreneur, mechanic, or taxi driver, took up the ordeal. After Nerio had fainted in the former year at the point or station that Jesus encountered his mother, the organizers of the latter thought the better of it and proceeded immediately to raise up an image furnished by the rector of San Lucas. Again in 1967, the omens were not good. *El Universal* tells how a horse ascending the hill ahead of Jesus broke loose and fell backwards, "almost crucifying" Jesus, the writer noted with evident glee at his choice of words. *Excelsior* in the same year then describes Nerio fainting and being carried away on a litter, an image again replacing him. (The year 1968 was extraordinary in this respect, because there was actually no crucifixion even of a wax or corn figure, and we shall return to that event shortly.) Thus not until 1969, when a new Jesus, Pedro Guillén, replaced Nerio, is it clear that the person representing Jesus actually did mount the cross and join the thieves, yielding the classic figure of Golgotha to the immense crowds and to the greedy television cameras (*E*).

In these years reporters had concentrated on the athletic prowess of each individual Jesus, the weight each bore being a statement about pretensions, the failure to mount the cross an ultimate judgment not only about Jesus's individual strength, but about the success of Iztapalapa itself in pulling off the spectacle. In the opinion of most contemporaries, there was a definite reason for such failures: the Way of the Cross itself was little short of a battlefield, and the first victims of this disorder were the Jesuses themselves. At every step of the way, but especially when they had to rise up from a fall, they were met with what seemed to bystanders to be particularly violent beatings by the soldiers (*U*: 1968). Manuel Nerio had fainted in 1968, the *El Universal* chronicler said, because the crown of thorns had dug into his scalp so deeply but also "because he had been beaten so severely." For all the playacting, the Jesuses were simply exhausted by the time they neared the peak of the Cerro.

A scarcity of police was no longer the problem. Precisely in these years the Comité began to enumerate for reporters the numbers of the forces of order, and they escalate along with everything else in the whole last third of the century. Over the years, large contingents came to man the barriers that now separated the audience from the esplanade during the judgment and sentencing of Jesus. Guarding this esplanade could at times seem the very essence of police authority.[38] But the place of true combat between the police and the audience was still, as it had been in earlier periods, the Way of the Cross itself. And what a crowd it was. Between 1963 and 1970, that path affords perhaps the grimmest picture of the Iztapalapan record, one full of conflict and violence.[39] The soldiers of the play and the formal forces of order were essentially two sides of the same coin, and their radical increase in these years made for an annual conflict, as the exploding population of the borough in the streets strained to see their savior pass by on the way to his death. The procession of 1966 was perhaps the most brutal. Centurions and their horses trampled bystanders who were attempting to see or touch Jesus passing by, hitting men, women, and children while some 200 policemen made themselves scarce. One source says that in this case, the audience was the victim of the actors (E). So great was the disorder, said *Excelsior* in 1967, that Jesus's guardian angel received more blows than the lord himself.

Yet here again, our writers link this very disorganization to the affective expression from the people who lined the route of the *Tres Caídas*. Not only did the procession in 1968 provoke tears in hundreds of people (E); when the centurions beat Jesus along the same route, bystanders as in the past yelled something like: "Don't strike him! Leave him alone!"[40] The event had not lost, would not lose, its ability to move the Christian audience. Nor were the streetwise reporters slow to critique appearances that might discourage such devotion. Thus the Holy Thursday reporter for *Excelsior* in 1967 complained that Manuel Neria "did not look like the Divine Redeemer," but he was pleased to report that the girl playing Mary had as her main task crying without any external help.

The great procession slowly rose up out of town to finally reach the spot where, from that day to this, Jesus and the two thieves would be "crucified," through the agency of metal brackets that support their arms and bodies. This area was, however, even more difficult to police than the area downhill, and so many fights broke out that it was an embarrassment that had to be corrected, as the *El Universal* reporter wrote in 1965. A somewhat ill-tempered reporter for *Excelsior,* observing the panoply on Good Friday of 1967, compared the Cerro to a public garbage heap, and described again the trampling of the thousands of people who had long since staked out their places on the hillside to observe the procession up the hill and the great crucifixion of the three men at its crest.

The average reporter did not realize, however, that the crowding and confusion of the Way of the Cross in this period, as earlier, were one of the conditions for the persistent religious enthusiasm that they report. For every reporter who could write that a performance was "tumultuous but reverent" (U: 1964), thus pointing to this fusion, ten others indulged in the customary complaints of disorder. Yet around 1967 and 1968 observers were distinctly gratified by the course of events. The curate of

San Lucas, for instance, thought the events of 1968 were much better ordered than in previous years. The police commandant on Good Friday of
the same year was quite as gratified. He told *Excelsior:* "Previously, no decent person dared come here on Good Friday. And now you see not only
entire families, but many tourists."

In the light of such sentiments, and of the obvious benefits the celebration brought to the borough, the attitude reported by the *Excelsior*
Good Friday reporter of 1967 to the effect that some people (still) favored doing away with the ceremony, was definitely minoritarian. What
rather rose to the surface were sentiments like those of an *El Universal*
reporter writing in 1964, on 21 March. He began by imagining that
Iztapalapa could become "one of the most important pilgrimage centers
in the whole country," because more and more people were coming to
venerate the Señor de la Cuevita or Santo Entierro, which was now said
to be *muy milagrosa.*[41] (This is the first and indeed only reportorial claim I
can find that this statue was miraculous.) The writer then proceeds to
narrate a legend of this statue's origins, also the first of its kind. Finally,
the reporter recounts how on Good Friday evening the image of the
Santo Entierro presided over a procession in which the corpse of Jesus
was followed by penitents, the apostles, virgins, Jews, and allegorical
cars, with 8,000 neighbors from the barrios falling in behind. All of this,
our writer makes clear, he had from the representative of the organizing
Comité. Was this not one more reason, he concluded, for the government, and especially the Department of Tourism, to provide substantial
subventions for the event, so that in the future there will be "greater media attention, [as Iztapalapa] is converted into an international tourist attraction"?

Obviously, this reporter had made his choice: the passion of
Iztapalapa, and not that of Cuajimalpa or any other pueblo of
the Valley that wished to compete with Iztapalapa, was the
one ready to rise to international status in an age of globalism. The years
1963 to 1970 had indeed seen the emergence of competitive Jesuses
ready to outdo the Iztapalapan forerunner through increased mortificat-
ions. That pueblo had responded by converting their Jesus—long since
no child innocent—into an athlete distinguished by his weightlifting abil-

ity and endurance. This might not be realistic; he is not like the Jesus of biblical times, whose very defenselessness and helplessness had been integral to his man/Godhood. The new model is rather a macho hero who, in Guillermoprieto's words, only wants to die for his people's salvation.[42] But it was this strong, assertive Jesus who could bring Iztapalapa the international attention it now yearned for.

8

fOR SALE: THE HUMAN INTEREST
Of A WORLD SPECTACLE

"Today, in the Coliseum of the city of Rome, the highest dignitaries of
Christianity will relive the fourteen stations of that transcendental moment in the life of humanity."

With these words, Mexico's Channel 2 invited readers of *El Universal*
to tune in that Good Friday morning of 1978. Viewers would see not just
the pope, but the institution of prelacy itself converted into so many divine fishermen witnessing their master's suffering. The strong theatrical
tone of the advertisement reveals how successfully the television medium, at least, was changing ecclesiology into dramaturgy and corporeal
imitation into virtual images, thus rendering it ever more difficult for the
lay Iztapalapans to hold their own in this thespian battle. Yet the Mexican
church had itself come to terms with its new thespian mission and identification, and no longer wished the Holy Week festivities to go away.
Instead, that establishment was taking up the role of dramaturge everywhere and preaching the moral value of such theater. How times had
changed!

The decade before us, 1971–1982, is crucial for understanding modern
passion theater. On the one hand, this is a period in which the reporters
from the capital further broke down and described individual elements
of Iztapalapan life. We learn a great deal more about the organization of

the play, the parts that the different neighborhoods *(barrios)* now played in that organization, the sums of money that had to be raised each year, and gain more insight into town mythology. On the other hand, the attempt to present the spectacle as an aesthetic form tempted certain power brokers in the city to imagine that the town image during the passion presentation could be sold for a fixed price to a single outside buyer, as if this seething "inferno," in one reporter's word, were one single commodity. The resulting fiasco mirrored similar notions in Mexican national life during this decade, which began with the looting of Mexico's newly discovered oil reserves and concluded, at the end of the presidency of José López Portillo y Pacheco, with the forced devaluation of the peso and the *fin de siècle* impoverishment of much of the country.

It is the ambivalent sense of values, which draws one's attention now toward particulars, now toward the totality of the Iztapalapan passion, that is the center of our concern in this chapter. The input of the church in driving this ambivalence completes a triangle of concerns before us. The tortured relations between the local church and the lay presenters of this spectacle led to a fissure that threatened town order itself. In the course of this decade, the first hints appear of the realization that, ultimately, the church—no longer antagonistic to the play no matter what the text—would have to be let back into the spectacle if the town was to exploit its festival to the fullest.

The recent history of the church's involvement in the Iztapalapan passion begins with the fateful Way of the Cross in 1968 when, the Jesus of that year being unable to reach the place of crucifixion, the local churchmen failed to step in and provide the organizers with a figure of Jesus to affix to the huge cross, as they had in previous years. To the shock of contemporaries, there was no crucifixion on the afternoon of Good Friday, 1968; Gestas and Dimas hung alone alongside the naked cross planned for a Jesus at the top of the Cerro de la Estrella. What lay behind this debacle, and what happened when that representational element was omitted that was the very goal and essence of the Iztapalapan passion? *Excelsior* suppressed the whole matter, but, fortunately, *El Universal* answers these questions to our satisfaction.

As had happened repeatedly in recent years, Jesus (Manuel Nerio), fol-

lowed on the Way of the Cross by "members of various religious con-
gregations," (E)[1] fainted short of reaching the top of the Cerro "because
of the lashes that the centurions had given him" (U). But this time the
parish priest Antonio Herrera stepped forward to tell the crowd that
he would not provide the expected Jesus sculpture: "You came to be
amused, to feel folklore, to divert yourselves, rather than to participate respectfully and in silence to commemorate the road to Calvary.
God wills that which has happened. You will not have a crucifixion. The
cross will remain empty, and nothing will take Jesus's place. Pray and
sing with me."

Many on the Cerro were dumbfounded, breaking out in tears and
blaming the priest "for having interrupted the staging of the Via Crucis."
Worse: since there was no Jesus on the cross, his Seven Last Words could
not be intoned there. Instead, to hear them many had to return to the
church of San Lucas to take part in the so-called Mass of the Seven Last
Words.[2] With the church uncommonly full of people assisting in the
Good Friday liturgy, the Stations of the Cross were carried out along its
inside walls at about 4 P.M. In short, in 1968 Good Friday church services
supplanted a central part of the popular spectacle on the Cerro de la
Estrella. Not to mention the Japanese diplomats who were present: even
some of the people in the church, El Universal continues, were not happy
that Jesus had not been crucified on the Cerro, obviously a powerful image of Christian emotiveness! On the other hand, many others thought
with the priest that people indeed had to stop visiting the Cerro for diversion and instead be respectful. God, it is implied, had caused this to
happen, and the reader can well understand why Father Herrera had
been so gratified by this outcome of the 1968 passion. The church had
proved that it was obviously still a player in the Iztapalapan passion, up
to and including determining its outcome.

To this event can be traced the beginnings of a counteroffensive by the
churchmen and traditional Catholics against what they thought had become of the Iztapalapan spectacle. Although neither the churchmen nor
lay traditionalists remotely wished to return the passion to its earlier
state—all were reliant on the numerous tourists who each year aug-
mented town income—they did want to regain a more traditional model
or liturgy for these days. And nothing showed their determination, nothing proved the decisiveness of these years, than the events of the follow-

ing year 1969, recorded by both our periodical sources in their customary Holy Saturday stories.

The *Excelsior* reporter was in Iztapalapa first thing that Good Friday morning of 1969, and found the streets and squares empty "except for some people who made their way to the church of the Cuevita, where the parish priest of [Iztapalapa], Antonio Herrera, would celebrate his own passion, as the faithful put it"—rather than the lay passion, the writer means us to understand. Something unusual was clearly afoot. That reporter did not know what Herrera's service might be, but he did know of another rite that the priest would indeed stage in the Santuario later that day, after the famous lay crucifixion. "What is certain," he said, is that padre Herrera "just as he has done for several years, did celebrate the last station of the Way of the Cross [the burial or Santo Entierro], which in Iztapalapa is called 'Los Nazarenos,' in the atrium [of the Santuario]." (*El Universal* added that "Los Nazarenos" was put on "by some penitents of Iztapalapa.") In short, at the beginning of this report there is already an intimation that Herrera was again at the work of reestablishing clerical influence. For some years he had been trying to bring "Los Nazarenos" or the ceremony of Santo Entierro to the Santuario after the *Tres Caídas* had ended in the crucifixion, but now there were suspicions that he was staging some other rite much earlier, at about the time the well-known passion was about to get underway in the great esplanade at the center of town.[3]

The truth was that, on that morning, the customary permission for the play to begin had not yet been granted. This was an almost annual cliffhanger in which the clergy held out as long as it could to obtain the best terms from the town and the organizing Comité. Unlike in previous years, when the text of the play was the matter formally at issue, in 1969 money was what held up the decision to go ahead, and specifically, the procedure by which funds garnered from the spectacle would pass to the Committee for the Reconstruction of the parish church of San Lucas. The particulars of the disagreement are obscure, but the result was that this churchman, who was the parish priest of San Lucas, lost his role in handling income from the performance. Padre Herrera had to step down from his position in the Comité Organizador, and this allowed the lay members to pass the monies directly to the committee charged with the reconstruction. According to *El Universal*, this agreement was achieved when the governmental Delegate of Iztapalapa mediated between the priest and the Organizing Committee.

With that agreement in place, the Delegación government gave the go-ahead signal for the annual spectacle, and the esplanade near San Lucas promptly came to life. "But," *Excelsior* reports ominously, "the tension among the people was tangible." There was obviously one group of laity at the (otherwise empty) San Lucas in favor of "La Pasión," and another at the Santuario approving of "Los Nazarenos."[4] The danger of conflict between the two groups was patent. "Sixty grenadiers placed themselves at strategic spots to prevent one of the contending groups from trying to subvert order," the reporter noted, then specifying those spots. Various Secret Service agents, *Excelsior* continues, stood guard at the entrances of the Santuario and of San Lucas.

Surely, the *El Universal* reporter could be forgiven for reserving judgment when Herrera, despite everything, assured him that "there is no dissension." In fact, this long-time curate disappeared from Iztapalapa without a trace in the months after the 1969 spectacle, and was soon replaced by a new parish priest. Herrera had clearly launched a tradition-based protest against the great street pageant, perhaps related to the traditionalism that arose around the Christian world to counter the reforms of Vatican II. In any case, from that day to this, such traditionalists have consistently attempted to maintain something of a separate identity from the established pageant.[5]

Curiously, the crisis of 1969 seems to have established, once and for all, and for one and all, the unavoidability of the Iztapalapan performance. One writer in *El Universal* proclaimed in 1982 that "the Iztapalapans refuse to bury their traditions." What he meant was that this holiday had become central to the city's existence. As another writer of the time paraphrased his sources, "the passion, so say the residents, is something that has noticeably evolved. Its value as an element of social cohesion cannot be overstated" (*E:* 1980). The clergy would not be denied its part in this chorus of affirmation, and from the mid-1970s its spokesmen regularly broadcast one boilerplate message, obviously received from above: there really was nothing wrong with the Iztapalapan passion. After all, it was "mere theater," a "theatrical recollection" positively contributing to a good Christian life since almost all the actors do

it as a type of penance and go to communion before the representation"
(*U*: 1973, 1976). In order to take part in it, citizens had to have their confession heard and receive communion, and that was good.

This ecclesiological reasoning is surprising enough: one would not expect to learn that play acting, the *bête noire par excellence* of traditional
churchmen, was now viewed as a means to increase the faithfuls' reception of the sacraments. In approving the play, that clerical position does
not attach any moral utility to the *imitatio Christi*. Rather, the traditional
requirement that the Comité imposed on its putative actors to take the
sacraments is what is valuable and redeems the performance. Needless
to say, this clerical rhetoric is unconvincing: the actors had taken the sacraments in this way for decades without the play having been acceptable
until now.

Just as amazing is the clergymen's newfound admiration for the
mandas or vows that were such an important part of the exchange system inherent in the play. I can find no clerical interest or involvement in
these *mandas* before this point. The faithful swore to a certain supernatural and practically to the play's organizers, we recall, that they would participate in the passion for a certain number of years on the condition that
the divinity fulfill their request, or in thanks for having done so already,
and this allowed the organizers to plan. As I have earlier indicated, the
basis for participation in these passions was not really to afford penitents
the opportunity for the "remission of the temporal punishment due to
sin," to cite the traditional clerical formulation, but rather a simple payback (the verb *pagar* is quite customary) of a debt incurred by the penitent himself in making the vow, to a supernatural who held his or her
marker.

Doubtless the understanding of these payments was different for the
clergy and the populace, the former insistent on the actor's guilt, the latter rooted in notions of contract. What is so interesting about the new
clerical approval of the plays is that it *de facto* involves accepting a popular rather than a theological understanding of the vow. This novelty is
quite striking, since the *manda* system itself works without the sacra-
ment of confession or the participation of a confessor. The clerical appeal to the "pagan" play to stimulate laymen to go to confession is,
surely, no historical accident. For in the last third of the twentieth cen-

tury, ecclesiastical authorities have had to face what for them is a more general crisis. Ever fewer of the faithful are having their confessions heard.

What really renders this ecclesiastical argument moot lies, in fact, in the age of the processional "penitents." The churchman who approved these *mandas,* after all, did not live in the 1920s, when one could postulate that penitents above the age of reason were actually repenting their sins. The whole movement of the Iztapalapan spectacle from the 1950s has, we have noted, been toward the assumption of roles by actors rather than by those who for religious reasons assumed a sacred role, and this dynamic is nowhere clearer than among the body of Nazarenes who accompanied Jesus on the Way of the Cross. Those who "played Nazarenes," in the words of one reporter (U: 1971) were by now mostly children, not adults. In other words, they played as if they were repaying *mandas* but often had not made any such promises on their own because of their tender age. Indeed, I encountered at least one case in which a child took up his cross and crown of thorns to fulfill his *mother's* vow to a divinity (U: 1979). Consequently, from a purely formal point of view, the priest's praise for the *manda* as a type of repayment through (self-) punishment for one's sins does not concur with the times and does not ring true.

This passage from a religious experience to a theatrical one, or, as it was conceptualized by one contemporary, from religious sentiment to folklore (U), was not smooth at all, for if not among the priests, then surely among the bulk of the population in attendance, it was expected that those who played the roles would experience them. One of the striking aspects of the decade of the 1970s is revealed in an *El Universal* report of 1977, which states unequivocally that two of the lead actors had not sought the parts out of religious motives. The reporter writes that Carlos Rivas Fragoso had wanted to play Jesus for three years, "for no other reason than that he knew that he would be the center of attention of the neighborhood." "He had little interest in religion," the writer continued, "and knew the Bible just as little, even if a vague religious sentiment that he got from his parents led him to put himself forward as a candidate." Sofia Gutiérrez was no whit better, according to our source. At seventeen years of age, she was not very religious at all. But "her ostentation, the simple purple dress on which her father spent 2,500 pesos, and her pride" stood her in good stead when Pedro Guillén, one of the organizers, met her and decided "that I looked like the Virgin," as she told the reporter.

Clearly, a complementary relationship was developing between the organizers' determination to present a whole spectacle as an aesthetic unit, and a felt need on the part of readers for human interest stories through which they could get to know and to like or dislike the various actors. We see it in metaphors of behavior: on the one hand photographers offer to take a snapshot of a visitor next to the Virgin Mary (U: 1982), while on the other a Mary Magdalene armed with her own camera moves along the Way of the Cross snapping pictures of the outside world looking in on her (U: 1975). This human interest urge comes out still more clearly in the reportorial attempts, before the performance had begun, to interview the upcoming Jesus and even his family. The best example of this at the time involved the family of the same Rivas, this time playing Jesus in 1979 (U: 12 April). We learn that Rivas was a twenty-year-old taxi driver—an occupation he shared with several others in this decade—who did not have an athletic build. His spiritual guide is the current parish priest of Iztapalapa, padre José Socorro Quintana. The sister of "Christ" is one Rosaura, and he has a brother named Antonio, who speaks with the interviewer about the cross, which he thinks weighs more than 100 kilos. More than 5 meters long, it was made by an out-of-town carpenter. Antonio then shows the reporter the crown of thorns, and notes that it has enormous spines. "Clearly, we will cut the spines in the interior part by half so that they do not stick in him, for no one wants to really hurt him."

The cross "lies against the outside wall of an apartment that contains the image of St. Paul. We have this image because my papa is the mayordomo of the barrio. The image is the one that belongs to the barrio [and] each of the Iztapalapan barrios has its image and its mayordomo. Since my father is the mayordomo, we will keep the image for a whole year.[6] We are required to venerate it here," Antonio continues, and so the Rivas Fragoso family has assigned a whole section of the house "in which the altar and the image of St. Paul stand alone." The interview ends with Antonio once again expressing pride in his father's office, telling the reporter that both he and his brother Carlos, the once and future Jesus, were attending the tryouts for roles (ensayos) in the house that had held them for so long, that of the Cano family in the Callejón de Aztecas.

This interview is interesting precisely because a newspaper thought that the family vignette of the Rivases anchored in their neighborhood would appeal to its readership. From a single passage in *El Universal* in 1964, we know that the participation of members of each Iztapalapan neighborhood in the passion presentation was now, and for the very first time in the history of the pageant, a desideratum, but until this 1979 story there is no indication that these barrios played any perceptible role.[7] Now life in these eight traditional barrios starts to make itself felt in the reports, and in subsequent years, as we shall see, these neighborhoods slowly became an institutionalized part of the passion activities, even as the identity of the play as dominated by a few historic families yielded to modernity. Before 1964, the newspapers give no evidence that the barrios as organizations mattered to the passion of Iztapalapa. Now they do.

The makeup of the Comité Organizador is a second aspect which the newspapers of this decade record with individuality and detail. This history is not easy to document with the institutional precision one would wish, for the Comité has maintained its internal history as a closely guarded secret and books of the Comité have been unavailable to this researcher. But the newspapers of these years do, as indicated earlier, often record the names of each of the main players, and by the decade at hand, these lists resemble the cast lists of motion pictures and legitimate theater productions. From them, one can now study who has held particular roles in the last fifty or sixty years.

It turns out that the leading Roman and Jewish roles were and are usually retained by the same persons year after year. Thus the famous tryouts held each winter are mainly for the Christian roles, with the Jews and Romans doing the judging. Particular roles tended to pass from one member of a family to another. The most important discovery is that until 1988, the dominant family in the history of the presentation has been the Guerra family, the very family that hinted at one point that it might have been involved in the movement of the play from Chimalhuacán to Iztapalapa at the end of the nineteenth century.[8] In short, until yesterday, so to speak, not the neighborhoods but a group of important Iztapalapan families has defined the institutional infrastructure of the town's renowned passion play.

The stellar position of the Guerra family in the history of the play is second only to that of the Cano family. From the time of Martín Cano, the president of the Comité Organizador and Iztapalapa's *comisario ejidal* in 1955, this family has been associated with the ceremony because its house in the Callejón de Aztecas, number 7, has been, as *El Universal* put it in 1989, "the seat of the actors of the passion for forty years." But in terms of influence, the Guerra appear to have been unequaled, as already noted by *El Universal* in 1963. Recording the fact that Antonio Guerra Juárez had in that year made his debut as Pontius Pilate, the reporter observes that Antonio's grandfather, José Guerra, had previously played that role as long ago as 1940 (actually 1938), so that the Guerra family was actually "in charge of" the role. What the journalist did not spell out, because everyone knew it, was that the person who played Pontius Pilate, the single most important heraldic role in the passion (Herod being the only contender) was at that time usually simultaneously the director or principal organizer of the play itself, that is, the head of the Comité.[9]

For whatever reason, Antonio did not, alas, repeat either role in 1964, for his father (?), Santiago Guerra Guzmán, succeeded him as Pilate in that year and as Comité head no later than 1967.[10] This obviously powerful leader left a mark on the passion like no other single person. Every succeeding year until 1981 saw Santiago play Pilate, supervise the performance, and struggle with churchmen as the performance rose to great prominence during his tenure, all the while furnishing the press with interviews and this scholar with much crucial information about the whole event. He lived to express his pride in the play's having gained international recognition (E: 1980). Then as the spectacle moved further into its baroque phase, José Guerra Serrano, identified as the third generation of the family to participate in the play and as the son of Santiago Guerra, made his first appearance (U: 1978). By 1982 he was playing Pontius Pilate (U), and in 1983 he directed the performance, continuing in those dual roles through 1986. In 1987 still another and the last Guerra to ascend to these honors, José Luis, emerged as head of the Comité, with the responsibilities "that his ancestors of four generations have passed on to him."

It is unnecessary to do more than cite the journalists themselves in our decade in order to demonstrate the hereditary character for the other main non-Christian roles, for the Iztapalapans were anxious to broadcast these longevities. In 1978 *El Universal* cited Porfirio González Cedillo in his role as captain of the *sayones* as one of several Iztapalapans who had played the same roles for almost half a century; the same newspaper had documented him by name in that role as early as 1969. The merchant Juan Morales Guillén, 41 years old, told *Excelsior* in 1971 that he had played the role of the bad thief Gestas for 18 years, while his good-thief partner, Hilario Hernández, 43 years old, had hung on the cross in this role for 17 years. Tomás Alvarado Cedillo, whose family had long been involved in the pageant, served as Judas for at least 17 years after he began in 1970 (*U:* 1987). Behind the stage, the chief make-up artist of the production was Martín Guillén Luna, who in the 1971 *Excelsior* is said to have held that job for some 23 years. And as we have already seen in the case of the father who in 1961 passed on his role as a Roman to his son, the less illustrious non-Christian roles probably had a similar longevity among their actors.

Particularly noteworthy among these records up through 1982 is that not one of these actors was identified by his barrio, as we do find to be the case in more recent records. This could indicate that the majority came from the area immediately around San Lucas or the Santuario, in the heart of town, but in any case, the absence of such a barrio identification does make it clear that their residence—and some of these actors were also members of the Comité—was not an essential part of their institutional identity.[11]

Thus just as the individuals playing Jesuses became the stuff of human interest in this decade, so the main players of the passion also became individuated and their names recorded. A third general arena where individuation can be observed is in the increased attention that the financing of the whole festival received in the press. This had presumably become a matter of interest to the newspapers' readers, and has remained so till the present. In 1976 the Comité estimated the total cost of the pageant at 100,000 pesos (c. $8,000 US), 40,000 of which was raised by the organizers (*U:* 16 April). Two years later, the same body came up with a total figure of 175,000 pesos, but after a major devaluation, so that the sum approximated the previous one (*U:* 1978). In 1980, a more substantial worksheet was given. The total expenditure on the ceremony was, the reporter quoted, on the order of 500,000 pesos (c. $19,000 US). To meet those costs, the Delegation taxed some 1,500 traveling salesmen

100 pesos each to raise 150,000 pesos. The delegational government itself chipped in 10,000 pesos, and the rector of San Lucas his "customary"
2,000 pesos (U). All three sources amounted to 162,000 pesos, seemingly
a poor bargain. But the question ultimately was how much money visitors expended in Iztapalapa on Holy Thursday and Good Friday, and
here the news was encouraging. The *El Universal* reporter estimated that
if there had been half a million visitors in all in 1980, and each person
left behind 20 pesos, the town took in something on the order of 10 million pesos. That was a sum that certainly encouraged everyone to plan
for an even bigger crowd next year!

Since in this matter of money the Comité estimated 500,000 visitors
for all of Holy Thursday and Good Friday 1980 to assess the town's
financial gain, we have clearly arrived at the point where the thorny
problem of actual attendance at the passion must be addressed. Let me
be frank. The attendance figures reported in the press at least in the last
third of the twentieth century are grossly, and increasingly inflated, de-
serving no more credit, in fact, than the accepted mythology concerning
the date of origin of the passion.[12] True, these figures can be compared
over time to gauge whether attendance was increasing or decreasing, but
even that is guesswork. The most that can be done is to lay out the dis-
tinctions that were at times made by reporters, report their figures, and
leave it to the judgment of subsequent visitors to the site.

Until 1982, the figures reported each year can be assumed to be those
for Good Friday alone—those on the Cerro combined with those in the
town center—since reporters were rarely there on Holy Thursday in that
period. From 1920 until 1950, five crowd estimates range between 15,000
and 40,000. From 1952 till 1965, the seven estimates range from 30,000 to
300,000, with a mean figure of 250,000, after which they fall off to a
mean of 50,000 until 1970. In the decade 1971–1982, the total figures in
the two papers are as follows:

	Excelsior	El Universal
1971		50,000
1972	400,000	280,000
1973		
1974		100,000
1975	250,000	
1976		750,000[a]

	Excelsior	El Universal
1977	1,500,000[b]	
1978	400,000	400,000
1979		100,000
1980	1,000,000	500,000
1981		600,000
1982	200,000	500,000

a. "Exceeding all predictions"; U.
b. Estimate of the subdelegate; E.

Then suddenly, in 1983, *Excelsior* reports 1,000,000 visitors on Good Friday alone, and from that year almost to the present, the figure given has with rare exception exceeded a million, the maximum figure being 3,000,000 in 1987, and the mean figure for Good Friday being in the neighborhood of 2,000,000. The one major exception to these generalizations is 1992, when, as sorrowful reporters let it be known, only 300 people visited Jesus in prison in the Cano house, barely 20,000 saw Jesus sentenced in the main square, and "very few" people were on the Cerro before Jesus arrived to be crucified (U). A total figure of as low as 250,000 was bandied about in that year, even if the authorities wanted to believe that something approaching a million people had indeed come (E). All this, everyone complained, after a recent past in which up to 3,000,000 visitors had come! The years after 1992 saw a recovery, to be sure, with the mean number through 1999 running around 2,000,000, but the Iztapalapan estimators continue to believe that the peak of attendance had been reached in 1987.

A review of these figures shows that the decade 1971–1982 registered an ascendancy of claimed visitors, figures which then exploded in the following decade, 1982–1992. Closer attention to the figures for 1971–1982 gives us some additional insight into these crowds, even if the figures themselves are much inflated and only have relational value. Though the figures sometimes came from some authority, as often as not the two newspapers reported wildly different numbers for the same year, probably received from different authorities with varied interests. It is these relations which are interesting. In 1971, for example, *El Universal* reported that tourists made up 30,000 of the 50,000 present, the remaining 20,000 being locals (by way of comparison, *Excelsior* in 1974 reported the population of Iztapalapa at 250,000). In 1973, *El Universal* reported 30,000 people in the main plaza for the judgment and sentencing, but 250,000 on the Cerro for the crucifixion, while in 1978 the same figures ran 100,000 and 300,000 in *Excelsior*. The numerical preponderance of the population awaiting the crucifixion over that at the esplanade is certain, and had in fact been assumed throughout the century. Finally, a comment on Holy Thursday crowds. Up until 1982 the size of the crowd that witnessed the Holy Thursday events was reported only in 1978 (12,000 in the esplanade, *E*), to rise, often ridiculously, thereafter. The 20,000 whom *Excelsior* registered in 1984 (*E*) gives way to millions reported in *El Universal* in 1989 and 1992, alongside which the 200,000 figure reported by *El Sol de México* in 1999 seems the soul of reason. The point is that Iztapalapa even today remains only moderately successful in drawing visitors on Holy Thursday, and despite one aborted attempt to stage the Resurrection on Easter, on that feast as well (*E: 1982*). For visitors, Good Friday and its crucifixion remain the essence of the holy season at Iztapalapa.

Readers will not err if they suspect that most of these inflated figures in the last third of the twentieth century, surely enhanced by the competition with other passion spectacles studied earlier, also reflect interests of one or more of the groups determined to produce a large turnout. The problem, however, is that such suspicions cannot often be proven. Still, the immense figure of one-and-a-half million visitors given out by the subdelegate of Iztapalapa in 1977 did indeed emerge in an identifiable political context, to whit, the one known political (as distinct from ecclesiastical) scandal in the history of the passion, involving nothing less than the sale of exclusive photographic rights to the whole pageant to a foreign cinema operation in that year.

The very daring of this sale tells us something about the drive for aesthetic unity that characterized the play in the latter part of the twentieth century, for without such unity, even the idea of selling a play of the streets as if it were an indoor theater production would have seemed risible. Again, context. These were years in which the Iztapalapan organizers advertised a total picture of a previously neglected world-historical site, doing so at times by planting "news" stories they themselves had written, in short, advertisement for tourists. In 1969 *El Universal* passed on the rector's vaunting of the ancient if decrepit church of San Lucas, the third oldest in the Americas. Then in 1976, the same paper let readers know the morning of Good Friday about the archaeological dig on the

Cerro to locate "the alleged Treasure of Cuauhtémoc." And finally in 1979, *Excelsior* printed a tourist screed presumably authored in Iztapalapa itself, with the headline "Población fundada por Izcóatl," the last sub-heading reading "Iztapalapa en Semana Santa: Espectáculo Único en el Mundo." The content pushed the recently constructed myth of the ancient origins of the spectacular. Reporters from all over the world would be there, the statement naively proclaimed. An aggressive adver-tisement campaign was afoot to identify the great and simple clarity of this passion.

Now to the other sales attempt. On Good Friday, 1977, fistfights broke out near the esplanade among the photographers. The background was filled in by *El Universal* and *Excelsior,* whose reporters explained that some element of the Mexican government—either the Dirección de Cinematografía, the Ministry of Tourism, or the Iztapalapan delegate Ricardo García Villalobos himself—had accepted $10,000 US from the Witold Film Board of Canada, associated, we are told, with one of that country's universities[13] in exchange for the exclusive right to film the Iztapalapan pageant! Mexican photographers were physically prevented from taking their pictures that Good Friday, and blows were struck. The subdelegate of Iztapalapa confirmed the story. He insisted that no harm had been done the Mexicans. Money alone mattered, he said, and it would defray the expense of the performance. The delegate denied that he himself had gotten a penny *(un solo quinto)* but, in the event, he "vio-lently prevented any Mexican photographers or cameramen from print-ing [*imprimieran*] scenes from this representation,"[14] causing the *zipizape.* To add to the humiliation, *El Universal* reported that the Canadians pro-ceeded about their work wearing red bracelets that carried the official seal of the Mexican government, while demanding that the native pho-tographers produce their own bona fides.

Needless to say, by the following year 1978 the authorities were deny-ing everything (U). There never had been any exclusive right to record the pageant. The $10,000 dollars had become 10,000 pesos, and the Ca-nadian firm was but one of several that had sent offers the delegational government's way, others being *Time-Life* and *The National Geographic.* It was all above board, said the authorities: there was not and never had been a sale of anything. Out of gratitude *(en agradecimiento)* the Canadi-ans gave 10,000 pesos to the Comité Organizador, but this was not a payment for anything. With this money one has now been able to buy a steel platform and better equipment. "That's the whole story!"

Immediately after the event in 1977, the head of the organizing committee, Santiago Guerra Guzmán, had denied knowing anything about it (E), and three years later, recalling the alleged "scandal," a Comité spokesman said he did not know if U.S $10,000 had been handed over to the Secretariat of Tourism, and he issued a blanket denial that the group he represented had realized any economic benefit from the pageant (E). Thus though the details of this escapade remain hidden, clearly the play, by now quite vast in its dimensions, was sufficiently under the control of the authorities that they could potentially sell it like a play in a theater, with cameras being checked at the door and resistance being almost futile. It is hardly surprising that in 1981 this delegate remained in office, and there is no evidence that anyone was punished. Indeed, by 1991 the governing Partido Revolucionario Institucional (PRI) openly proselytized its own interests during the ceremonies.[15] The scandal itself remains a unique, and perhaps the most bizarre event in the century-long existence of the pageant.

This affair was hardly history when another scandal erupted in Iztapalapa, if one of a more predictable and familiar type, that is, yet another bout between the organizers of the pageant and the local clergy. Recall that in 1969 the former rector, Antonio Herrera, had vacated his post after beginning a counteroffensive against the established pageant which, but for the police, might have ended in a riot. The new parish priest in the limelight, José Socorro Quintana, showed early signs of wanting to compose differences. To the surprise of all, on Good Friday 1971 he appeared on the Cerro de la Estrella and, with a microphone, proceeded to interpret homiletically the crucifixion that was taking place before all eyes, just as in ages past. *Excelsior* was astonished. "Never before had an Iztapalapan curate participated in this ceremony" on the Cerro, he remarked.[16] Even more encouragingly, the priest was also heard to remark positively that the whole pageant was "very folkloric." As late as 1976, *Excelsior* has the rector of San Lucas satisfied with the pageant and predicting its still greater success in years to come.

But promising beginnings soon led to the usual stalemate, probably caused in part by the Comité's continuing refusal to allow the priest to censor the text it had prepared, but also by the curate's determination—

if we are to believe the sources—to butter his own bread while he could. As reported in 1980 in *Excelsior*, the padre had first come up with the idea of initiating a passion play on the Iztapalapan model in his birthplace in Jalisco. As always, the Comité fought such attempts to export the play.[17] Next, obviously trying to capitalize on his uncle's position, Socorro Quintana's "nephew" pushed in vain to have himself made the Jesus for the pageant that same year, even after the Comité had rejected the suggestion (*E*); *El Universal*, in fact, says that Socorro wanted the right to appoint actors of his choosing to all the roles. "These are problems that arise every year," one of the organizer's said wearily, "but this year they were about to get in the way of the festivity," and he accused the priest directly of wanting to boycott this "distinctly popular" tradition for the sake of "economic interest" (*E* and *U*).

The upshot of this friction, which the Comité declined to detail, was that Socorro refused to donate to the Comité the clergy's customary 2,000 pesos to defray the total cost of the play. As we have already seen, however, that contribution was a relative pittance, indeed as early as 1946, without mentioning the church, *Excelsior* had said that most of the money to carry out the pageant came from the people of Iztapalapa and its Delegación.[18] And so now in 1980, the organizers, and especially Santiago Guerra, could boast to the reporter that "the opposition of the clergy did not represent a real obstacle, because we have the support of the Delegación and Gobernación. . . . In fact, the passion . . . is a product that has evolved noticeably, and its value as an element of social cohesion is imponderable"(*E*).[19] This is perhaps the most radical anticlerical statement in the record: the church had lost its economic wedge, and that signaled the end of its ability even to delay the events.

In the eyes of some other contemporaries, however, the most serious upshot of this latest ruckus was that Socorro Quintana simply walked away from the pageant, so that the headline of *Excelsior* in the same year 1980 screamed "No Ecclesiastical Authority Participated in the Organization." It was clear that the church's financial contribution to the Iztapalapan production was trivial; it remained to be determined if the church's other benefactions were of as little moment as the Comité in 1980 seemed to think.

Regarding the spectacle itself during the decade 1971–1982, the first observation is that the noise is predictably modern. Gone are all signs of native instruments, not long after that antiquity began to be revived else-where, as for instance in the neighborhood of San Angel (U: 1963). Now the Zumpangueña Orchestra played all-European instruments on the Cerro (U: 1973), while the noise of merchants crying "Agua fresca de limón" was so loud as to interrupt the discourses of the Sanhedrin in the main plaza in 1973 (U). Salespersons were everywhere.

But the most striking aspect of the reporting on the passion play in this decade is the continued insistence of the players and of the reporters on the violence of the performance. The sentiment behind this message was evident. It was taken for granted, of course, not only that "at Iztapalapa, they don't nail the hands," in one reporter's words (E: 1985), but that all whipping and other violent contacts were feigned rather than real. Yet reports in this decade dwelled on actual violence. Thus El Universal in 1972 observed that Jesus "undoubtedly suffered" from his formal flagellation after being sentenced, and in 1984 Excelsior recalled that in 1981 one of Jesus's two flagellators, outraged that he himself had not been elected to play Jesus, had to be restrained from brutally whipping Jesus. Similar observations were made on the Way of the Cross, El Universal insisting in 1977 that the Jews and Centurions had whipped Jesus de verdad. Thus it made sense to the writer in Excelsior in 1974 that Jesus "almost always having been hurt" by these officials, "the public immediately took steps to avenge these offenses on those who had hit him." In fact, the reporter took that crowd revenge as a proof that, despite everything, the Iztapalapan procession was indeed a religious and not merely a "pagan" event.[20] Finally, Excelsior in 1972 quoted Juan Morales as telling the reporter: "I am Dimas, the Bad [sic] Thief. I am 41 years old and I have played my role for 18 years. Say how we suffer de verdad, see how marked up is Jesus from being flagellated during the Way of the Cross, and look at how Gestas, don Hilario Hernández, suffers. Labor union leaders ought to come here to see how we suffer."

A questionable but perhaps real increase in violence, or at the least the notion that the Iztapalapans were pushing the limits of the permissible, must have been driven by the competition and challenges such statements offered to others. Before all, in order of importance, film and television provided that competition. Indeed, in a remarkable statement of 1976, the reporter from El Universal explained the crowd's unengaged reaction to the Iztapalapan presentation as follows: "The unfeeling masses were unimpressed, because they have seen the bloody spectacles in the mass media."[21] That statement says it all. No matter how "realistic" the Iztapalapans tried to be in presenting the passion, movies and television could always outdo them. This may have moved the Iztapalapans toward ever stronger punishment to awe their viewers.

Though print and visual media were certainly important in this regard, in these plays that at best ludically represented violence, actual brutality also marked some important non-Mexican passion plays that became famous in the 1960. I mentioned especially the extreme flagellation at Santo Tomás, Colombia, and the equally horrendous flagellation plus actual crucifixions at San Pedro Cutud near San Fernando north of Manila, both extensively reported in our Mexico City newspapers. There is no reason to doubt that representations of this type also had some influence upon the Iztapalapans as they prepared their own plays in these years. Indeed, contemporary newspaper evidence from outside Mexico City suggests, as we saw at Cuajimalpa, that an increasingly realistic brand of *imitatio Christi* was taking root around the capital, which I would call toying with crucifixion. Thus in Guadalajara in 1978, *Excelsior* has a Jesus tell how "they bind me to the cross with curved nails to make it seem that they are nailing me." And in 1990, a Jesus at Tlalnepantla near Chalma who insisted repeatedly that he was not in it for the money said that he stood "ready to be really crucified if someone would offer up golden nails"(E).[22]

Thus the competition from contemporary media as well as from other Mexican passion plays seems to have pressed the Iztapalapans at least toward more of the semblance of violence. That violence cannot however be seen purely as the result of contemporary context. No matter how difficult it may be to demonstrate, the peninsular and indigenous backgrounds to this violence must be considered. Take for instance the already described practice of cutting the back of flagellants with glass so as to facilitate demonstrable bleeding by these actors, which is found in Colombia, the Philippines, and in New Mexico. It presumably arrived in these various parts of the world penultimately via Mexico—even if to date I have not encountered the practice there—and just as surely originally from Spain, where it had in turn arrived from Italy (see Chapter 1).

A record like this causes us to suspect Spanish roots of other penitential practices, up to and including actual crucifixion. Historical scholarship has been unable to locate any tradition of actual crucifixion either in early modern Spain or Mexico, and the Filipino cases mentioned above seem to date only to the 1960s or 1970s. Nevertheless, a persistent rumor in Mexico and among the Maya does want us to believe that in the old days, some communities actually nailed the boy playing Jesus to the cross on Good Friday.[23] Nor is the rumor absent in central Mexico, and the long-term presence of such rumors is itself worthy of note. Writing in 1927, for instance, the ethnographer Frances Toor stated matter-of-factly that "there have been instances when living Christs have been nailed to the cross," and later ethnographers have added to this supposition without proving the case.[24] At this point, I wish to emphasize that I have not found the slightest indication of such a practice in Iztapalapa itself.

A particularly suggestive *Excelsior* story of 1966 does, however, move us again to entertain the hypothesis that actual crucifixions may indeed have had deep historical antecedents. It concerns 23-year old Jaime Castellano Mesa of Poza Rica (Veracruz). Three years earlier this "fanatical youth," as he is called by the newspaper, had promised to fulfill his vow *(cumplir una penitencia)* once Mary healed his skin disease. It was now healed, so the boy sought permission from his parish priest to carry out the vow, which was to have a friend nail his hands on each of the three coming Good Fridays. After failing to dissuade the boy, the curate gave his permission, and the boy proceeded, intending finally in this year 1966 to deposit the last nail on the main altar of the Basilica of Guadalupe "to recall his promise," keeping the other nail as a memento. It is not hard to imagine earlier times in which the proper payback for a vow would have been an actual crucifixion for an equally devout member of the faith.

A second characteristic of this decade, though not as significant as the first, also requires mention: the tendency of the play and the reporting to cut the distance between the past as performed and the political present. Perhaps the most indicative of these jarring closures of time and space is the report that the delegate—the same one who had allegedly been involved in the scandal of 1977—"made himself present in his role as a public functionary, within an act [of the play] which, basically, has a religious meaning" (U: 1979). Thus the spectacle now largely being financed by the Delegación, the distance between church and state might be collapsed in this way, after more than a century of strict constitutional separation. But at another level, the Iztapalapan spectacle had for decades closed this distance. As early as 1939 *El Universal* called it "most curious" that the multitude took part in the ceremonies, "calling Pontius Pilate the President of the Republic." And exactly half a century later, in 1989, the same newspaper cites the new head of the Comité Organizador as saying that by mistake, the herald announced Pilate's sentence of Jesus in this manner: "I Pilate, President of the Mexican Republic, determine that. . . ." The same association occurs elsewhere as well. Obviously this was not a mistake, whatever witticism was involved, and no matter how far we may be from grasping the subtle message linking the thespian representation to the state.

One last curious anachronism of this type again suggests that often enough, the Iztapalapans in playing the passion were also commenting on contemporary events. It occurred in an interview that *El Universal* took from Ubaldo Salazár, who was "possessed of his role" as Jesus in 1976. "I deny," he proclaimed to the reporter, "that my apostles are subversives or guerrillas. They are instead humble working people who, like me, search for peace. . . . I am neither a communist nor seditious, as the pharisees accuse me of being." This eminently contemporary language almost certainly refers back to a charge the "Jews" had made against Jesus before Pontius Pilate, to the effect that Jesus preached that his sect did not have to pay taxes. Indeed, it was said that Jesus was sentenced not just because he called himself the son of God, but because he had not paid taxes to Rome (*U:* 1991). That charge had in fact found its way into the thespian action as the cortège ascended the hill to the Cerro de la Estrella, as *Excelsior* reported in 1972. Turning their horses against the public, the Romans yelled: "Long Live the Roman Empire! The people must pay their tribute to Caesar! The man of Galilee condemned to death!" I will not quibble with those readers who, searching for hidden meanings, might also see in these words a sly protest against the tax exemptions of the Mexican clergy.

I have sought to describe the ambivalence and ambiguity with which the Iztapalapans presented their spectacle three-quarters of the way through the twentieth century. On the one side, the play had reached the point where it, indeed the town itself, might be marketed as a singular spectacle, but on the other, that pageant had itself become a matter of contention for the citizens of the town. On the one hand, the play had assumed large proportions in every way, but on the other hand, it was susceptible to the fierce competition that it faced not just in Mexico, but in the Christian world at large and particularly from the mass media, which could surpass the violence of the trial and crucifixion of Jesus every time. And perhaps most important, though by now the Iztapalapan church could no longer inhibit the course of the town festival, its absence raised prospects of future troubles not just regarding morals, but the order of the performances as well.

There were different attitudes concerning the importance of church participation. In 1978, El Universal posed to the head of the Comité, José Guerra, the problem of a text which, without the input of a priest, threatened to wander too far from the biblical story of Jesus. To that Guerra replied, "we adhere to [the story] better than does Zeffirelli."[25] The same paper's 1981 story painted a more serious situation, one in which, without the priest present (we recall that he had departed), the actors did not present elements of the story in good order. Indeed, imagining Jesus's historical crucifixion to have been a solemn event, that reporter now speaks of the "absolute disorder" of a fiesta that "was totally foreign to the historical truth of what actually happened." The only ones who benefited from the performance, he concluded, were the merchants. (As if they had been absent from the original procession to Calvary!) Such were the traditional lines of the question of legitimacy in Iztapalapa at the end of our decade. Those postures might seem antiquated. In 1979, an experimental group in Mexico City was performing "Jesus Christ Superstar" (U: 12 Apr. 1979).

9

AS THE PARENTS LOOK ON:
NEIGHBORHOODS AND NIÑOS
AT THE CENTENNIAL

The worst of times . . . the best of times—the years from 1983 to 2000. A horrendous earthquake struck Mexico City in 1985. The country at large remained in the midst of an enduring economic crisis, compounded by widespread corruption and electoral fraud, as the PRI tried by all means to hold on to power in a country that had had enough of its rule. The beneficiary of the crisis was PAN; its slow but remorseless rise to power sent a member of that party to the presidency at the end of 2000. Even before that, Iztapalapa had directly felt the new political winds: the standard-bearer of the leftist Party of the Democratic Revolution (PRD) had become the mayor of Mexico City, and thus a functionary of the same party, feared by the pious, came to lead the local Delegación. Iztapalapa had other worries. Modernity had brought festive competition from abroad and from other media to this now overpopulated sector, but also great poverty and with it a reputation for crime and lawlessness. In this political windstorm, each passion might turn out to be Iztapalapa's last.

In the face of these superstructural realities, the town would exert itself as never before to hold on to representations of its past and thus to its future. And so despite the end-of-the-century gloominess, the Iztapalapans looked forward to a bright future for their passion play, when the city would realize all the potential that its promoters, from

Iztcoatl to the subway of 1994, had promised it. Inevitably, changes kept altering the play. Whereas in the past the play had been conceived as a vehicle for the fulfillment of individual vows, it now began to be seen as a collective representation to the divinities. Secondly, whereas the ideology and execution of the festival had always been the task of a group of old families, the play now became a federative undertaking, with the neighborhoods or barrios of Iztapalapa becoming an integral part of the shaping and performance of the play for the first time. The local church, the Comité Organizador, and even the political parties were all affected by this simultaneous move toward neighborhood particularism and ideological collectivism. With those cards on the table, as we turn one last time to the actual performances themselves, we discover a third characteristic of this period. In this score of years, it almost appeared as though the Nazarenes, those young cross-carrying and crown-bearing children, had, both in numbers and significance, come to replace the Iztapalapan Jesus at the center of the visual field of the performance. The "star" (U: 1987) of the previous *Tres Caídas* had yielded to the great collectivity of the children. In this total theater, young people more and more appeared to dominate a religious exchange system, an *imitatio Christi* still created and manipulated by their elders.

Having curtailed their reporting of the official ecclesiastical liturgies of Holy Week in previous decades, *Excelsior* and *El Universal* remained loyal to the pageant of Iztapalapa right through the end of the twentieth century. As always, that favoritism is best measured simply by comparing the amount of space given to the events in the Holy Saturday issues of the two newspapers. Thus in 1991, *Excelsior* places its Iztapalapan story side by side with its story on the official ecclesiastical events in the city, as though they were of equal significance, while in the next year *El Universal*, in a whole page given over to passion pictures, placed one of the archbishop in the cathedral at the bottom of the page, while six others above on the same page were all of Iztapalapa. Pictures were so much more engaging than text, a living passion much more exciting than solemn liturgy (see fig. 20).

In truth, many of the traditional events downtown were in rapid decline. The first of these was the characteristic Mexican celebration of the

Seven Houses on Holy Thursday evening, when traditionally ladies and gentlemen would dress up in their Sunday best and visit seven different churches, each of which was decorated with a magnificent "monument" of oranges and flowers and objects of precious metal surrounding the exposed host. By 1995, "few [were] visiting" these churches (*E:* 14 April); the rite was largely moribund in center city.

The second traditional set of rites were the Holy Saturday celebrations, called until the mid-1960s "the Saturday of Glory." As we have seen, in 1956 Pope Pius XII dictated a change in the spiritual significance of this day by ordering that henceforth Holy Saturday be observed as a day of mourning for Jesus's death rather than, essentially, as the celebration of Jesus's resurrection, which is how in fact that day was popularly considered not only by Mexicans, but by the writer's Irish-American culture when he was growing up. The decline in the day's celebratory tone, at least in the Valley of Mexico, was assured, because most pastors followed the pope and refused to allow their churches to be used for celebrations on that day. This could only have compromised the celebrations at the end of Lent. Another Holy Saturday rite, this one with little ecclesiastical flavor, was also attacked in the period we are examining. This was the Burning of Judases, the large exploding dolls made to look like hated political and cultural figures, one of the most significant festivities of the City of Mexico in the nineteenth and twentieth centuries. After a deadly explosion of the rockets in the Merced Market in 1988, a law was passed that forbade inserting explosives into these figures (*El Sol de México:* 1999). With the passage of that law, the rite of the burning began to die out. Already in the 1970s the premier maker of these objects, Pedro Linares, had warned that the production of Judases and of the rattles (*matracas*) used on Good Fridays had decreased (*U:* 1976, 17 April; *E:* 1977, 10 April), but the warning did not stop its decline. Today, these dolls can still be found in a market or three on Holy Saturday, but, with rare exceptions, they pack no explosives. Photographs of an occasional Judas can find their way into the newspapers if they resemble some particularly hated political figure, like former president Carlos Salinas de Gortari, but in general this Holy Saturday practice has expired as a living tradition in the capital (*U:* 1999), much to the regret of traditionalists.

Even as the burning of Judases and the rites of the Seven Houses declined, however, another, seemingly secular custom has experienced exponential growth in the last generation, to the dismay of all right-think-ing citizens. I refer to the practice of children, and also some adults, throwing water-filled balloons and buckets of water at passers-by on Holy Saturday mornings. The authorities have uniformly condemned this practice, which is particularly marked in the lower-middle-class sec-tions of the city, because of the city's endemic water shortage (*U:* 1982, 1994). Still, that has not prevented the Easter Sunday papers from carry-ing various photographs of the phenomenon.[1] The roots of this practice are uncertain. I once thought it related to the old gesture of Pontius Pi-late at Iztapalapa, when, having washing his hands of guilt, he threw the basin of water onto the crowd on Good Friday, but it is more plausi-ble that it originated in the ecclesiastical rite of the blessing of water on Holy Saturday morning, or even in the fact that Holy Saturday was the traditional day of baptism with water in traditional medieval Chris-tianity.

As these trends made themselves felt across the capital, the leadership of Iztapalapa often felt their borough was a backwater of the enormous city to which it was now so directly linked. When *capitalinos* looked south, they encountered a poor conglomeration steeped in urban prob-lems that seemed invincible . . . 363 days of the year. These "frictions," one reporter said, made this Delegación "the most conflictive in the Fed-eral District" (*La Jornada:* 1999), yet another polarity to add to those that had long separated the denizens of this borough from their nearby, more affluent, and better patrolled downtown counterparts. Iztapalapa was the center of the largest precinct in the whole federal district, the same paper noted in 1999, with the second highest number of Catholics. It was number one not only in population but in crime. In another article in the same *La Jornada,* Josefina Quintero commented that Iztapalapa, plagued by criminal struggles over drugs, was wracked by unemployment and dissension, and she put nicknames to some of the unemployed leaders of the gangs that made life unbearable every one of those 363 days: El Pato, El Marín, El Soñador, El Escuincle, and La Singer.

But on the 364th and 365th days of the year, says *La Jornada* in this same issue, things changed, as the Iztapalapans, in this paper's words, "followed their savior." The view that the town was ignored except on these two days was echoed elsewhere. The Delegación addresses none of our needs except during those two days, the economist Tito Domínguez, playing Judas, told *El Universal* in 1994.[2] So bad was the economic crisis during most of this period, indeed, that one priest in Iztapalapa cried out that the Mexican worker suffered his Way of the Cross every day.[3]

In short, we often encounter in these years a sense that the passion play merely covered over functionally the harshness of the unbending realities of Mexican life: poverty, corruption, and again, poverty. A cartoon in *El Universal* in 1989 shows a threadbare Iztapalapan man having his picture taken during Holy Week. He protests to the photographer that he is not dressed up to look poor; rather, his clothing shows the poverty that is his real fate (fig. 21). True, one does find the positive when one looks for it. One politician thought—wrongly—that while the precinct of Iztapalapa was well known for its high crime levels, "there has never been any significant violence during Iztapalapa's Good Friday celebration" (*The News:* 1999), this apparently being its own reward. Another reporter happily pointed to the excavation of antiquities on the Cerro de la Estrella by the archaeologist Manfried Reinhold (*E:* 1984). Indeed, still another writer (*E:* 1992) told her readers they had not seen anything yet: this was the last time the Cerro would look as it does, she wrote, for by next year, a brand new *Centro Ceremonial* seating 250,000 would be in place. Pure fantasy, to be sure, and more realistically, a reporter in 1995 opined that Iztapalapans might think themselves well off indeed when from that same Cerro they had to look through the capital's ever-present layer of smog to find downtown. In truth, Iztapalapa, like most of Mexico, stood immobilized through this period of economic crisis, and that was difficult indeed for this still poor, formerly indigenous town.

Surely in part as a result of these difficult conditions, at the end of the twentieth century some important changes emerged in the mythology and ideology of the Iztapalapan passion. The decisive development occurred in 1985, when, for the first time, the Comité, and thus both newspapers directly located the origins of the town's passion play in the gratitude Iztapalapans had felt after 1833, when God is said to have saved the city from the cholera epidemic. Early in this work, I characterized the story of the plague origins of the Iztapalapan passion as an outstanding example of how quickly, especially when driven by competition, a legend can grow and almost overnight be granted a "time out of memory" status, not only by simple citizens, but by scholars as well.[4] Indeed, not only did this story soon become canonized; it spilled over elaborately into new rites and legends. We now read an account according to which "pure women" during the passion pageant thanked God for having saved the city in 1833 (U: 1994). Still more striking, in 1996 we hear Jorge Ávila, the head of the Comité, warn the Iztapalapans that cholera might return if the passion play was not maintained (Dallas Morning News)! This narrative theme or thread of an invented origin for the passion itself converted into a cultic reality is certainly a valuable document in the history of religion.

The emergence of this legendary linkage is significant because it marks the passage in Iztapalapa from an individualistic to a collectivistic comprehension of what its citizens were about each Good Friday. Recall the vow or *manda*, the contractual basis for the pageant's continuity: an individual promises a divinity (and through it, the Comité) to take part in the passion for a given number of years if that supernatural fulfills the devotee's request. Alternately, the individual is the benefactor of a *milagro*, and is thus obliged to pay back the divinity with a set amount of participation. The basis of this contract, I have insisted, is reciprocity rather than any theology of guilt for sins committed, although the sacramental clergy's insistence on the guilt of its lay flock often clouds the operative principle of *do ut des,* so that in the popular formulation we occasionally encounter a nonsense phrase like *en expiación de pecados para cumplir alguna manda* (in atoning for sins to fulfill some vow) (E: 1987). Above all, this contractual principle is eminently individualistic in character, involving an agreement between one divinity and one mortal, rather than between a supernatural and a collectivity. Let me be clear: until about 1980, I found no evidence to support the idea that the collectivity of Iztapalapa had contracted with a supernatural.

Thus the 1985 story that the collectivity had responded to God's suppression of cholera after 1833, and Ávila's assertion that the cholera could return if Iztapalapa did not honor the Cuevita and the via Crucis, mark a new stage in the history of the pageant. The passion of Iztapalapa would continue to determine the individual fates of thousands, to be sure, but now, the great passion play might also steer the collective fate of the city itself. In the light of the centrality of the passion to the totality of the residents, who could doubt it?

Indications of this new collectivistic overlay are not wanting. With the economic crisis affecting everyone, for example, the pageants appeal to

God for its alleviation (*E*: 1986).[5] But the decisive example of this move to collectivism is certainly the assertion that every year, at the moment of Jesus's crucifixion on the Cerro de la Estrella, some type of meteorological event—usually rain but sometimes wind, thunder, and lightening, hail and the like—struck the event and bystanders, adding an aura of "magic," in one writer's word (*E*: 1992), to the total performance. *El Universal* carries the first notice of rain at the moment of crucifixion in 1967, with similar reports in the same paper in 1969, 1976, 1981, 1989, 1990, as well as reports of its absence in 1982, 1991, and 1999. *Excelsior* as well often reported these and similar meteorological events (for example, 1987, 1989), and passed on the Comité's spokesperson's claim in 1989 that a meteorological event "always" occurred when Jesus died on the cross. Such an occult significance for the Iztapalapan passion was qualitatively new in its history. These accounts do appear modeled on the biblical account of darkness, tremors, and winds at the moment of Jesus' death (Matt. 27.51). But it is clearly significant that in the midst of these lay rites, a macrocosmic linkage of Iztapalapan forms and actions with general heavenly events was bruited about among the populace and by the newspapers as well.[6] Indeed, on the basis of these records it could be argued that the more secular the culture, the greater the collective understanding of the passion became in these years, and the more likely that the heavens themselves would respond.

What is particularly fascinating about this new sense of collective meaning in the town passion is that it emerges at almost the same time as an important institutional innovation. We have noted that until recently the barrios had deserved no mention at all in accounts of the town spectacle. Now, however, the passion comes to appear organizationally as the federated result of the barrios of Iztapalapa working together, rather than as the product of some old families that, united in the Organizational Committee, had guided it through the first century of its existence. To oversimplify: once the governmental Delegación of Iztapalapa had taken over the funding of the spectacle, the barrios challenged these families as its organizational nexus.

It may be surprising to learn that, at least as far as the passion play is concerned, the barrios have only recently emerged as part of the institutional history of Iztapalapa, so accustomed are we to assume that organization always proceeds historically from small to large.[7] But Nabor

Reyes, who was born in 1892, told an interviewer that at that date the city was not even divided into the so-called "traditional barrios," but only into the moieties Zomulco and Atlalilco.[8] The records of our two periodicals would seem to bear this out. The first use of the word "barrio" in Iztapalapa's Holy Week records occurs in 1964, when, as noted, *El Universal* recorded that on Good Friday night, that is, after Jesus had been crucified and the Comité's pageant was over, the Santo Entierro followed a procession of some 8,000 neighbors from all eight barrios of the town. There is good reason to suspect that the clergy, and specifically padre Antonio Herrera, had organized this procession, given that the Santo Entierro or statue of the Cuevita was buried in the Santuario.

It appears therefore that at this point the barrios had no direct institutional link to the great Iztapalapa pageant. Perhaps that had changed by 1979, when the mayordomo of the barrio of San Pablo and father of Carlos Rivas, that year's Jesus, was attending the tryouts to select players for the varied roles, conceivably as a representative of that neighborhood. And things had definitely changed by 1987, when Hugo Valdés was selected to be Jesus in the tryouts "which the Comité Organizador carries out in the eight barrios of Iztapalapa each year" (*U*), a barrio system first mentioned in this account. Perhaps there was no mandatory division of roles among the barrios at this point, but apparently the Comité had now taken steps to attract candidates for the nonhereditary available roles. Pontius Pilate, Caiaphas, Annas, and Herod were roles that continued by force of custom to be hereditary, and were—significantly—said by the same source to be held by younger people. But the secondary characters were assertedly chosen, as always, by their qualification or merit. Valdés made an interesting choice for Jesus in any case. He was a 23-year-old engineering student and businessman who was a veteran of American-style football and allegedly had ten years behind him with the White Burros team. Even more interesting, Valdés is identified as a parishioner of the barrio church of San Miguel, perhaps the first person elected to a role in the passion play with that important residential fact added to his identity.

Without a doubt it is in the 1990s, however, that the linkage between barrio and festival is solidified and elaborated, and certainly the agency for the first major development in this bonding was none other than the Iztapalapan church. To explain this development, I must begin at the end and move backwards. I have made it clear that, traditionally, the events of the Iztapalapan passion began the evening of Holy Thursday, in earlier times in the atrium of the church of San Lucas, and later in the esplanade off that atrium. But at the end of the 1990s, an old ritual but one new to Iztapalapa came to precede the procession to San Lucas. A mass was celebrated at about 4 P.M. in the Santuario, called "the Mass of the Seven Houses," which was conceived as a type of good-luck sendoff for the coming events (E: 1994). This church service was followed by a procession "to the Seven Houses," which were, our sources assure us (U: 1992; E: 1993), equivalent "to the traditional eight barrios of Iztapalapa." This procession involved visits to the various titulary chapels or churches of these barrios. It then concluded with the long-established procession to the somewhat refurbished church of San Lucas, whose curate (in 1993) gave a special welcome to the apostles (E).

This incident telegraphs another important development of recent years, which is that, at variance with the past, local churchmen had now become an integral part of the whole lay spectacle (this subject will get its full due later in the chapter). What is crucial at this point is that the "Seven Houses," an ancient practice that was largely moribund in the capital itself, "few visitors" (E: 1995) making the trek to seven of the center's churches to wonder at their increasingly lonely "monuments," had now been introduced perhaps for the first time into Iztapalapa, obviously by a clergy determined to reliturgize Iztapalapan life, but more significantly at this point, as a means of integrating the relatively recent geography of the barrios, and some of their chapels and churches, into the total processional life of the Iztapalapan Holy Days. While the ideal of participatory inclusiveness had been about since the 1960s, now the processional reality of that inclusion was established. Thus in 1999, *La Jornada* reported matter-of-factly that the actors for the play were chosen "by friends, *compadres,* and family members of the leaders of the eight organizations that represent the inhabitants of the barrios of Iztapalapa." Tomorrow, that report added glumly, the gang wars between the neighborhoods start again.

It is not clear that Iztapalapa took the next logical step and made the Comité itself representative of the eight barrios, but the group certainly was coming ever more under government control. By 1989 the Comité had converted itself into a civil association, a status that increased its responsibility toward the citizenry as a whole,[9] and by 1992 bore the exalted title "El Comité de Organización de la obra teatral" (E). In the last year of the century, the PRD (Social Democrat) federal deputy argued that "the citizens and mayordomos of the eight barrios ought to take part in the Iztapalapan Passion of Christ, for they would bring greater representation and moral support to it" (Reforma). He drove the message home: "The presidents of the barrios, the mayordomos, ought to participate in this civic act. They have a greater and a legitimate representativeness, and further, they provide a very important moral support for it. And it does not seem to me that [the Passion] should be run by a group that is listed as a civil association." With this swipe at the Comité as presently constituted, this party official urged in vain that it be broken up and reconstituted out of its eight barrio parts. The Comité might itself be wracked by disunity at this time—just like the PRI, some reporters quipped (Novedades, 1999)—but it would remain, at least for the present, "a type of senate of those native to the central barrios" (Últimas Noticias, 1999), in short, a family organization. Yet even though this goal has not yet been achieved as this is being written, the emergence of the barrio as a constitutive part of passion organization is a major characteristic of the Iztapalapan event at the end of the twentieth century.

The integration of the so-called rite of the Seven Houses into the Iztapalapa proceedings on Holy Thursday, as well as the blessing the curate of San Lucas was ready to give the apostles in these years, is imposing evidence of just how far the church had moved in accommodating itself to the requirements of this "pagan" performance, and it is to this continuing saga of church-state relations up till the millennium that we now turn. Toward the end of the last century, church-state relations were significantly modified by still another legislative move toward accommodation with the church. In 1992, a series of decrees made it possible for priests and nuns to vote and to wear their habits in public.

As early as 1969, we recall, padre Herrera had "celebrated his own passion" on Good Friday morning and with "Los Nazarenos" had led the celebration of the Santo Entierro that evening, evidence of an attempt by the church to build up a type of dissident theater to compete with the great pageant. By 1986, that competition was out in the open. Alongside the procession of the Comité, which at noon brought hundreds of Nazarenes to the main esplanade to begin the famous Iztapalapan "pagan-religious celebration," marched another procession featuring an "image of Our Lady of Sorrows [Dolores]" (E: 1986). The use of an image explains the import of this competing march. "This was the official liturgy," the reporter explained, "the celebration of the faithful of the church of San Lucas, whose parish priest has always denied permission for the celebration." But, he concluded, "the [city] representation was carried out, with or without [the clergy's] permission. . . . Holy Week in Iztapalapa has the greatest resonance of all. It is better than Madrid's. The tradition is 143 years old, and its customs have become law."

This forceful defense of the Iztapalapan festival, accomplished by comparing it favorably to Madrid's rather than to the relatively minute goings-on in the church of San Lucas, should not conceal what lay in the future. In general, from then on open confrontation was out, accommodation of ecclesiastical activities was slowly in. One straw in the wind of this general movement was *Excelsior*'s first-time reference in 1987 to the lay Way of the Cross in the streets and up to the Cerro as so many "stations," a para-liturgical term that previously had usually been reserved for activities in churches, so that henceforth the open-air *Tres Caídas* procession was to some small extent imaged as an ecclesiastical procedure. The best example of this sense of accommodation in these years is provided by an exchange in 1989 between the Comité Organizador and the priest in charge of the Santuario, Francisco Orozco Lomelí,[10] to the end, as always, of gaining permission to perform the play. The public relations officer of the Comité reported to *El Universal* that

[the members of the Comité] manifested and recognized that the representation of Ixtapalapa was of a pagan character. [But the priest] contested this. He was not certain of that, since they carried it out with faith, and that was sufficient to be able to put aside such formalities. . . . He recognized that this was a theatrical representation of the type he called "theater of life." He stated that Ixtapalapa is an area rife with conflict, yet for these days [of the celebration] the gangs (*chavos bandas*) make a ceasefire, and even work together for [the success of] the celebration.

Clearly, this priest saw no need to attack the main event head on, as long as the Comité Organizador did not directly contest clerical, or "the faithfuls'" attempts to stage their own Holy Week. In this atmosphere, *Excelsior* could consequently state in 1990 that the Passion and Death of Jesus, in addition to being performed in the streets and on the Cerro, were also performed in San Lucas, as if there was some equivalence between the two. From 9 o'clock that Good Friday morning, this paper states, while an (alternate) group of Nazarenes entered the church, those coming to the esplanade to watch the judgment and sentencing of Jesus in the established drama could observe "another Christ, that of the dissidents," "standing in the church door with a face bloodied from the lashes he had received." "Within this ancient parish church," he continues, "they celebrate the whole Way of the Cross, as they have done for some fifteen years here, from the time a group of persons decided to separate themselves from the traditional [events] because, they said, in them everything has been emptied of virtue." From the same year's account in *El Universal,* it is also clear that after the crucifixion on the Cerro, a Procession of Silence or Santo Entierro brought the body of Jesus—presumably a copy of the by-now famous Cuevita—back down the hill not directly to the Santuario, but first to the central esplanade, "where the festivities culminated," only then to be processed on to the Sanctuary and burial. For the first time on record, this post-crucifixional event, the elsewhere time-honored, quasi-ecclesiastical Santo Entierro, was now considered part of the main spectacle.

At the very least, by this time it is evident that churchmen were theatrically performing parts of the passion narrative within their churches. Thus in 1992, at least 100 persons "opposed to paganism" and wanting to avoid participation in the "blasphemous" rite so disrespectful to the Catholic religion (*E*), gathered in San Lucas to watch the dissidents stage their own Last Supper in the choir of the church (*U*), while in 1995, the Jesus of the main festival was having the Washing of Feet performed on his own person during the opening ceremonies at the Santuario (*E*: 14 Apr.). In 1992, the curate of San Lucas may still have refused to permit the city celebration (*E*: 1993), but at the same time, the representative of the San Lucas Parish Council—the first reference to such a body—assured newsmen that the faithful there had no quarrel with the pueblo's festival—which aimed at drawing tourists—but were only fulfilling their own avocation, "which is religious, of the church" (*U: 1992*). The same determination to cover up the ancient animosities is apparent in the following year 1993, when the priest at the Santuario described the *buena convivencia* that existed between the church and the pueblo. After saying his mass there, padre Gerardo Alemán expressed his satisfaction that "this pagan legend" continued, and noted that his colleague Miguel Trejo, the parish priest of San Lucas, even welcomed the apostles to his church (*E*). In the light of the history of the Iztapalapan passion, all this is striking indeed.

Still, the churchmen and the "devout"—apparently so called to distinguish them from an irreverent laity that performed and followed the street passion—were quick to publicly condemn the latter and maintain their own theater. The preacher in the Santuario on Palm Sunday 1995 spent his time "reviling these [upcoming] performances as pagan and as unauthorized by the Catholic church" (*E*). Then on the following Good Friday some 500 dissident Nazarenes carried a figure of Jesus—again a statue!—through some of the streets around San Lucas, before entering that church for the so-called Mass of the (Seven Last) Words. But the matter did not stop there, for the Nazarenes followed this up by distributing a manifesto which reproached "this production that makes Iztapalapa famous. It has robbed religious sentiment of its virtue . . . involved ever more the Delegation of the Federal District, and nourished ever more the dominant merchandising sentiment" (*E*). It was in the context of such sentiments that on August 6 of the same year, surely these same dissident Nazarenes, certainly at one with the parish council and the rector, erected a monument in the ancient atrium honoring the Society of Nazarenes on its centenary.[11] Having "flourished for ages," as *Excelsior* said with resignation in 1995, this division still remains in place.

Thus at the end of the millennium, the church itself had come to be a part of the theatrical production of the passion, even as, allied with a small part of "the faithful," it continued to protest against the allegedly profane performance of the pueblo. To some extent it can be said that two unequal theaters competed with each other for audiences, at least down in the town valley and in the streets between the Santuario and San Lucas. For *Excelsior* informs us in 1998 (10 April) that while the clergy's strategy in this year's celebration was, on the one hand, to "sanctify" the coming celebrations with its opening mass at the Santuario, on the other it was determined to maintain its distance from the events on the Cerro de la Estrella. In truth, the history of struggle between the Iztapalapan church and pueblo had been long and often fraught with tension and confrontation. It was, after all, the early laws against the church that had given the live performance of the Iztapalapan passion its form and distinction. Now, early in its second century, following the example of the popes and its own archbishops, the church had taken its own role within the great theater of historical imitation. It now "joined in the fun," if I may so express myself, even as the laity itself, still proud of never having allowed the clergy to change the play's text (E: 1995) but having long since shed most of its early profanity, had grown serious about the play.

The years 1992 and 1993 marked a watershed in the history of the passion play. Not only was it in these years that the pueblo first felt the sting of declining numbers of visitors. It also now began to take stock of its historical memory. In 1992 the book *Semana Santa en Iztapalapa* was published, with many pictures and several essays celebrating primarily the Iztapalapan, but other Mexican passion celebrations as well. Then in 1993, after a sponsored competition to assemble old photographs from scrapbooks and from occasional newspapers, the same editor and patrons brought out *150 Años, 150 Fotos,* an invaluable collection of black and white photographs that is the *sine qua non* for any visual overview of the passion through the decades. Although the notion that the passion had been performed for 150 years was a myth, one in fact only recently generated, that should not blind us to the real achievement of the previous century. A vestigial, backwater Aztec village in the swamps of the Valley of Mexico had, with enormous energy and with the most tenacious attachment and duty to its past, preserved a communal ritual expression, a funny if solemn recreation of the passion of its lord, even as this village slowly but explosively grew into a major city ever more a part of the great city of Mexico. No wonder that Iztapalapans at the end of this twentieth century developed a proud if at times outlandish estimation of the importance of their passion play. The actors scorned the passion play performed in the Philippines, where, I might add, women were prominent among the Jesuses who actually had themselves crucified (E: 1995); theirs and no one else's was the best in the world. And *Excelsior's* reporter in 1998 went along with the new globalism of the Iztapalapan viewpoint. "This is a celebration," he proudly if naively proclaimed, "known in all corners of the planet"!

Given the tenacity of this institution, no one can easily predict its future. It must appear an anachronism to many Mexicans in this age of instant communication and secular concerns, just as it had for other citizens and reporters since mid-century. But just as surely, the play continues to hearken visitors and viewers back to an earlier time when humans sacrificed themselves to the Gods for their devotees and vice versa. Still, the duty of the historian remains to describe and analyze the state of the play itself at the end of the millennium, and we begin by noting that conflict accompanied the publication of *Semana Santa en Iztapalapa* in 1992. As *El Universal* reported on Good Friday of that year, on the previous Holy Wednesday the Autonomous Metropolitan University (UAM) and the Delegación had presented *Semana Santa* to the public without making it clear who would get the proceeds from its sale. The Comité Organizador demanded royalties *(por regalías)* from the delegational authorities, noting that by licensing the traveling salesmen, the leaders and functionaries in the Delegación had taken in some 862 million pesos. For their part, the vendors verified that figure, complaining that each and every one of the 1,500 licensed salesmen paid the Delegation half a million pesos per license, plus a quota of 50,000 pesos each day, plus 18,000 pesos to the leaders, for a total of 568,000 pesos from each merchant, or 862 million from 1,500 of them. "We too are in business," the merchants insisted.

In describing this literary-financial dispute over the book's revenues, *El Universal* of course repeated the charge, so common in our period, that the pageant had been overwhelmed by merchandising. The Holy in Holy Week had been lost. Those who gained the most from the passion, our reporter wrote, were the "leaders of the merchants and the delegational bureaucrats." Then in a 1994 interview given to the same paper, Judas (the economist Tito Domínguez) gave a wider context to the situation. He spoke out against his town being carved up into spots for peddlers. Instead of the pageant being "an act of the people," he said, "it has become a circus, where we [the Iztapalapans] are the clowns." This spokesman, later head of the Comité Organizador, had a warning for this new world of globalization. We must not lose our traditions, he said, "and especially now, with the Free Trade Treaty, which can diminish our culture."

The pageant that presented itself to the eyes of visitors in these latter years of the century was by any measure baroque in size and splendor, even if, as we have observed, there was a definite softening of attendance first reported in 1992. From this point of view, 1987 and 1988 seem to have marked a high point. *Excelsior* cited the head of the Comité to the effect that the performance of the former year was the best attended and organized ever, while the same paper in 1988 reported that that year's pageant was "perhaps the best representation of the century." How to explain this seeming complacency? Certainly one of the main reasons for these optimistic assessments rests in the fact that the number of various types of police on the scene had grown almost geometrically in the eighties. One paper spoke of up to 5,000 forces of order being present on the ground (*La Jornada:* 1997), while overhead three helicopters circled over the crowd to monitor its comportment. There were police who spoke foreign languages for the tourists (*E:* 1968), and all manner of armed men guarding each and every theatrical precinct from intruders. To be sure, reporters, photographers, and ordinary people continued to register reports of vicious fistfights, especially on the road leading to the Cerro (*Mexico City Times:* 1997), and to express their hatred of the "hysterical," "brutal" police, the "true beasts" (*E:* 1998) who repressed such encounters (*U:* 1988). But all in all the reporters were inclined, especially in the 1990s, to comment that there were often more police than there were visitors (*U:* 1990). This was clearly an exaggeration, but an indicative one nonetheless.

Reports on the actual events of these years are not identical to those of previous decades, for there is a significant shift of human interest and of reportorial attention. We recall that in earlier decades, the attention of reporters and presumably of other witnesses to the Iztapalapan passion was quickly drawn to the person playing Jesus, for the obvious reason that the pageant was about his passion and death. But in the period at hand the Jesuses of Iztapalapa were beginning to lose their starring position, as the expectations, or in the reporter's words the by-now worrisome "indifference" of the crowd, came increasingly to concern reporters (*U:* 1984).

In the early years of our period the newspapers took a bemused, at times ambiguous attitude toward the Jesuses of Iztapalapa. Thus in 1983 the *El Universal* reporter sardonically advised Jesus, the 15-year-old Victor Manuel Valle Martínez, to look to the future: he will be famous from now on and the whole world will salute him. "Today you are The Elect" (*El Elegido*), he told his *Cristo adolescente,* and all the people are "avid to see you fall." The newspaper's indirect reference to Servando González's film *El Elegido* (1977), which cast Jesus and the other Iztapalapan players as denizens of a deeply superstitious past,[12] matched by its recognition that the town's Jesuses benefited from their performances, have a realistic modern touch, to be sure, but in the end, the reporter noted that Valle Martínez did finish his task and was crucified.

To be sure, subsequent reports can be traditional in their reports about the Jesuses. In 1986, for example, *El Universal* called that year's Jesus "El Casto" because of the claim he was still a virgin, while in the following year the same paper featured a Jesus ready to carry a cross "as heavy as the very body of Christ" and who knew his Bible, "which will permit him to identify with the biblical personage." The Jesus of 1989, Alberto Dirbas, insisted that his fellow actors treat him harshly, for this would make his hardship "a little bit like the suffering of Jesus" (*U:* 29 March), and indeed as late as 1995 it is said that the flagellation of that year's Jesus was "more real than ever" (*E*). We recall the Cuajimalpa Jesus cited in *El Universal* in 1971 and 1974 who demanded the same brutality from his fellow actors, and to the same end, and are aware that through such protestations and behavior Iztapalapa still meant to compete with other towns in drawing a crowd.

Certainly the most fascinating reports about Jesus in these years, those in *Excelsior* in 1991, bring out vividly the still-present tension between the blessed if not good life one expected from any given Jesus and the theatrical undertaking all realized they were involved in. On the one hand the story *Excelsior*'s reporter filed on Holy Thursday of that year described a populace outraged by Alberto Ramírez's decision not to play Jesus barefoot if it was hot the following day. "This is a play (*actuación*), not a self-mutilation," Jesus had protested, to which some retorted: "This is a Christ [determined to be] comfortable" (29 March). Yet on the following day, Good Friday, another *Excelsior* reporter watched the people respond to that very same "comfortable" Jesus as if a self-mutilation was indeed in progress. "It was almost impossible to appreciate the procession. One saw how much the people exerted themselves when Jesus Christ passed. His body whipped, his head crowned [with thorns], drops of blood flowing over his face, the skin showing on his knees, his sight gone, and his weak voice brought tears to those who were present."

This survey of reactions to the Jesuses of these years might make it seem that not a great deal had changed over recent years, but reading these accounts year by year leaves a different impression. In sum, there appears to be an incremental readiness to put the actor's personal religiosity into question and, perhaps most important, there is a distinct absence of the type of human interest stories about the persons playing Jesus in these years. Again, there are pearls of reportage still to be encountered, such as *Excelsior*'s remark in 1998 that that year's Jesus was 13 years younger than the real one. But it remains clear to this reader of the sources that the Iztapalapan Jesuses were declining as objects of human interest.

To a certain extent, reporters in these years seem to have filled a small corner of that void with trivia. Some of it informed the reader about technical aspects of the spectacle: a microphone hidden in the lance to pick up Jesus's last words as he hung on the cross (*U:* 1986); artificial or even real blood[13] in small bags hidden in the spines of the crowns of thorns (*U:* 1999); the Thirty Pieces of Silver Judas got for betraying Jesus, at one point ironically identified as "devalued pesos" (*E:* 14 April 1995), and in 1999 as chocolates covered with shiny papers embossed with coin images (*La Crónica de Hoy:* 1999). Another tidbit let readers in on the fact that a small globule of fake blood was concealed in Jesus's crown of thorns to aid the appearance of bleeding (*U:* 1999). Still other morsels from these years recorded hilarious moments in the midst of the religious theater that show that not all the mirth of the original plays had vanished. Thus in 1985 a Route 100 bus, its horn blaring, had an encounter *(encuentro)* with Jesus and his cross. The satiric headline in *Excelsior:* "Iztapalapa Could Have Lost Its Tradition, Jesus of Nazareth About to Be Sent to the Red Cross." The comedic headline was of course a play on *the encuentro* between Jesus and his mother Mary on the Way of the Cross. By now the erstwhile "reverent and decorous" passion of Iztapalapa could be considered by the press itself as the stuff of ridicule. In fact, in the same year 1985 *Excelsior* referred to the pageant as "at times, like vaudeville." In 1999, certainly without being aware of the historical ramifications of what it reported, *Reforma* observed offhand that by racing around ecstatic at being released from prison and ripping fruit from the trees in the esplanade, Barabbas garnered more attention than did Jesus at his judgment. In this industrial-strength festival, such small peeks into an ancient past were indeed still possible.

Despite their charm, such trivia do not in themselves make up for the void created by the decline of Jesus as the center of attention at Iztapalapa. Earlier, the figure of Jesus had benefited from a calculated journalistic determination to discover human interest in the characters of this play, and above all in that of the Christian lord. In more recent years, there was an unmistakable turn toward the notion that now Iztapalapa as a collectivity, in addition to Iztapalapans as individuals, had made a vow to its divinities and would benefit from their attention. Seeking to understand the dynamic character of this great ceremony, I suggest now that the emotional void caused by the decline of Jesus as superstar was filled by a new emphasis on the ever younger age of the actors. And, within that generational superstructure, that an undoubted explosion occurred in both the numbers and significance, both collectively and individually, of the Nazarenes involved in the passion.

Sensitivity to the age factor had existed from the early days, to be sure, and by the end of the twentieth century one could even follow a *cursus honorum:* a six-year-old child could start off as a shepherd, fulfill his own penitential *manda* at eight (having reached the so-called age of reason), be a Jew at ten, soon to attain the age for being a Roman (*U:* 10 April 1998). Thus it is true that since the earliest days of the pageant, particular roles had been reserved for persons of a certain age.[14] Yet historical developments did take place in this matter. The ages of Jesus and Mary were raised in mid-century because a child Jesus did not suit the crucified Jesuses one saw in churches, and just recently, an Iztapalapan had observed that even the older Jesus of the latter part of the century was not the age of Jesus when he died. Finally, we have noted that the age of the Nazarenes had already begun to decline after mid-century.

More recent annual reports out of Iztapalapa show an unmistakable emphasis upon the young age of several groups of players. A precursor of this tendency occurs in 1971, when *jóvenes* or young people are said to represent the pueblo of Jesus (*U*). By the 1980s these signs are everywhere. Thus in 1987, *Excelsior* pictures a group of *jovencitas* dressed as nuns, and in 1995 it describes another group of young girls as the Jewish pueblo. *El Universal* in 1987 in turn states flatly that Pontius Pilate, Caiaphas, Annas, and Herod were played by *los más jóvenes,* a remarkable departure from earlier practice, when these roles were always played by adults of even advanced years. What is important here is not that any given role was certifiably held by younger players than it had been in the past; though plausible, our evidence cannot prove the case. Instead, it is the emphasis on age which cannot be denied. How to explain this turn to youth? To some small degree the reporters may have been reflecting the new attention to the younger generation typical in and after the 1960s. I would argue, however, that the change is of major social significance, often encountered by historians of formal behavior and festivals, where the age profile of festive players drops significantly as a traditional culture develops into a modern one.[15] What happens at this juncture is that the adults who had usually played such parts as a form of social contract become disinclined to do so any longer, increasingly considering that procession or fiesta is "kids' stuff." The adults do not, however, typically walk away. They rather guide or constrain their children to perform in public as the older generation had once done.

The influx of children was most visible among the Nazarenes, the segment of the Iztapalapan passion play that more than any other has filled the void left by the decline in attention to Jesus. To be sure, in the records of these last decades of the century one still occasionally encounters the statement that this prominent group was composed of *niños, jóvenes y ancianos* (U: 1971), and I have indeed observed mature men playing Nazarenes during my visits to the celebration. But by this date, the overwhelming number of Nazarenes are children and young boys. Thus not surprisingly, reporters now began to zero in on young, individual Nazarenes to record the many experiences that had led these boys to join the group—as they had done earlier with Jesuses. These writers were also struck by an accompanying "fanaticism": now parents constrained their children to carry out vows they had promised supernaturals to fulfill themselves. Children would pay back their parents' own debts.

In addition to expanding, the hometown pageant turned into a regional phenomenon. In 1998, *Excelsior* in its Good Friday issue explained that while previously the Nazarenes and Virgins in the processions had all been natives of Iztapalapa, they were now "all *jovencitos* of Iztapalapa, Tláhuac, and Iztacalco," the latter two towns respectively to the south and north of Iztapalapa itself.[16] Only the central characters, this reporter continued, had to be from the eight barrios of the delegational seat, but otherwise, all eventual participants were now welcome—as long as they paid the required registration fee of 20 pesos.[17] Now youngsters came to

Iztapalapa from out of town and followed the signs that read "Wood Crosses for Rent to Nazarenes" (*El Heraldo de México:* 1999), availing themselves of such merchants' goods.[18]

After decades of competing with Iztapalapa for visitors in Holy Week, people from the small surrounding towns, or at least some of their youngsters, now traveled to the great festive center on this sacred day. The practice of outsiders coming to a nearby center to join in a passion performance was certainly not new. In 1986, for example, *El Universal* reported that each year, inhabitants of Chinameca (Mor.) came to the same Tláhuac for the purpose of carrying out flagellations. But if only because of the enormous size of Iztapalapa's performance, a visit there was something else. Thus for all intents and purposes, Iztapalapa's passion at the end of the century bode well to become an expression of regional religious theater. Doubtless the new receipts these new recruits brought into the Comité made this turn of events attractive for the Iztapalapans, but the jury was still out on the long-term utility of this new openness. Nevertheless, the recruitment of the Nazarenes in this period must be seen in a regional context.

Most importantly, the geographic expansion must explain in part the stunning increase in the number of Nazarenes marching bearing their crowns of thorns and their crosses in the Iztapalapan passion. Their gargantuan presence is best expressed by an image created in 1999 by *El Universal*. Readers recall the sequence of events in the now-classical passion play: Jesus was tried, sentenced, and then finally whipped 40 times in the great central esplanade. Then a procession formed that slowly moved through the small streets in town till it began to climb up the main thoroughfare that led finally to the Cerro de la Estrella and the crucifixion. That was the established image. In 1999, however, *El Universal* noted that the Nazarenes had already started up the hill to the Cerro before Jesus had even been judged in the esplanade—this is how massive the total phenomenon had become. Clearly, there were now so many Nazarenes that if they had not started up long before his judgment, Jesus would not have been crucifiable until the following day![19]

The rise of the Nazarenes as an ever more imposing part of the total spectacle can be followed in the newspapers. They were first counted in 1961, when *El Universal* said 50 or more Nazarenes had marched. In 1964 *Excelsior* reported 100 of them, and from then through 1978, the figures in both newspapers ranged between 100 and 400. In the last score of years of the twentieth century, the numbers, at times provided to the papers by the Comité, at other times estimated by the reporters, were as follows:

1982	2,000	1990	500
1983	750	1992	200 (E: "peregrinos o nazarenos")
1984	700	1993	4,500 (E: 9 April: aged from 8 to 105)
1985	1,200 (E: "nazarenos o penitentes")	1995	500
1986	500	1996	4,000
1987	3,000 (U: 17 April: none over 20 years of age)	1997	2,000–3,000
1988	2,800	1998	2,500
1989	3,800	1999	4,300

Clearly, an explosion in the number of Nazarenes had taken place in this period, as well as a decline in their average age. No longer were they few, adult, and hooded as in the early part of the century, but legion, juvenile, and determined to show off their innocent machismo by carrying heavy crosses and wearing crowns of thorns. Here, in short, is an insistent representation of publicly self-mortifying childhood in a culture whose quotidian reality was marked by the ever-present threat of gangs and drugs. In 1988, *Excelsior* told how those taking part in the via Crucis "usually flagellate themselves in a type of solidarity with the Christ of Iztapalapa," perhaps referring at least in part to some of the Nazarenes. And in 1989, the pavement turned so hot that it was martyrdom to walk on it, *El Universal* reported, but the 3,000 and more Nazarenes had nevertheless promised to go barefoot. This phenomenon of innocence mortified requires some analysis.

It appears that the year 1987 marks the turning point after which reporters repeatedly concentrated on human interest observations about individual child Nazarenes. *El Universal* in that year describes what it called the youngest Nazarene, one-year old Mario Giovani, sitting on his cross while sucking on his milk bottle (fig. 22). In the same article the writer also provides what amounts to an honor roll of those Nazarenes carrying heavy crosses, naming them and giving the weight of their crosses (for example, 70 kilos, 100 kilos, and so forth). Perhaps most fascinating in this report is the writer's affirmation that two other (named) Nazarenes carried the crosses that the Iztapalapan Jesuses had borne in the two previous years. Clearly, the organizers had saved the artifacts and now used these child Nazarenes as bearers of the institutional history of the pageants.

From this point on, reports at the end of the century are marked by attention to the identities of representative Nazarenes. These players had never before been identified by name. Thus in 1989 *El Universal* furnished its readers with personal vignettes of two such Nazarenes, the one 11, the other 26 years old, standing on the Cerro de la Estrella awaiting the arrival of Jesus for his crucifixion. The reporters had a specific illustrative end in mind: whether these children were acting out the role of Nazarenes freely, or under the constraint of their parents and, more generally, of the adult world.

If I am not mistaken, this problem of choice, so richly documented in our sources and so central to our understanding of the festival at the end of the century, was first broached in *El Universal* in 1990. The periodical's reporter laid it out only partially, simply stating that some of the children refused to fulfill their parents' wish (that they take up the role of Nazarenes in the pageant), while others played along with the parents' "caprice." The same paper highlights the conforming youngsters again in 1994, referring to the dozens of one- to four-year olds out in front of the procession, "disposed to fulfill the promise made by their parents." Obviously a one- to four-year old cannot freely "dispose" to do anything, and the writer makes clear that it was the parents and not any child who had made the promise or *manda* in the first place. Still in the same day's paper, the writer provides a human interest story to help explain this mechanism of child sacrifice. This mother's child had almost died of dehydration, so here was the same boy this Good Friday carrying out for the first time the *manda* that not he but his parents had made: to participate in the passion procession for three years. The same writer cited another mother telling how her child had almost died at birth, "and so I promised that my little ones will process the eight barrios for three years." These exchange dynamics were archaic; they were not new in the history of Christianity. But in our context they do represent a novelty, because previously, children had not dominated the penitential scene.[20] And clearly, these children did such things, this mother was frank to admit, "without knowing why."

A fundamental change in the nature of the promise's execution had taken place as the age of the Nazarenes declined in the last third of the century. These children were obviously not *penitentes,* because many of them commonly had not reached the age of reason. They were, as our sources might say, "playing" Nazarenes (*U:* 1971), and in that role they soon took over responsibilities their parents had incurred to fulfill their own *mandas* to participate as Nazarenes in the spectacle, a form of exchange comparable to that taken over by legatees in traditional Europe, who assumed the duty of paying off a testator's debts.[21]

What was different, of course, was that these responsible parties were often children who did things "without knowing why" and often enough, as children, were not free to refuse. Let us not exaggerate. We do find boys operating in the light of reason and making consequential promises, like the boy mentioned by *El Universal* in 1986 who promised to carry a cross if his father returned, or the one mentioned in *Excelsior* in 1999 who became a Nazarene to thank God that his father came through his operation well. "I promised," he said, "and here I am." And there are young men who later insisted that they had operated freely when much earlier they had made a vow. The *Dallas Morning News* in 1996 told of a 19-year-old boy who carried a heavy cross whose weight, he thought, was "just about right" for his sins. He hoped that this fifth year of fulfilling his *manda* would be sufficient for God to spare his mother's life. Thus the origin of the *manda* he had undertaken at age fourteen had to do with his mother's illness, not his boyhood sins. And finally there were those cases where it is not clear whose will was done, like 12-year-old Tomás López, who carried a cross so that his father would find work (*U:* 1986).

By this point in time, in fact, a debate had begun in Iztapalapa as to the meaning of this phenomenon of self-castigating children. In 1997, for example, *Novedades* described *pequeños* two years old and up who took on the role of Nazarenes "because of their parents' faith that by making this sacrifice, the *niños* would then be less ill." But most people did not accept that explanation, the reporter continued, "the majority insisting that it was the children themselves who wanted to participate." Obviously, observers like this reporter were describing adults who, like the mother who helped her 12-year-old Nazarene son Juan Luís carry his five-kilo cross (*U:* 1999), blindly maintained that tiny *pequeños* freely willed their own mortification.

It was in 1999, the last year of the century, that this matter came to a head in the pages of *El Heraldo* through three interviews with local women done by that paper's reporter. Amelia Contreras Cano, for one, piously recalled the good old days, when, she said, one had to be eighteen years of age before participating in the passion, because that was when young people became "canonical Catholics." Today even 13- and 14-year-old girls of the pueblo take part in the religious festivities, she bemoaned, and they are often constrained to do so by family tradition. "Imagine!," she exclaimed, horrified at the thought of young teens playing the luscious roles of the women of Herod's and Pontius Pilate's court, a righteousness the more wounded by the fact that she had, she claimed, herself played the Virgin Mary in 1969.[22]

The same Contreras went on to deplore the loss of reverence that had occurred in the last ten years. Today, thousands of Nazarenes think that the weight of the cross they bear measures the extent of their faith, even if they only carry it for a short time. As this woman notes, in fact a custom had developed by which, no sooner on their way, some Nazarenes found themselves unable to continue. "So they got help from three, even up to six, friends." Our source thus confirms another variant of the cultural exchange of pain, perhaps new to the Iztapalapan passion and now practiced by some Nazarenes, but in fact an age-old penitential practice by which Europeans for centuries had thought to pay off debts by having others carry out physical penances. We have this in the words of erstwhile Nazarenes, as paraphrased to our reporter by a second female complainant: "How much will you charge me to carry out (*pagar*) my *manda*," one Nazarene asks another, "without my having to carry the cross and do the procession barefoot?"

Finally, in the same *El Heraldo,* a third woman spoke out forcefully against the exchange between parents and children. "How is it possible," she asked, "that a father begs his small son to pay off his own guilt by carrying a cross weighing 35 kilos and walking barefoot over a boiling pavement? It is a bestial act!" The customs of the Nazarenes, she concluded, "had been converted into fanaticism." The characterization of the processional actions of the Nazarenes as fanatical is all the more significant when we recall that at this date the pageant was, by the agreement of one and all, as much or more secular than religious.[23] Clearly, María Estela Barrera Díaz saw deeply into this seeming paradox. It must be remembered that the word "fanaticism" in the Iztapalapan reporting uniformly refers to excessive *religious* enthusiasm, for instance, self-flagellation. In effect, Barrera described a type of religious devotion in which some adults manipulated and abused essentially sacrificed children. Our reporter in fact concludes his account by describing just such a child to his readers. We see a boy eight years old carrying a 25-kilo cross. His feet are wounded and bloody. He "begs his father: 'I cannot do it any more, everything hurts,' to which his father replies: 'Put up with it. Much of the procession still lies ahead of you.'"

In the last score of years of the twentieth century, the play of Iztapalapa presented itself ever more severed from the thousands of visitors who observed it. Largely gone were the crowds that had earlier battled with police in the narrow streets of the via Crucis, and barricades reserved the great esplanade for the actors and photographers alone. In 1986, *Excelsior* asks us to picture the very crosses of the Nazarenes lined up side by side to keep away crowds, and in 1990 the same paper described a great chain of guards resisting spectators who threatened to penetrate into the plaza. The image *The News* in 1997 drew up was of a sea of spectators outside the magic circle, each armed with a five peso periscope allowing them to peer across the divide to see their spectacle (fig. 23).

To be sure, traditional sentiments are still alive, and it is clear that the emotive power of this gargantuan spectacle had not run aground. *Excelsior* in 1995, for instance, insisted that the flogging of Jesus was "more real than ever." In 1986, *Excelsior* could still assure us that "the veracity of [some of] the actions provoked gestures of grief among the spectators," true "outbreaks" of emotion, and in that same year *El Universal* described the Virgin Mary, lots of women and children, and even some men who "really cried" on seeing the crucifixion. Finally, in 1997 there were those on the Cerro who at the last moment cried out "He's innocent!" (*El Nacional*). But the more general tenor of the reporting in these last two decades of the century is more exactly captured by *La Prensa* in 1989. Sadly and very different from other years, its writer said, "no one was seen to cry at the death of the son of God." It was too hot.

At least combativeness was no longer the main order of the day. Traditionalists might bemoan the decline of earlier attempts to bring order, such as an earlier rule that women were to wear mourning clothes and men purple belts as signs that they had neither drunk nor blasphemed before the play (U: 1987). But more typical of these years were the 250 volunteer *pentatietas* so determined to keep order, El Universal reported in 1983, that they tried to stop Barabbas from carrying out his tomfooleries, even though that zaniness was canonical![24] With a police force on hand whose size at times seemed to dwarf that of the thespian corps, these years increasingly witnessed less "the struggle between good and evil," as *Excelsior* might still characterize the play in 1999, than the resounding victory of festive law and order on the eve of the electoral overturns of 2000.[25]

The fact was that the Iztapalapans, especially in the years after the Delegación assumed such a significant role in the play's financing, had developed a keen sense for protecting and improving the reputation of the town, and of Mexico itself, through the image it projected to viewers, both those present and those watching on television. This may explain why, unlike Oberammergau, the Mexican spectacle, despite the horned caps worn by the Jewish priests and the malediction directed against the descendents of all Jews,[26] appears never to have been marred by serious anti-Semitism. For instance, while the apocryphal figure of the Wandering Jew is present in the text of 1945,[27] he is not mentioned till 1976, when the *El Universal* reporter describes how Samuel Belibeth pushed Jesus to the ground, the cross crashing down on top of the Christian savior in an action so realistic it moved children to tears. Again in 1997 and for the last time, the same scene reemerged in the newspapers, when *La Prensa* wrote how Jesus denounced Samuel "and your race" upon their meeting. It must be said: the theme of deicide is present in the Iztapalapan sources, but it is muted, and there is never any suggestion in the records of this play of that prejudice being directed against any contemporary Jews. Probably in part because of the secondary status of the clergy in the town's passion, virile anti-Semitism has proven a nonstarter.

Freed of this cultural encumbrance, as well as of much of the ancient racism that had marred early urban attitudes towards Iztapalapa, those active in the play among the two- and a half million inhabitants of the Iztapalapan delegation concentrated on what mattered, trying to counter the town's recent reputation for poverty and crime by getting out the message of a positive identity. The newspapers chipped in, reporting the ambassadors who continued to visit, like the one from Helsinki in 1995 (E), proudly vaunting the scientific visitors from Cracow who came to study the event in 1986 (U, E), and especially emphasizing the television reach of the performance. In 1985, Excelsior said that 500,000 had seen the television transmission, and in 1989 the same paper estimated that 50 million Spanish speakers had seen it via the Morelos satellite. Indeed, in 1993 Excelsior claimed that this passion play had been directly transmitted to the Vatican.

Perhaps the most telling image of this calculated aesthetization of the performance was provided by El Universal in 1999. For the Good Friday procession, we learn, citizens decorated their barrios with purple and white crèpe paper. "They tied oranges and melons to the trees, so that from Calvary [itself] such details would show up on television. To the same end they also cried out from the rooftops . . . , asking the photographers to snap their pictures." The Iztapalapans had long since learned how to gain recognition for their town. Now they thought to shape their total community into a single television snapshot. Perhaps the son of God on the cross of the Cerro would see his pueblo and do its bidding.

On Good Friday of 1987, Excelsior published a remarkable article by Mario Aguilera that attempted an overview of the "masochistic" tendencies of some Mexican religious celebrations, where Christians "martyred themselves." It stands alone among the journalistic sources I have seen as an implicit critique of such practices, the author wondering at the start if these religious zealots did not cover their faces "so that we would not be able to see their masochistic smile." The author passes in review some of the more sensational sites of such self-mutilation: Atotonilco (Gua.), where penitents crowned with thorns locked themselves up without eating for 24 hours; Taxco (Gue.) with its bloody chains and cactus crosses and barrels, the "castigations of God" at Huaquechula (Pue.), with weighty crosses that often do irreparable harm, and finally Cuajimalpa, where for much of Good Friday and led by the parish priest, groups of actors alternately whip each other—the Christians the Judases, then the Judases the faithful.

Iztapalapa, by far the largest of these Good Friday celebrations, goes unmentioned in this report. Throughout its history, that town had made it seem that the passion's retribution was terrible, that the flagellation was, as one reporter stated, "as real as ever" (*E: 1995*) even though it was since the beginning supposed to be faked. The constant tension between what appeared and what is, a tension expressed in the town's reactions to the competition all around it of real violence or the technically superior appearance of violence in the news media, had produced over time a miracle of civic striving. (For the sake of verisimilitude the citizens tied their very oranges and melons to trees!) That more than century-long effort had at first conquered the capitaline opposition of the mestizos, then converted the erstwhile opposed priests into one of the festival's greatest champions, and finally offered to the world an image of the children of the community sacrificing for their parents. It was, is, an amazing accomplishment.

The student of the passion returns to Iztapalapa in the new millennium. As usual, he first goes there on Palm Sunday, and then again on a weekday before Holy Thursday, to sense the town once more in its pre-festive "narcotic peace," in Frances Toor's felicitous if no longer fully appropriate phrase.[28] Few of the peddlers have yet arrived, so one may stroll leisurely from the subway station to the great esplanade. There the carpenters and painters, and especially the audio technicians testing their amplifiers, are still busy with final preparations, hammers contesting unequally with boom boxes for attention. This is the day too for a leisurely stroll to the Santuario and San Lucas and, behind the esplanade in the reconstituted marketplace, for a relaxing outdoor lunch with friends. Entering the relevant delegational offices, however, one becomes aware that the impending passion is indeed the local order of the day, with clerks hurrying to get out last-minute propaganda and to make final preparations for the anticipated appearance of the Jews and Romans of yesteryear. One gathers that all will be ready.

Then on Holy Thursday and Good Friday, the student returns to observe one last time the continuities and register the changes in this great reenactment of the death of the Christian hero and the life of the community.

The number of visitors attending the passion ceremonies at Iztapalapa continued its significant decline into the new century. More than any other factor, this reality helps explain the major emphasis in the newspaper coverage of 2000 and 2001, which discusses the role of the Nazarenes in the representations and the influence of the church in Iztapalapan festive life. The concern at low numbers is already evident in the reports of Holy Thursday activities in 2000. *El Universal* notes that few people went to the sermon at San Lucas, and that in the outside activity there was "little new and fewer people" (21 April). *Excelsior* reflected this disappointment, saying that the some 20,000 people there on that day "was a poor number for an event that usually attracts the multitudes" (21 April). All hope, therefore, was placed in an expected turnout of over a million on Good Friday, and in fact, *El Universal* reported a crowd of 1,500,000 that day, with *Excelsior* seeing some 200,000 people on the Cerro alone.

These Good Friday claims were surely grossly exaggerated, as usual, if we compare these claims to those made by reporters in the following year 2001, where one finds a new journalistic realism in the face of no longer controvertible decline. *La Prensa* estimated some 50,000 visitors in Iztapalapa for Holy Thursday, "less of a crowd," it admits, "than one had hoped for." Indeed, it continued, there seemed to be more merchants in town than tourists. Again they pinned hopes on the following day, and sure enough, *Excelsior* reported in its Holy Saturday edition that some two million had been there on Good Friday, *El Heraldo de México* reporting a more modest but certainly still inflated one million. More reliably, the liberal *La Jornada* quoted the police to the effect that only 15,500 people had been on the Cerro to witness the crucifixion. Finally, unparalleled in the journalistic record, *Reforma* doubted the numbers published by the Comité and accepted by other news organs. While everyone claimed that two million people had been there on Good Friday, wrote its reporter, "there were not that many there" that day. In fact, in this year, "Iztapalapa's annual tidal wave came to little more than an intense swell, with no risk of drowning."

The numbers we have cited over the years leave little doubt, in short, that a diminution that had begun in the 1990s began to quicken in the new century.[29] Observers explained this trend by pointing to the hot weather on Good Friday in these two years, so that watching the representation on television became a particularly attractive alternative (*U*: 21 April 2000; *Reforma*: 2001). Only the future will tell whether this decline is temporary, but certainly the increasing secularism of Mexican society plays a role in it. For the same decline in numbers was also registered in the city's cathedral in the Zócalo. On Good Friday 2001 the temple's dean told the faithful in his sermon that Jesus's sacrifice on the cross had in fact been useless (!), since people continued to commit terrible sins (*Novedades*), but he could as well have condemned the poor attendance on that day. No less starkly than his dean, the cardinal-archbishop of Mexico sermonized that "the drama of the cross is a motive of scandal for the Jews,"[30] again without mentioning attendance. But the reporter who was present mirrored the prelatial disappointment, noting that these sermons took place "before hundreds of the faithful, not the thousands one might have hoped for" (*E*). It is clear that some of the decline in numbers at Iztapalapa and at the churches downtown was due to a general decrease in attendance at religious services.

Yet it would be wrong to conclude from this evidence that the status of the church was in decline as well. As we have seen, the fortune of this corporation had in fact slowly begun to improve around mid-twentieth century, and after 1992 the clergy could once again move about in public in clerical dress. One earnest of that recuperation emerges clearly from our sources in the new millennium, and that is a noticeable increase in the newspaper coverage of ecclesiastical events, at least during Holy Week. In other words, especially *Excelsior* and *El Universal* appear to hint at a reversion to the habits of an earlier age, when the cathedral and parish churches in town counted for as much or more in newspaper reporting than the visual magic of Iztapalapa.

On Good Friday 2001, Iztapalapa itself presents much more striking evidence of the resurgence of the clergy. For the first time in the whole history of the pueblo's passion, *Excelsior, El Sol de México,* and *Reforma* all report that a member of the church hierarchy, Marcelino Hernández Martínez, attended the Good Friday spectacle there, where he was welcomed by the lay authorities. Hernández was the bishop of the seventh vicariate, the area of Mexico City including Iztapalapa, and this year as in previous ones he had blessed the actors at the Santuario on Holy Thursday, notably bringing with him the greetings of the cardinal-archbishop (*La Prensa:* 13 April)! But now Hernández appeared in public at noon the following day, Good Friday, accompanied by the delegational authorities (*E*)! A major turnabout for the church, by any reckoning. *El Sol de*

México has the delegado assert that in the future, prelates might want to get involved in preparing and realizing the passion event, while *Reforma* claimed that that step had already been taken. For the first time, it said, the church and the pueblo had joined forces to concretize the staging of the Iztapalapan passion.

Whatever the reality of this situation, the recognition by the Mexican hierarchy of the Iztapalapan passion remains a remarkable denouement of a spectacle whose very essence had always been its laical nature and that laity's historic resistance to clerical control. Needless to say, it remains to be seen if the clergy will come to control the reenactment in the future, and there is no evidence to date that the clergy has successfully interfered with the preparation of the text upon which the performances have always rested. What is more important is to ask why this has happened. Surely the growing influence of the church in Mexican society at large must form part of any answer, but I would hypothesize further that the delegational authorities, and perhaps the Comité as well, had found in the church a guarantor of the great Iztapalapan passion play at a point when its continued popularity was in question. But it will not have escaped the reader's attention that that guarantee is possible because, since mid-century as I have argued, the clergy itself had learned to downplay liturgy and foreground its own theatrical character.[31]

What the episcopal vicar and the delegational authorities saw in these early years of the new century was an outsized production—"the biggest theater in the world" (*E:* 13 April 2001)—whose very size would now necessitate a significant modification in the execution of the via Crucis, the last major change that I observed in the performances of the new millennium. Central to this shift are two issues involving the Nazarenes that we have already hinted at in the last chapter.[32] The first was an increasing skepticism regarding the financial management of the spectacle itself. Encouraged by the fact that the Comité was now a civil association, and thus more accountable to the public for the financial management of the play, *El Universal* on Holy Saturday 2000 published a blistering article attacking the Comité on these grounds. Between the funds provided by the Delegación and the merchants, most of the expenses of the passion were covered. Yet the Comité, now a civil association called Semana Santa Iztapalapa, received a lot of money from the merchants and charged each and every Nazarene 20 pesos for participating. How was this money disposed of? "No one," the paper complains, "knows how the money is managed." When asked, different members of the Comité gave contradictory answers, and though the delegate was aware of the complaints to this effect, there was no evidence that they were being investigated. This, the paper concludes, has been going on for the ten years since the establishment of the civil association! It is not clear if or how this suspicion of scandal is related either to the fact that the established head of the Comité, Jorge Ávila, was replaced in the following year by the economist and long-term Judas or devil of the play, Tito Domínguez, nor to the subsequent history of the Nazarenes. But it is part of that history.

In addition to increased skepticism, there was further evidence at the beginning of the new century of the production's increasing infantilization. Reporting on the Palm Sunday festivity 2001, *El Sol de México* describes fathers and grandfathers instructing their children that the man they saw up front surrounded by other children, was *Diosito* or *Padre Dios* (9 April). And more to the point, *Excelsior* describes the Holy Thursday procession to the Seven Houses in 2001 as made up of children, two to four years old (13 April 2001), many of whom were carried by their fathers, uncles, and other relatives. *El Sol de México* said that most of those who joined the procession that same day were children. Clearly aware of the changing age patterns, the writer further claimed that in Braga, Portugal, all processants on Holy Thursday were children (13 April 2001). The body of Nazarenes was by now mostly made up of juveniles and children.

The significant modification to the spectacle resulting from these changes was already hinted at in 1999 in *El Universal*'s report that the Nazarenes had started up the hill to the Cerro de la Estrella before Jesus had even been sentenced, whereas customarily this group had waited in and around the esplanade for Jesus to be condemned before starting his via Crucis. In 2001, the organizers, in a decisive change, carried through this 1999 feature to its logic conclusion. The organizers had decided that because they took up so much room, the presence of the thousands of Nazarenes with their crosses in the esplanade during the judgment and sentencing of Jesus was no longer tolerable. "It was necessary to reserve the stage for the principal personages and not take up room," it was explained (*U*). Since they could not be in the esplanade for the sentence, logistics made it impossible for them to march through the many small streets of Iztapalapa immediately behind Jesus, nor with him up the streets leading to the Cerro. The only thing they could do was to process up to the Cerro, as we have seen, even before Jesus was sentenced, traversing the via Crucis without their savior.

Outrage against this ordinance marked the accounts of *El Universal* and *Novedades*. Both papers noted that accompanying Jesus throughout his travails, until death, had been of the Nazarenes' essence, so that the *mandas* or vows that the Nazarenes made would otherwise be only half observed. But the visual impact of their absence was what rankled most. They would not be seen as they marched through their barrios. If their blistered feet did receive care from the Red Cross, it would no longer be in the esplanade. "No longer could one see the purple rows in the streets," *El Universal* mourned, "the wooden crosses that advanced in zigzags together with the actor Jesus." The Nazarenes would ascend the Cerro before Jesus or not at all. Historically, the crowds on the streets had tried to join behind Jesus to stay close to him. Now, many Nazarenes who tried to join the procession behind Jesus, instead of preceding him, joined the attacks on the police.

There was only room for actors and grenadiers around Jesus, *Novedades* remarked more profoundly than its reporter knew, but none for the faithful child Nazarenes. This was a violation of inveterate custom, the paper added, while *El Universal* observed as well that something essential had gone out of the spectacle. For decades the Nazarenes had been the principal personnel in the representation, and among the actors who had actually suffered. Now, it seemed, this youthful body of thespian penitents, who, for all their centrality to the Iztapalapan spectacle, had never been meant to represent actual historical individuals or groups, yielded their place to the grown actors on the stage. It remains to be seen if this dramatic innovation, which has made of the Iztapalapan affair much more of a staged theater piece, will be sustained.

Yet let there be no mistake. Despite the secularization of modern life, and in the face of modern skepticism viewing it as more a commercial undertaking than a religious one,[33] the Iztapalapan passion retains to this day its power to move the people's religious feelings. More than a century after its commencement, things are not, to be sure, what they once were, and especially the rhetoric has changed. Now reporters label the great performance a form of "popular religion" rather than a native expression (*U:* 2000). But complaints of disorder could still be heard, and that disorder might, as always, still be the product of a religious sentiment itself staged by the thespians, as when in 2001 the "Jews" yelled at the passing Jesus: "Long live Barabbas . . . , Death to the King of the Jews" (*E* and *El Heraldo*)! As always, irreverence remained the precondition of awe. No surprise, therefore, to find in this same year a woman trying to break through the barricades to offer Jesus some water (*E*). *Excelsior* in 2000 noted that still "the religiosity of the pueblo overflowed," while for all his thespian professionalism, the Jesus of the passion might yet be viewed as "almost an actor, almost God" (*U:* 9 April 1993). And just as one might have noticed a century earlier, in 2001 there were "mothers who covered their children's eyes so they would not see how the main personage was punished by means of flogging and humiliation" *(Novedades)*. The passion of Iztapalapa continues to instruct us in empathy for the innocent victims of our history.

CONCLUSION

The presentation of slavery [auctions] at Colonial Williamsburg has
. . . become routine, and the results have been astounding. Visitors
get caught up in the re-enactments. Some offer to help slaves escape. Others protect slaves from abusive masters. Some turn on
slave owners, and not merely to debate the issue; several visitors
have had to be physically restrained. . . . The actors—mostly young
black men and women—have been caught up in it as well. They report that while playing slaves they were often treated as slaves, not
merely by visitors but by others as well, setting in motion nightmar-
ish fantasies.[1]

My last visits to the passion play of Iztapalapa and one final reading of
this history of its great play leaves me less with a desire to summarize
than to interpret Iztapalapa's place within the complex of historical
reenactments. What does this play about the last days of a man/God tell
us about collective attempts to remember through reenactment?

Throughout the modern period, the determination of the Mexican
church and first the colonial, then the national state to control the streets
of its towns and dioceses has remained the coercive context for understanding Mexican culture's passion plays. From the late sixteenth till the

twentieth century, the archbishops of Mexico attempted to suppress native plays commemorating the passion and death of Jesus. During the
viceregal period, when prelates feared that the indigenous peoples still
represented a threat to Spanish culture, they tried to prevent passion
plays in the native tongue from being translated into Castilian, whence
they might corrupt the creole and the Spanish-speaking mestizo population. Later in that same period, the same prelacy, allied with the colonial
state if not necessarily with parish priests on the ground, further resisted
indigenous performances of the passion, because in telling the Jesus
story, native leaders, dressed as caped soldiers or *sayones*, publicly represented their own public face, their own native political and social structures. That is, once they took the suffering Jesus as the alter ego of their
exploitation, these native Americans, through enacting the Jesus story,
claimed their own processional right to roads and streets festively made
native.

By the nineteenth century, it was the turn of the new, postcolonial Mexican state in competition with the church to itself lay claim
to those streets by outlawing outdoor religious ceremonies. It was in fact
within the context of state laws directed against the church that the lay
Iztapalapan passion developed. That pueblo created a passion play that
was purely secular in the sense that neither a priest nor a statue but a lay
native played Jesus without the church assuming any determinant role in
that reenactment. Over time the actors in this play ceased to be mostly
indigenous and the play itself came to be thought of as a largely folkloric
re-creation performed by a mestizo population of modest means, a view
that led to another type of opposition to the continuation of the play.
The modern Mexican state, which wished to project a worthy public face
to the world, for long decried passion plays, and especially the one at
Iztapalapa. This raucous play could never rival Oberammergau, and annually humiliated Mexico in the eyes of the world. It should be suppressed.

Only in the second half of the twentieth century did the Iztapalapan
passion play become important enough to the economic life of the
Iztapalapan borough and even of the capital as a whole that press and
citizens began to unequivocally support its performance. It was now
viewed as an event that could be backed not only by the government of
the capital and the Delegación, but eventually by the clergy itself. Now

freed from many of the anticlerical laws that had hampered it for almost a century, and inspired by the very popes to convert themselves to some extent into Holy Week thespians, the clergy of Mexico elsewhere took the lead in resurrecting or developing passion plays. Toward the end of the twentieth century in Iztapalapa itself the churchmen slowly infiltrated back into the organization and performance of the passion. Thus as great a product of lay culture as was the Iztapalapan spectacle, one can only understand it by recognizing that from its beginnings, it stood under pressure from church and state, and, in the later period, from other competitive towns and media.

The fact that the Iztapalapan passion attracted tourists has been a powerful argument for supporting the play through private, and soon through governmental funds. This economic incentive should by no means be seen as at odds with the religious motivations for performing the play. The exchange of spiritual values never operates apart from the exchange of material ones; both are part of the same process.[2] Seducing visitors to a town for spiritual gain is one side of a coin whose inverse is the chance to improve one's material fortune. Departments of tourism and of devotion, in short, function in a similar fashion. True, Iztapalapa had few significant relics or miraculous statues to attract visitors, but rightly regarded, its passion spectacle itself became a devotional object that brought untold thousands to its gates. The pueblo did its utmost to encourage the flow of tourists. The total town functioned much like a sacred frame, especially from the 1960s when from one side of the frame to the other stretched a huge esplanade.[3] Across it marched scores of solemn actors, but also bevies of beautiful Miss Iztapalapas, annual athletic Jesuses bearing record-sized crosses, and hundreds of often child Nazarenes leaving behind an indelible image of crosses and crowns of thorns. Attractive to audience and the worldwide camera alike, this seductive painted panel, enriching itself and challenged by audience, constantly reminds us of the centrality of the tourist to the "center out there," in Turner's happy phrase.[4]

As important as are the phenomena of outside pressure and tourism to understand the shapes this historical reenactment took, it is the means by which the living audience and players annually reconstructed and relived the death throes of Jesus that afford the deepest insights into the phenomenon of remembering. Early on, the newspaper *Excelsior* characterized the Iztapalapan Good Friday event as a "reconstruction," to be sure, but also as "a total historical resurrection, in which no important detail is lost."[5] But the Iztapalapan passion, rightly understood, while definitely a quasi-fictional and variable reconstruction for an interested audience, was also something more. That savior's suffering and death was one with which many poor and fated Iztapalapans could well identify, as if both, like death itself, were out of history. For here, again and again, one witnessed the horror of an innocent's sacrificial death.

The leading students of historical memory all agree that our memories respond to and are shaped by contemporary concerns, no matter the fervor of our conviction that what we remember corresponds to what actually happened.[6] That view certainly corresponds to what we know of the Iztapalapan passion. First, the fundamental text of the play, as we have seen, has not been the Bible but Pérez Escrich's novel. Second, the Comité Organizador has now and then modified that text, leaving out one part or the other as it appeared less attractive to the audience. Further, year after year the visuals of the passion were always slightly changed by the Comité. True, it was often said that such modifications made the presentation "more realistic," but in fact, a determination to represent certain socially relevant contemporary realities also has often come to the fore. The juvenation of the play that I have documented comes to mind, as does the fact that Jesus was rarely played by anyone remotely approaching the age of 33, Jesus's age at death. Certainly the very presence of the penitential Nazarenes in the procession of the Three Falls is the least realistic representation of all, for, as we have shown, the Nazarenes did not act historical roles but represented the contemporary community that performed the passion. In short, they were the living devotees in a moving *Andachtsbild,* the type of devotional images easily found in churches in which the living are shown kneeling before a historical reenactment.[7] All these instances demonstrate that the Iztapalapan passions were particular social and political constructions of the historical death of the God Jesus, each a complex blend of many historical, social, and political messages.[8]

Still more penetrating evidence of the constructed nature of these plays is to be found in the performances themselves. I refer specifically to the latent or real violence between actors and audience that has played so large a part in the Iztapalapan passion, which can be said to concentrate in one image three systemic conflicts in Mexican passion plays. The first of these is the spatial struggle of the outside with the inside, shown in the greater violence outside pueblos have used in their passion plays so as to compete with Iztapalapa through crowd-pleasing realism. A second systemic conflict is a diachronic battle between generations, otherwise called acculturation, which we have seen in the violence visited by the older generation on the younger: early on in the hints of a type of child sacrifice, and later in the century in the evidence that children were expected to suffer while paying off not their own debts but those of their parents. A third and final systemic conflict is again in the realm of time, seen in the fact that, suspending the time of the passion, the Iztapalapan stage managers *slowed down* the procession to Golgotha so that the audience and *sayones* could attack each other along the route and thus generate religious sentiment. By identifying the contours of such conflicts, modern media have facilitated the consumption of such violence.

In all these areas, the plays calculatedly departed from what might be imagined to have been a realistic representation of the passion. Even more significantly, they crossed purposes with what would have been an ordered representation of the passion and death of Jesus, in favor of one that allowed these conflicts to dissolve into "disorder." That is, contemporary generations, regions, and politics entered into the fray, so that any given play was more complex than the literal conflict between good and evil, between Jesus and Barabbas. Indeed, at all these tension spots we have noted what amounts to a confrontation of the present with the past, the pace slowing down or picking up so as to produce affect. Sometimes manipulated to this end, powerful contemporary sentiments of love and hate came to the fore, and those who believed that the crucifixional past was past were dismayed.

The reporters often said that the actors and audiences got the past wrong. But did they? Throughout this work, I have noted that complaints about social "disorder" were commonly if often unconsciously coupled with the observation that the religious behavior of the audience "went overboard" *(desbordado),* just as certain sacred behaviors of the actors were said to be "grotesque." The characterization applied to the wild man Barabbas, but in the clerical mind it applied as well to a "grotesque" live Jesus actually mounting and being suspended from a real cross. In short, beneath much of this criticism is the theme that there is no room for profanity in showing the fate of a God, which ought to be solemnly and reverentially represented. What was, in fact, at issue was that audience and "Jesus" might actually reproduce the horror and fascination that made up the historical crucifixion, the authorities fearing the audience and the clergy a humiliated "Jesus."

I have earlier highlighted this fundamental conflict between a clergy identified by solemnity whose *imitatio Christi* is essentially liturgical and immobile in character, and a laity identified with profanity whose *imitatio* must by definition be theatrical and thus its reenactments highly mobile in nature. Now I would draw out another conflict between the different social classes: the middle and upper classes, which tend to be triumphalist in nature and to celebrate the Resurrection of Jesus, and the lower middle and lower classes, which annually reenact the suffering and dying Jesus. Poor Iztapalapa was and is largely made up of these survivors, in the early passions, the dirt-poor Nahuatl speakers despised by their mestizo betters, in more recent ones denizens still stereotypically despised as the criminal dregs of the megalopolis. The image that these people see each year as the savior is dragged through the streets has been and is congruent with their own experience of scarcity, injustice, brutality, and early death, as Good Friday preachers have so regularly noted. This is a reconstruction much different from that of the long-lived members of the better classes, who will not know such a prompt death. Reconstructing suffering and death is in itself a curious epistemological notion. But for those more open to that fate, the experience of an Iztapalapan passion surely provides a momentary identity across time, beyond the easy notion of reconstruction, especially when the victim is a living offering with whom one can bargain.[9] When the woman pushed past the Romans to bring "Jesus" a cup of water, she commiserated at once with a long-dead hero, a contemporary young cabdriver, and with her self.

APPENDIX

NOTES

BIBLIOGRAPHY

INDEX

Appendix

GOOD FRIDAY CALENDAR

1885 April 3	1915 April 2	1945 March 30	1975 March 28
1886 April 23	1916 April 21	1946 April 19	1976 April 16
1887 April 8	1917 April 6	1947 April 4	1977 April 8
1888 March 30	1918 April 6	1948 March 26	1978 March 24
1889 April 19	1919 April 18	1949 April 15	1979 April 13
1890 April 4	1920 April 2	1950 April 7	1980 April 4
1891 March 27	1921 March 25	1951 March 23	1981 April 17
1892 April 15	1922 April 14	1952 April 11	1982 April 9
1893 March 31	1923 March 30	1953 April 3	1983 April 1
1894 March 23	1924 April 18	1954 April 16	1984 April 20
1895 April 12	1925 April 10	1955 April 9	1985 April 5
1896 April 3	1926 April 2	1956 March 30	1986 March 28
1897 April 16	1927 April 15	1957 April 19	1987 April 17
1898 April 8	1928 April 6	1958 April 4	1988 April 1
1899 March 31	1929 March 19	1959 March 27	1989 March 24
1900 April 13	1930 April 18	1960 April 15	1990 April 13
1901 April 8	1931 April 3	1961 March 31	1991 March 29
1902 March 28	1932 April 25	1962 April 20	1992 April 17
1903 April 10	1933 April 14	1963 April 12	1993 April 9
1904 April 1	1934 March 30	1964 March 27	1994 April 1
1905 April 21	1935 April 19	1965 April 16	1995 April 14
1906 April 13	1936 April 10	1966 April 8	1996 April 5
1907 March 29	1937 March 26	1967 March 24	1997 March 28
1908 April 17	1938 April 15	1968 April 12	1998 April 10
1909 April 9	1939 April 7	1969 April 4	1999 April 2
1910 March 23	1940 March 22	1970 March 27	2000 April 21
1911 April 14	1941 April 11	1971 April 9	2001 April 15
1912 April 5	1942 April 13	1972 March 31	2002 March 31
1913 March 21	1943 April 23	1973 April 20	2003 April 20
1914 April 10	1944 April 7	1974 April 12	2004 April 11

NOTES

Introduction

1. On which see Chelkowski, *Ta'ziyeh,* and *Staging a Revolution;* Fischer, *Iran,* 170–180.

2. The classic work is by Halbwachs, *On Collective Memory;* also Connerton, *How Societies Remember;* Gillis, *Commemorations;* Kaplan, *Farewell, Revolution.*

3. Herodotus, *Persian Wars,* bk. VI, chap. 21; see the Introduction to Aeschylus' *Persians* in *Complete Greek Tragedies,* 216–217.

4. Toor provides several examples in colonial and postcolonial New Spain; *Treasury,* 193–207. For the practice in Europe itself, see e.g. Trexler, *Public Life,* 224–240.

5. Elaborated upon in Trexler, *Religion in Social Context,* 183–226.

6. See, for instance, the seminarian who told the faithful of the pueblo of Milpa Alta, Mexico, that one was actually whipping Jesus when one sinned; in the Mexico City daily newspaper *La Jornada,* 27 March 1997.

7. See, for instance, the condemnations by the late nineteenth-century dean of Canterbury, F. W. Farrar, cited in Thurston, *Lent and Holy Week,* 394–395. Earlier, the seventeenth-century Ingolheimer Jesuit Jakob Gretscher (also Gretser) was the sworn enemy of such Protestant divines; see his *Opera Omnia,* especially vol. 4, containing all his writings defending flagellation.

8. The distinction is found in Thurston, *Lent and Holy Week,* 394–395. Needless to say, the same distinction has been made between northern and southern Europeans, northern and southern Americans and, as this book will show, between the rich and the poor.

9. See recently Constable, "Ideal of the Imitation of Christ," in his *Three Studies.*

10. Certainly the forms of peninsular devotional practices had a continuous influence on American ones, and that influence will be noted in the work that follows. However, *native* passions, the historical grounds of this work, must largely be explained by the dynamic content of American life.

11. See the dramatic description of these political events in Krauze, *Mexico,* 693–733.

1. Passion Theater

1. *Egeria: Diary,* 8–23, and for the Holy Week account, 104–114. For a Palestinian carrying crosses for rent to today's Christian pilgrims, see the photograph in the *New York Times,* 11 November 2000.

2. Folda, "Crusader Liturgical Processions," kindly made available to me as an unpublished typescript by the author. Folda notes (18) that the sites of the via Dolorosa established by the crusaders were significantly different than those described by Egeria more than 700 years earlier.

3. Constable, *Three Studies,* 150.

4. Dinzelbacher, "Diesseits," 160–161. Thurston, *Lent and Holy Week,* 394–395, with many texts referring to Jesus's suffering.

5. Ibid.

6. Daxelmüller, "Der Untergrund der Frömmigkeit," 141.

7. Antoine Collet was tried by the Inquisition in the 1570s for arguing in this fashion; Flynn, "The Spectacle of Suffering," 156.

8. Dinzelbacher, "Diesseits," 179.

9. "Ex caritate nimia"; *Legenda Maior,* chap. 3; see also Trexler, *Religion in Social Context,* 387–418.

10. Daxelmüller, "Untergrund," 142.

11. Ibid., 172, 169.

12. Ibid., 173.

13. Constable, *Attitudes,* 22. For Damian, see Trexler, *Religion in Social Context,* 183–227, at n42.

14. De Boor, *Die Textgeschichte,* chap. 4; see also Drumbl, *Quem quaeritis,* 361–362.

15. Toschi called the resurrection "the protoplasm of liturgical drama"; Toschi, *Le origini del teatro italiano,* 50.

16. See Sticca, *The Latin Passion Play,* 167; Drumbl, *Quem quaeritis,* 365.

17. Ibid. My reading of the play suggests that a figure rather than a live Jesus

may have received the blows of the Romans and Jews; see, for example, Sticca, *The Latin Passion Play,* 167. See further Allegri, *Teatro,* 200. Note that already in the eleventh century, the abbot of this monastery had been praised by no less a figure than Peter Damian for the flagellation the Monte Cassino monks practiced on each other.

18. Ibid., 127.

19. Jacobelli, *Risus Paschalis,* 26. The usual source cited for this practice is the German humanist Oecolampadius, but its use reaches from the Carolingian age to the early twentieth century.

20. Romeu Figueras claims that in France and Catalonia the passion was more important than the resurrection, but then states that Castile favored the latter; "Passione," 7:1748. Bernardi speaks of the "separation between the Easter liturgy of the elite and the passional devotion of the common people," between "the dramaturgy of the real presence in rituals, founded on the triad of prayer, adoration, and thankfulness, and the dramatic imitation of the humanity of Christ, which has as its themes laughter, suffering, and violence"; *La drammaturgia,* 41–43. Bynum shows how late medieval theologians (slowly) adapted to the popular will; "The body of Christ," 439, with several references to this effect.

21. Drumbl, *Quem quaeritis,* 250, 262, 365.

22. Since the story itself is so implausible, this thespian character of "Jewish malfeasance" may rather point to a passion play performed by Christians that in this early period did not have the approval of the ecclesiastical authorities; see Trexler, *Religion in Social Context,* 183–226, at n61.

23. Henderson notes that the statutes of flagellant confraternities always carry the justification "per memoria della passione di Cristo"; "The Flagellant Movement," 157.

24. Terrugia, "In quale momento," 436, 446, 458–459, and examples of the dialogues at 446.

25. Frank, *The Medieval French Drama,* 146; Stegagno Picchio, "Passione," 7:1743.

26. The best general institutional information on passion plays is in Young, *The Drama,* 1:112–149, 492–539, and in Meersseman, *Ordo fraternitatis,* especially for Dominican performances. A good local history is Henderson, *Piety and Charity.*

27. Rubin, *Corpus Christi;* Dean, *Inka Bodies.*

28. For England, Bevington, *Medieval Drama,* 536. Knudsen notes that in the Alsfeld play (near Bad Nauheim, Germany) spectators "were to understand how much Jesus had suffered"; "Passione," 7:1749. Of course, some of the many tor-

tured Jesuses in late medieval paintings document dramatic customs, as well as vice versa, a fact undeveloped by Marrow in his fundamental *Passion Iconography.*

29. Without references, Frank argues that most were performed on Easter; *Medieval French Drama,* 29. The passion was commonly performed on the feast of Corpus Christi as one among many plays narrating the total *Heilsgeschichte.* See also Cohen, *Le livre de conduite* of Mons. This passion play was done in July, and all the dated passion plays Cohen lists for that city fell in summertime.

30. Cohen provides examples of invitations sent out to different towns to attend the passion plays; ibid., lxvi.

31. Knudsen, "Passione," 7:1749. A recent collection of papers on German passions is Henker et al., *Hört, sehet.*

32. Knudsen, "Passione," 7:1748–1749.

33. Romeu Figueras, "Passione," 7:1748; see however the more generous view of Shergold, *A History of the Spanish Stage,* 28–29; also Donovan, *The Liturgical Drama,* and Webster, *Art and Ritual.*

34. Such authors appear unaware of the main lines of the scholarly discourse regarding the origins of passion theater, beginning with Drumbl and his commentators. As an example of such imprecision, Stern, for example, indexes as "passion plays" several works that on examination deal only with post-passion subject matter; *The Medieval Theater,* 381.

35. "Representaciones de la Pasión de nuestro redentor Jesu Christo e otros auctos e remembranças de la resurrección"; cited ibid., 256.

36. This was a first step by which the layman, playing one who took down Jesus from his accustomed cross over the altar, might come to participate in the ecclesiastical liturgy within a church. For the 1582 description, see Chapter 2 below.

37. The liturgical piece is called the *Surgit Christus in sepulchro;* Romeu Figueras, "Passione," 7:1747–1748.

38. Romeu Figueras, "Passione," 7:1748.

39. Del Encina, *Obras dramáticas,* nos. 3 and 4.

40. Romeu Figueras, "Passione," 7:1748.

41. See Burkhart, *Holy Wednesday,* 21.

42. Llompart, "Desfile iconográfico," 191.

43. Oviedo does not say the Genoese introduced flagellation into Spain, as Llompart has him doing; *Memorias,* 1:55–56, on "Disciplinantes y mercaderes" (no. 22). Oviedo's subtly ironic commentary suggests that, though the Genoese view flagellation as restitution, they would be better off to pay their debts in cash, and then flagellate.

44. Dickson, "The Medieval Origins," 18, citing the *Fonti per la storia d'Italia* 85, vol. 2:389–390.

45. See in general Grendi, "Le confraternite ligure," 19–52. I have profited from a conversation with Angelo Torre on this subject.

46. Bernardi, *La drammaturgia*, 102; see ibid., 290, for the less persuasive view that the *casazza* came to Sicily from Spain.

47. The decree of Charles III, dated 20 February 1777, banned public flagellation and thus over time effectively put an end to the classical flagellant confraternities; *Novísima Recopilacíon de las leyes de España*, vol. 5 (Madrid, 1807), 347. Public flagellation still survives, however, in the town of San Vicente Sonriso, north of Madrid. It has recently been studied in unpublished papers graciously forward to me by their author, Del Rio, "Flagelación en San Vicente," and "Disciplina." It is well known that celibates in the arch-conservative Opus Dei use flagellation as part of their pious activities; see that group's *Constituciones*, article 147. For the confraternal foundations of the earlier time, see for example Flynn, *Sacred Charity*, 127–134; Moreno Navarro, *Cofradías y hermandades*; Sanchez Gorillo (fl. 1632), *Religiosas Estaciones*, 151–194; Puyol, *Plática*, which was originally published in *Homenaje a Bonilla y San Martín*, 1: 241–266.

48. Gerbet, "Les confréries religieuses," 77, 86, 99.

49. Munuera Rico, *Cofradías y hermandades pasionarias*, 35.

50. Cited in Puyol, *Plática*, 10–11.

51. Cited in Llompart, "Desfile iconográfico," 180.

52. There was a period in the seventeenth and eighteenth centuries when it was the mode for young aristocrats to beat themselves in public, so as to attract women by such knightly prowess. And it is also possible that the French visitor was bringing his own homegrown prejudices to bear on the Spanish situation.

53. Seville's synodal constitutions of 1604 recognize that some confraternities rented flagellants because not enough of the brothers were willing to scourge themselves and rather barred that practice as indecent; *Constituciones del Arçobispado de Sevilla*, c. 95rv. And far to the north, in his 1605 account of Holy Week in Valladolid, the Portuguese Pinheiro again says that if a brother of blood cannot carry out his discipline, he rents a servant or friend to do the job; *Fastiginia*, 46.

54. The term "Cyrene" also evokes the image of a live actor helping to bear the cross of a wooden Nazarene statue during a traditional passion play. See for instance the Cyrene in the play at Papalotla described in chap. 7, n6.

55. Puyol, *Plática*, 22.

56. Flynn, *Sacred Charity*, 132–133.

57. Exemplified in the 1565 Compostela statutes, cited in Puyol, *Plática*, 19.

58. For further information, see Webster, *Art and Ritual*.

2. The Passion Plays of New Spain

1. The Franciscans promptly introduced other established peninsular ritual and doctrinal festivals as well, celebrations beyond the reach of the present study. See for example Curcio-Nagy, "Giants and Gypsies," 1–26; Harris, *Aztecs, Moors, and Christians*.

2. Gage, *A New Survey*, 263.

3. Said of Sinaloans in 1635 in the *Archivo general de la Nación* [AGN], *Misiones*, vol. 25, f. 272v.

4. *Colección de documentos inéditos*, 13:379.

5. For conflicts with the natives' own exquisite ceremonialisms, see Trexler, *Church and Community*, 471–492. The celebration of Holy Thursday by soldiers in the field remained a custom; see for instance the 1598 account of Juan de Oñate's troop in Pérez de Villagra, *Historia de la Nueva México*, 101–103. The troop erected the traditional monument, conceived as Jesus's burial place, and put a guard of soldiers around it. Then the members of the troop whipped themselves. Interestingly, Oñate himself went to a private place to flagellate, Pérez de Villagra claiming to be the sole witness. But on such unseen witnesses, see Trexler, *Religion in Social Context*, 335–373.

6. Espinosa, *Crónica*, gives scores of examples of clergy inspiring laity through flagellation. This one work may stand for the many resting on that foundation.

7. The author contrasted the harsh life of the Franciscans with the soft one of the Dominicans; Chimalpahin, *Relaciones*, 251, 257.

8. The following information, unless otherwise noted, is in Grijalva, *Crónica*, 214–234, 283. The paraphrased text cited below is ibid., 221–224 (bk. 2, chap. 21).

9. In the viceregal museum at Tepotzotlán hangs a painting by the nineteenth-century painter Carlos Clemente López featuring Roa. Wishing to show the natives how Jesus had suffered, Roa stands on fiery logs while carrying a cross. The caption adds that another friar roasted live animals to show the natives the pain of hell.

10. This is an example of the standard clerical warning to the laity not to imitate the actions of spiritual athletes. A skeptic will suspect that Grijalva and/or Roa mimicked their whole scene of torture from the early churchmen mentioned by Grijalva.

11. For priests playing Jesuses in modern passion plays, see further below. The topos occurs repeatedly in the early missionary histories. Thus Mendieta, *Historia eclesiástica,* 433, has "the priest and his ministers, who represent Christ and his apostles"; this is repeated by Torquemada, *Monarquía indiana,* 3:226, and 227, where at the Washing of Feet "the [Franciscan] guardian presides, stands there in place of Christ."

12. See Trexler, *Religion in Social Context,* 292–333.

13. See further below; also Espinosa, *Crónica,* 311, 504, 515 on Cyrenes beating friars.

14. See Klein, "Impersonation of Deities," 2:33–37; also Gruzinski, *Les Hommes-dieux.*

15. The following is based on Horcasitas, *El teatro náhuatl,* 252, 335–336, 79–80.

16. Stens, for example, refers to an unpublished ms. of a passion deposited at the Anthropological Museum in Mexico City (*Archivo Histórico,* ms. 464); *El teatro franciscano,* 403. Quite as promising is another Nahuatl passion probably of the sixteenth century discovered in the *Archivo de la Fiscalía de San Simón Tlatlauhquitepéc* (Tlaxcala) by Raul Macuil, who is preparing an edition with Castilian translation.

17. The Holy Wednesday play translated along with a fine essay by Burkhart, *Holy Wednesday,* was, as the author notes, not a passion play but mostly a dialogue in which Mary tries to persuade Jesus not to go off to Jerusalem *(el despedimiento),* while Jesus says he has no choice but to go and meet his fate. It does contain prophetic flash-forwards of elements of the passion, but of course no scenes of it. Indeed, it has no scenic content at all.

18. The following is from Motolinía, *Memoriales e Historia,* 50–51, 232–234.

19. The friars' clear fostering of women's devotion before their men signed on to Christianity deserves a separate examination.

20. The term was still in use in the eighteenth century, when the *tenebrae* or *tinieblas* ran from 4 P.M. till c. 10 P.M. on Holy Thursday; Castoreña y Ursúa and Sahagún de Arévalo, *Gacetas,* vol. 1, 33 (1722), 167 (1729).

21. Motolinía, *Historia,* 232.

22. See for example the third diocesan synod of Lima, which prohibited natives in their own towns from establishing confraternities and introducing flagellation at times other than those common among the Spaniards; *Limata conciliis,* 244.

23. See for example the warning against (Spanish) "representations and remembrances," nighttime services, etc. "that set such a bad example" in

Lorenzana, *Concilios provinciales,* 82 (First Council). For the prohibition directed toward the natives, see ibid., 194 (1565: Second Council).

24. Ibid.

25. For what follows, see Dávila Padilla (1562–1604), *Historia,* first published in Madrid, 1596. A half century later, Dávila's account was paraphrased but starkly abridged by Chimalpahin, *Relaciones originales,* 288.

26. Chimalpahin has this crucial information.

27. For an overview of these descents, see Webster, "The Descent from the Cross," 69–85.

28. That of Jesús de la Penitencia. Chimalpahin's statement that the Soledad was founded on 12 April 1591 must yield to Dávila's first-hand description. The Mexican foundation probably followed a few years after the establishment of a homonymous confraternity in Madrid in 1567; Burkhart, *Holy Wednesday,* 35.

29. Santiago Silva, *Atotonilco,* 281–283.

30. See the study of such imagery by the Pátzcuaro school; Orozco, *Los cristos de caña,* vol. 1.

31. Dávila, *Historia,* 563.

32. Ibid., 563, 567. On articulate, if not puppeted, images, see Webster, *Art and Ritual.*

33. For contemporaneity, this text should be compared to the 1639 text of Téllez (Tirso de Molina), *Historia general,* vol. 2, 620–622, probably referring to events of 1616–18, when Tirso found himself in Santo Domingo. The author states that the new confraternity of the Sorrows of Our Virgin Queen wanted "some of our transvested [*revestidos*] priests to represent some of the most tender and anxious [passion] scenes [*pasos*]" of the man / God while others preached. Yet what was actually represented was not the passion proper, but the descent from the cross and the encounter of Jesus and Mary on Easter; see also Rubio, *Semana Santa.*

34. Chimalpahin, *Relaciones originales,* 288.

35. Ibid., 289, 291.

36. Dávila, *Historia,* 569.

37. Mendieta, *Historia eclesiástica,* 433, and for what follows, 432–437.

38. Torquemada, *Monarquía,* 3:225–229.

39. Ibid., 3:113, in the midst of a fascinating discourse on the central role of women in the administration of this and other confraternities; see also Burkhart, *Holy Wednesday,* 86.

40. As Chávez points out, in Seville one finds a three-part division of labor, the brothers of Blood, who flagellate, those of Light, who carry torches, and the Nazarenes, who carry heavy crosses; "The Penitentes of New Mexico," 117. In

Querétaro (c. 1640) Holy Thursday was called "the night of the Nazarenes," so popular had that avocation become in this city; Espinosa, *Crónica,* 141. Further on that city and college in Cervantes, *The Devil in the New World,* and the same author's "The Devils of Querétaro," 51–69.

41. Torquemada, *Monarquía,* 3:581–583.

42. "Ordenó la Estación de los Viernes de Christo Nuestro Señor, en el discurso del Sermón, que se predica"; ibid., 3:581.

43. The Franciscan Roberto da Lecce employed such drama in fifteenth-century Italy, as was brought to my attention by L. Blanchfield. See also Matthew of Agrigento preaching dramatically in Aragon, cited in Delaruelle et al., *L'Église,* 650.

44. Torquemada, *Monarquía,* 3:581.

45. The following is based largely on Iguíniz, *Breve historia,* 85–93.

46. Of the 14 Stations of the Cross, most represent stops on the *via sacra.* The exceptions are Station 1 (Pontius Pilate's Condemnation of Jesus, performed in place), and Stations 10–14 (Jesus stripped and given vinegar, nailed to the cross, his death, deposition from the cross, and burial, all performed in place, on Golgotha).

47. See Iguíniz, *Breve historia,* 93. The chapel of El Calvario was itself leveled in 1859, right after the anticlerical constitution of 1857 went into effect; see also Marroquí, *La ciudad de México,* 2:19–35.

48. For example in Puebla; see Ruíz Martínez and Armenta Olvera, *Las capillas.*

49. Pérez de Ribas tells how this lifting of the veil affected the natives c. 1640; *Historia,* 3:323–325; see other examples further below.

50. Guzmán too dates the phenomenon of the via Crucis to the early seventeenth century; *Parecer fiscal,* preceding *Parecer prima.* Any list of preserved station chapels would certainly include the impressive ones stretching along the main street of Acámbaro, west of Mexico City.

51. Espinosa, *Crónica,* 182.

52. Ibid., 174. Of course, there are also instructions to others to spit on these saints, hit them, etc.

53. Margin: "Para qui se pregone en esta ciudad, que no salgan las cofradias del sangre ni se azote ninguno, so pena de 50 pesos." Text: "non que por . . . algunas justas causas y respectos que al presente occurren del servicio de dios nuestro . . . viene quieta semana sancta . . . por tanto mandavan y mandaron que . . . non aya diciplinas ni prosesiones en ningun manera de dia ni de noche en toda esta semana sancta, so pena"; *AGN, Ordenanzas,* vol. 1, ff. 150rv (16 April 1612); see also Chávez, "Penitents of New Mexico," 115.

54. Iguíniz, *Breve historia*, 30. For the variety of *exercicios e mortificación* practiced by the third order *inside* its chapel, see the Franciscan Vetancurt (1620–c. 1698), *Teatro Mexicano*, 38. M.-J. del Río kindly advises me of a further prohibition of flagellation or flagellant dress on Holy Thursday night in Madrid, dated 17 April 1680; *Archivo histórico Madrid, Cons. Lib. Gob. 1680,* f. 165. Perhaps this is the historical context in which flagellation, previously common on Holy Thursday, was later restricted to Good Friday.

55. Vetancurt, *Teatro Mexicano*, 39. I suspect that despite its name, the chapel was actually inhabited by natives and/or mestizos.

56. Ibid., 42.

57. Ibid., 42. Vetancurt says that the early missionaries instituted such spectacles because the natives only learned through their eyes, etc. As I point out elsewhere, such stereotypes were also employed in Europe, where the common people were similarly "idiots"; see Trexler, *Church and Community*, 575–613. Vetancurt points to the use of technical wizardry on Ascension Day, to raise Jesus up, and on Pentecost, to lower him down; *Teatro Mexicano*, 42.

58. Castoreña y Urúa and Sahagún Arévalo, *Gacetas*, 1:33 (1722); cited in González Obregón, *México viejo*, 475.

59. Castoreña y Urúa, *Gacetas*, 1:35. The image in New Spain of real soldiers guarding Jesus was as ancient as the Guzmán account of 1530. The tone and tenor of Castoreña y Urúa's account is strikingly similar to the newspaper accounts of Holy Week ceremonies in Mexico City in the first half of the twentieth century.

60. *AGN, Inquisición*, 1182, f. 81r; ibid., Huejotzingo, hearing of 5 March 1770, dating the Puebla decree also to 1765; again, ibid., 1072, f. 236r.

61. Lorenzana, *Cartas pastorales*, 65–72 (Edict XII, February 11).

62. "Todos los papeles por donde se ensayan los Exemplos de dominicas de Quaresma, Nescuitiles, y danzas, y demás"; ibid., 72. What is noteworthy in this decree is that despite its predictable antinative bias, Lorenzana's edict could, *mutatis mutandis*, have been issued two years later in Toledo, where Lorenzana had by then transferred, and be directed against Spanish "religiosity."

63. Some of these records, from *AGN, Inquisición*, 1182, have been published in "Las representaciones teatrales de la Pasión," 332–356. But those—at times significantly different—in *AGN, Inquisición*, 1072, have not found their way into print. I cite mostly the original documents. On these plays and documents, see Weckmann, *La herencia medieval*, 515, with bibliography; and especially Horcasitas, *Teatro náhuatl*, 425–430. See ibid., 429, for a map of the area in which these plays were performed. For sixteenth-century passion devotions at Huejotzingo, see the careful study of Webster, "Art, Ritual, and Confraternities," 5–43; also Estrada de Gerlero, "El programa pasionario," 642–661.

64. *AGN, Inquisición*, 1182, f. 81v, 82r.

65. Ibid., ff. 84v, 86r, 87r.

66. Ibid., f. 86v.

67. Ibid., f. 81r.

68. Ibid., f. 81r.

69. Ibid., f. 84v.

70. Ibid., f. 82r.

71. *AGN, Inquisición*, 1072, f. 278r.

72. *AGN, Inquisición*, 1182, f. 82r.

73. Ibid., ff. 84r, 88v.

74. Ibid., f. 88v. For the tendency of Spanish contemporaries to think that the clothing worn by church statues represented how these supernaturals had actually looked while on earth, see Christian, *Apparitions*, 67, 116.

75. *AGN, Inquisición*, 1072, f. 237r.

76. For this and the following on Huejotzingo, see ibid., ff. 235v–242v.

77. See, for instance, ibid., f. 238v.

78. The Ozumba text is in prose; ibid., 245r–254v. It does not contain dialogues or any exchange between actors. Caiaphas and Judas appear to be the only speakers. Finally, there is no internal evidence that the play actually was from Ozumba.

79. *AGN*, 1072, ff. 254r–275v.

80. Ibid., ff. 204r–220r. Most intriguing are the instructions regarding the crucifixion: "Se lebanta Christo, y se ynca y cruza los brasos asta que barrenan la cruz. . . ." "Se tiene sobre la Cruz y le claban una mano y con una soga ajen quiteran la otra para que alcanse y para los pilo mesmo, lo boltean con cruz y todo boca baxo."

81. *AGN; Inquisición*, 1182, f. 81r.

82. Trexler, *Public Life*, 1.

83. Castoreña y Ursúa, *Gacetas*, 1:33–35.

84. "Que en las processiones que se hacen en la Semana Santa no se permitan personas algunas que representen a los Apóstoles, Evangelista y Sibilas ni tampoco a Pilatos ni los Judíos; ni se haga representación alguna al vivo de los passos de la Passión del Señor, ni sacerdote alguno ni secular haga a Nuestro Dulcíssimo Dueño Jesús, representando passo alguno de la Passión; pues las processiones han de constar solamente de las insignias y passos de la Pasión de vulto, ya sean imágenes de Jesuchristo Nuestro Redemptor, de María Santisima Nuestra Señora, de San Juan e Santa María Magdalens"; Aranda Doncel, *La Cofradía de la Extirpación*, 93–94 (episcopal edict of 1744). For opposition to this edict and its reassertion in 1816, see by the same author "Ilustración y religiosidad popular," 315.

85. The majority of the following documents date to the period 1794–1798, and are found in *AGN, Historia*, 437 ("Noticias de las procesiones que hay en esta capital la Semana Santa," written on blue paper).

86. For the political and social context of these years of "enlightened rule," see Taylor, *Magistrates of the Sacred*, esp. 272–277; D. Brading, "Tridentine Catholicism," 1–22, and his *Church and State*.

87. *AGN, Historia*, 437, Inef. 1795, f. 1r (28 February 1795), and below, new foliation, f. 4r.

88. Azcapotzalco provides one of several examples: the Indians were not *armados*, but only assistants; ibid., ff. 10rv.

89. The list is in an undated, anonymous letter (a *quexa anónima*) of the poor to the viceroy; *AGN, Historia*, 437, f. 7r.

90. Ibid., ff. 11r–12r (10 April 1794).

91. *AGN, Historia*, 437, Indiferente 1795, f. 1r (28 February 1795).

92. Ibid., ff. 23rv.

93. Ibid., ff. 23rv.

94. Ibid., f. 30r; further below, f. 8r, in the context of the viceroy's upholding of the decree of 20 April 1795. A prominent exception is provided by the town of Silao, which in fact won back the right to the "processions and *armados* of Holy Week"; ibid., Silao, f. 24r.

95. See further below. References to such "representations" are in *AGN, Historia*, 437, ff. 4r–5v (24 March 1794) and f. 25r (Silao).

96. For its part, the government of Silao in conjunction with the bishop of Michoacán restored two of the processions they had previously outlawed, the Santo Entierro and the associated procession of Soledad; ibid., Guanajuato, Silao, f. 25r, 29r (1 July 1798). See also Brading, "Tridentine," 18.

97. See e.g. *AGN, Historia*, 437, f. 2rv (18 March 1794). A seventeenth-century case of the Propaganda Fide banning the *Moros y Cristianos* because it took food from the mouths of women and children is in Espinosa, *Crónica*, 174.

98. *AGN, Historia*, 437, f. 7r (undated letter of the poor to the viceroy).

99. See especially the extensive argument of the Silao authorities about devotion drying up when "these live representations of images are absent"; ibid., ff. 1r–5v (reason 2).

100. Ibid., ff. 8r–9r (letter of 11 April 1794). The curate of Tacuba swore that his parish had no custom of armed centurions during Holy Week: the Indians neither guard the monument on Holy Thursday night nor rent the things required of the *armados*. The *sayones* (from the Latin *sagum*) are military men wearing capes. Alongside lesser soldiers, they are standard figures in passion representations.

101. Ibid., 4r–5v (24 March 1794).

102. See further below.

103. *AGN, Historia,* 437, ff. 11r–12r (10 April 1794).

104. Ibid., ff. 5r–7v.

105. Ibid., ff. 2rv (18 March 1794, corregidor to viceroy).

106. Ibid., ff. 11r–12r (10 April 1794).

107. Cited in Brading, "Tridentine," 18. The archival reference is Archivo Casa Morelos (Morelia), eighteenth century, 648, Vicente de Loredo (31 March 1788, ten days after Good Friday).

108. García Cubas (1832–1912), *El libro de mis recuerdos,* 324.

109. The following is taken from Prieto, *Memorias de mis tiempos,* vol. 2, 11–14.

110. Opposite a drawing of a crucified man, the Mexico City daily *El Universal* claims on 21 March 1937 that in 1840 in Tacubaya the locals "did the same with Christ that they did with Dimas and Gestas," presumably meaning that their Jesus was also hung from a cross. I have been unable to confirm this story either in Prieto or elsewhere.

111. Mme. (Frances) Calderon de la Barca, *Life in Mexico.*

112. Ibid., 130.

113. My italics; ibid., 129f.

114. The reader will note the contrast between this procession of priests in the capital and the dramatic procession of natives in the pueblos in the following year. The Judases, which ended up being blown to pieces, were made to look like political figures who were enemies of the people, and in 1853, General Santa Ana issued a decree prohibiting such imitations; see *El Universal,* 21 April 2000.

115. Note that in the intervening year, Calderon had observed massive flagellation, carried out indoors, during the 30-day period of penance called the *desagravios;* ibid., 264–266 (30 August 1840), a rite conceived as appeasing a divinity whose image had been defiled. Public flagellation had largely disappeared in Mexico and Spain as the result of the fundamental 1777 edict of Charles III cited above.

116. Calderon de la Barca, *Life in Mexico,* 353. Obviously, the tradition she describes did not involve text spoken by the natives.

117. Ibid., 354.

118. *El Universal* in 1923 notes that in the old days, rich families put up such monuments in their own homes.

119. Ibid., 360–361.

120. Ibid., 362.

121. Ibid., 362–363.

122. Ibid., 364. A comparable account is given in 1860 by Hassaurek in his *Four Years*, 81–82, describing Good Friday in Quito. This was "a sermon illustrated by a regular puppet show," from the altar of a church. To the sound of sobbing and wailing, the figure of Jesus was taken down from the cross, then turned around so that the faithful could see the scourged back of the man/God. More shrieking. "At the same time, the figures which represented the Virgin and Mary Magdalene, which were stuck on pivots and managed from under the stage, began to move. Mary Magdalene clasped her hands, while the Virgin was wiping her eyes. But when the box representing the tomb was opened, and the corpse deposited in it, the two puppets rushed to the grave and fell down before it." A 1759 painting by Juan Patricio Morlete Ruíz in the Pinacoteca Virreinal of Mexico City features the scourged back of Jesus; reproduced in Armella, *Treasures of the Pinacoteca*.

123. Calderon de la Barca, *Life in Mexico*, 364–366.

124. Ibid., 361.

125. The issue of 26 March 1871 is cited in the daily *Excelsior* of 1 April 1972. *El Correo* engaged the subject because some purists were condemning attendance at the play of Mozo de Rosales, *El redentor del mundo*, first performed in Madrid in 1869 and published there in 1874. The *Excelsior* writer pointed out that Christianity itself had begun in Mexico through plays.

126. Republished in the *Obras* of García Icazbalceta, vol. 2, 307–368.

127. Ibid., 340–341.

128. On the reforms accomplished by public display, see Trexler, *Public Life*.

3. Iztapalapan Beginnings

1. *El Tiempo*, 26 March 1894; 11 April 1897; 10 April 1898; 15 April 1900. At the time, most traffic into this area was by water; see the description of the aquatic feast at Santa Anita each sixth Friday in Lent; Arenas, "Elegía." In the new century much of the waterway was drained so that the Canal de la Viga became the Calzada de la Viga, and trains became the favored means of arriving at Iztapalapa; see below.

2. "Ridiculizan al Hombre-Dios"; *El Mundo Semanario Ilustrado*, 2 April 1899.

3. Ibid.

4. Ibid.

5. The attempt was made by President Lázaro Cárdenas (1934–1940); *El Universal*, 25 March 1978.

6. See ibid. for a list of the towns that capitalinos favored over the decades; also *El Tiempo,* 14 April 1895.

7. Ibid.

8. For both, see *El Mundo Semanario Ilustrado,* 2 April 1899, and also the headline in *Excelsior,* 20 April 1919.

9. Obviously what men do in festivals is different than what an organizer may say he wants these men to do, but in what follows, it will become clear that a distinction between public and hidden transcripts or texts, though useful for students of theatrical texts (like Scott, *Dominance*), does not take the historian very far in explaining passion theater. See rather the approach to this problem in Trexler, *Public Life.*

10. *El Tiempo,* 11 April 1897, and: "a divertirse con los 'huehuenches' y enmascarados que hacían de Caifás, del Cirineo y de Centurios"; *El Tiempo,* 15 April 1900. For carnival *huehuenches* in this region, see C. Oehmichen, "El carnaval de Culhuacán." These *huehuenches* (the root of this Hispanization of the Nahuatl word references the elderly) were sometimes done by transvestites and were commonly obscene in content; see Aldrete Cossío, "Semana Santa en San Luis Potosí," 67. See also Toor, "Carnavales," 10 and Redfield, "El carnaval en Tepoztlán," 33, where, interestingly, the Tepoztlán *chinelos* who are the equivalent of the *huehuenches* were said by one informant to represent the pharisees "who denied Christ" (like Caiaphas). For Caiaphas as the "head of the *sayones,*" see further below.

11. "No puede negarse la belleza de tales representaciones sin aparato ni artificio"; *El Mundo Semanario Ilustrado,* 2 April 1899. One reporter urged knowing Christians not to go, but to leave such things to the rustics; *El Tiempo,* 26 March 1894. On curiosity, see *El Mundo Semanario Ilustrado,* 2 April 1899.

12. I have not found the text of this "circular." It is praised in *El Tiempo,* 15 April 1900: sermons had previously been given on the road to Calvary as part of the now-forbidden ceremony, but now many people went into the village churches to hear the same. In short, the archbishop delegitimated the public plays by forbidding priests to sermonize along the Way of the Cross, in keeping, I should add, with the state laws of the 1860s and 1870s analyzed just below.

13. For "los ministros obligados por la arraigada costumbre popular," see *El Mundo Semanario Ilustrado,* 2 April 1899. *El Tiempo* recognized that the government's readiness to tolerate different cults went back to the time of the viceroys; 18 April 1897.

14. *El Tiempo,* 11 April 1897.

15. See Chap. 1, above.

16. The implications of the 1874 law were already contained in the Reform

legislation of 12 July 1859, which declared mutually independent the business of the state and "purely religious business"; see *Leyes de Reforma*, 25. On the 1874 law, see Niemeyer, "Anticlericalism," 19. It was subsequently incorporated into the Constitution of 1917; Branch, *The Mexican Constitution*, 15, 116. Toor, *Treasury*, 211, got the dates of the law wrong. The author adds, however (218), that since then (and to her day), these passion plays were celebrated either within churches or their atria. The correct understanding of this is that since, for many years after 1874, the plays were thought to necessitate some level of sacerdotal participation, they had to be done in churches and not the streets.

17. Galván Rivera, *Colección*, 26 March 1875.

18. See above, n. 10.

19. Krauze characterizes these two papers as "the two most read and most independent" dailies of the early 1940s; more on these and other papers of the time in his *Mexico*, 500–502.

20. For the date of any given Good Friday, see the calendar of Good Fridays in the Appendix. Particular reporters tended to report for one or two consecutive years.

21. For the Oberammergau tradition, see Shapiro, *Oberammergau*, 44–48.

22. Luna Parra, *150 Años*.

23. "Un Drama Bíblico," 64–66.

24. The letter is printed (with defective punctuation) by León Rivera, "Benito Juárez," 142–143.

25. In some form, San Lucas dates back to the sixteenth century. Originally a Franciscan *visita*, it was converted into a parish of the secular clergy in 1570—a fact that did not prevent its rector from being a friar, as we see, in 1867. The Santuario is much larger than San Lucas, leading some reporters to mistakenly label it "the parish church." On the Santuario of Santo Sepulcro, see Rodríguez, *Iztapalapa*, esp. 12–13 for the (fabled) origin of the statue, a story repeated by Rodríguez, *Hacia la Estrella*, 94–95.

26. It is not clear, however, that the Jesus removed from the cross and the one carried in the subsequent procession were identical. They were certainly different statues imagined to be the one and same Cuevita.

27. León Rivera, "Benito Juárez," 142. That such indigenous living "thieves" were forgotten, so that they continued to hang from their crosses after Jesus's passion was over, was apparently a popular comical motif; see the instance in Iztacalco in the old days: *U:* 8 April 1966.

28. Yet the passion utilization of San Lucas might be deduced from the 1867 letter. That letter does refer to the procession of the Santo Entierro, and in the early twentieth century, it marched from San Lucas to the Santuario.

29. "Indicó que la representación no es originaria de Iztapalapa: 'En el siglo

NOTES TO PAGES 73-75 ⊕ 241

pasado se representaba en Chimalhuacán, y de ahí la trajeron nuestros ante-pasados a esta parte de la ciudad. Aquí se presta más por la cercanía del Cerro de la Estrella, que es perfecto para la crucifixión.'" Guerra continues by saying that the representation is based on the book *El Mártir del Gólgota,* and on passages in the New Testament; *U:* 1979, and see further below. Chimalhuacán is on the eastern shore of the former Lake Texcoco.

30. Among many editions, see Pérez Escrich, *El Mártir de Gólgota* (Mexico City, 1979); more on the publishing tradition below.

31. Boggs and Mendoza, "Representación," 139–178.

32. The priest Luis de Uriarte told the *Excelsior* reporter in 1957 that the trial and sentence part of the play *(el proceso)* came from Pérez's *Mártir de Gólgota.* In 1968, *Excelsior* states that the "libretto" for the play was more than a century old (it was!), but that its author was unknown (he wasn't). In 1979, the head of the organizing committee again credited Pérez Escrich; *(U),* as did *Excelsior* in 1982. Without elaboration, the same journal in 1986 says that a "nueva version" was being used for the play.

33. Boggs and Mendoza, "Representación," 140; see further on the tradition Mendoza, "Drama," esp. 249–255.

34. Though not found on any of the 44-page editions and otherwise unverifiable, Ozácar's name was furnished to Boggs and Mendoza by the editor, Vanegas Arroyo; "Representación," 140; Mendoza, "Drama," 251. His identity remains a mystery. However, in 1954 *El Universal* may have been referring to him when it says that the original organizing committee of the pageant adopted "the original [text], from an author of the beginning of the century, who probably was a scribe or amanuensis of one of the public offices of the neighborhoods of Iztapalapa. [Yet] others say that it was probably written by some *evangelista* [or paid scribe] of Santo Domingo." That church's square still houses such scribes and printers.

35. While Pérez Escrich's work in fact covers the whole life of Jesus, only the last part, which deals discretely with Jesus's passion and death, is utilized in the Iztapalapan passion.

36. See Chap. 1. Boggs and Mendoza note the derivative nature of the *Concilios;* "Representación," 140.

37. For "el Concilio—ahora Comité," see the interview in Luna Parra, *Semana Santa,* 173.

38. "Representación," 140–147. The writers worked from a "text dictated and orally reconstructed by Santiago Guerra, who played the role of Pilate, and Porfirio González, who played the role of Captain of the Executioners, based on the *Cuatro Concilios* and the *Mártir de Gólgota* by Pérez Escrich"; ibid., 139.

39. Mendoza, "Drama," 251; that canon is still in use today; *E:* 1993.

40. Compare the 1945 Iztapalapan text of Pérez in Boggs, "Representación," 153–158 (scenes 2 and 3), to Toor, "El Texto," 27–29.

41. Horcasitas, *Teatro Náhuatl*, 338. For Cuajimalpa, see *U*, 1973.

42. Fernández, *Cuaresma y Semana Santa*, 27.

43. Thus the Buenos Aires edition of 1942 may be suspected of having such a theatrical motivation.

44. Cf. *U:* 1951, where the "Sanhedrin" segment early in the play is distinguished from the "Pretorio," or judgment and sentencing part later on. The word "pretorium" usually identified the residence of the Roman governor, that is, Pontius Pilate.

45. The first use of the word "folklore" with specific reference to Iztapalapa is in *E:* 1939. Surely referring to the same prohibition as *E:* 1921, an editorial in *U* in 1923 says that after inveterate custom had lasted for many years, "the ecclesiastical authority had to put an end to the pantomimes that reproduced the passion and death of Jesus in all its scenes in the atriums of the outside parishes . . . , done by a personnel of aboriginal *sayones,* autochthonous philistines and apostles of pure Indian blood . . . [featuring] as well the redskin Judas de Kerloth, who more than once almost died, not by being hung from a tree but rather having been stoned by the public."

46. Gerardo Sánchez Sánchez, cited in Luna Parra, *Semana Santa*, 265.

4. From Native to Popular Culture

1. Bakhtin, *Rabelais and His World.*

2. Both these cited accounts say that Marcelino Buendía was the head of the Comité in that year.

3. Good Friday fell on 10 April that year. Zapata's forces had taken Chilpancingo (Mor.). He was in general quarters in Chilapa (Gue.) on 14 March, and at Tixtla (Gue.) on 5 April. In 1945, 77-year-old Francisco Alvarado told Vicente Mendoza that during the insurgent occupation of Milpa Alta in 1914, Zapata made that town's Good Friday procession possible. As a colonel, he, Alvarado, had seen to the performance of a particularly elaborate passion play not within the customary church grounds, but in the streets of the town; Mendoza, "Drama," 249–250. On Zapata's sympathies, see Chevalier, "Un factor decisivo," 172–173.

4. Luna Parra, *Semana Santa*, 163. The *Ley de Organización política y municipal del Distrito Federal* was enacted on 26 March 1903.

5. On the eve of Holy Week, the paper said that the festivities will take place ("se efectuarán") more often than in the previous four years; *E:* 11 April 1919.

6. This account is found in García Cubas, *Libro*, 324–341.

7. It was not uncommon to confuse the two main churches in Iztapalapa, and even to refer to the "Santuario of San Lucas." I identify and correct mistakes in this and occasional later accounts, for the parish church of San Lucas and the larger Santuario or Shrine housing the Señor de Cuevita are two distinct churches. One would think the "Monte de Calvario" must be the famous *Cerro de la Estrella* or Hill of the Star on which much later the thieves and Jesuses would indeed be crucified, the very hill that attracted Santiago Guerra's eventual thespians to Iztapalapa. Yet the *Cerro* is more to the north than east of the Santuario.

8. The first extant description of the Holy Thursday representations dates to 1930, as shown further below.

9. An account of c. 1935 distinguishes between one large platform and "algunos otros que son los llamados pretorios, a donde debe ser llevado el Nazareno"; Vázquez Santa Ana, *Fiestas y Costumbres Mexicanas*, 2: 321 ("La Representación de la Judea en Ixtapalapa"). On the dating of this source, see further below.

10. See Chap. 2 above.

11. See the description of Boggs in 1946, where an Ecce Homo, that is, a statue of a handcuffed and otherwise disgraced Jesus that caused Pilate to exclaim "Such a Man!" was brought to San Lucas from the barrio of Santa Bárbara and placed in its atrium; "Representación," 143.

12. For Milpa Alta, *E:* 1 April 1994. *Excelsior* in 1920 specifies that until just a few years earlier, it was the image that was feigned beaten and crowned. It then proceeded to the atrium of the Santuario where the Three Falls were reenacted ("y se detenía en capillas al aire libre para figurar las Tres Caídas").

13. These live figures do not appear in 1919 or 1921, but do so again in 1930; see further below. It is certainly significant that not just Jesus but mother Mary as well were played by children; see below.

14. See n. 12, above.

15. As will occasionally be the case in the following pages, the legal requirements and the practice described in the newspapers appear to clash. Did carrying this image of Jesus not amount to staging a "religious ceremony"?

16. An oral memory of these children records that they were transported on a litter; Luna Parra, *Semana Santa*, 173. A child as sacrificial "victim" was appropriate in a certain fashion, because, historically, Jesus was viewed not just as an innocent, but as someone who could not defend himself; see below, at the point when the Iztapalapan Jesus came to be played rather by a young adult.

17. "Los papeles de Pontio Pilato, Herodes, Caífas, etc. y los de sayones, son representados por los vecinos más ricos de la populación" (*E:* 1920). Epitacio

Ubaldo Granados, who played Jesus in 1945, recollected this time past when the passion was done in the Santuario and the Jesuses were children, while Jews, "romanos, vírgenes, y apóstoles" were "en su mayoría personas ya grandes"; Luna Parra, *Semana Santa,* 173.

18. See the story regarding the via Crucis of San Mateo Texcalya (Mexico), in *U:* 1982, where the crowd turned against Caiaphas for just that reason. Recall that Caiaphas from early on was represented as one of the most grotesque mask-wearers of the passion figures.

19. *U:* 12 April.

20. The postwar understanding of Jesus and his followers as themselves Jews has remained foreign to the Iztapalapan passion, which remains resolutely polar in this respect. I will of course mention the rare expressions of anti-Semitism encountered in the records of the Iztapalapan passion. They usually hint at clerical rather than lay origins, and of course the notion of election has Judeo-Christian origins.

21. "Durante su recorrido se rezaban las estaciones." Already in 1931, the *El Universal* reporter captures the transition away from outdoor liturgy when he says that those who observed the passage of its Jesus in the atrium of the Santuario were using prayers "similar to those of the Way of the Cross that are said in the churches."

22. Unless I am mistaken, *Excelsior* in 1920 reached still further back, when it described a past in which the Three Falls procession featured a wooden image of Jesus which, just as now the boy Jesus, stopped at a series of chapels to act out the various Stations of the Cross: "Se le conducía en procesión al Santuario, y se detenía en capillas al aire libre para figurar las Tres Caídas."

23. In other words, after the long hiatus of the mid- and later 1920s, the Iztapalapans in 1930 reverted to the established celebration of the crucifixion at the Santuario. Toor's original account in *Mexican Folkways* 6, no. 2 (1930), 95–99, is reproduced in Luna Parra, *Semana Santa,* 135–138. A slightly varied description is given in Toor, *Treasury,* 218–219. Note that the reporter of *El Universal* in 1921 did not know the town well, referring to the parish church of San Lucas as the Santuario, and to the Santuario as the "parroquia de Iztapalapa." As usual, I correct this confusion in what follows, after indicating the confusion.

24. Luna Parra, *Semana Santa,* 135.

25. According to this account, the actors playing the thieves hung there for three hours, just as they had in 1867; see above. Note also that the hour of crucifixion had been set at noon, so the Deposition took place at 3 P.M., following Joseph of Arimethea's request for the body; *E:* 1933. At this point in that year, the spectators flowed into the Santuario, where the Sermon of the Seven Last Words was pronounced, just as it had been in our core years (*E:* 1920).

26. See for instance Nahmad Sitton, "Los días santos," in Luna Parra, *Semana Santa*, 29–53.

27. A number of passion play masks from Tzintzuntzán, Michoacán, no longer in use in 1925 when Toor attended the local passion, were reproduced by that author in her "El uso actual," 120. Unfortunately, the Brooklyn Museum of Art, which bought them from Toor, has now lost or destroyed them.

28. *Excelsior* says in 1957 and 1974 that this regime was still in effect, although by the later date individual actors were increasingly buying their own outfits, as documented further below. For the used-clothes renters of the eighteenth century, see Chap. 2 above.

29. *El Tiempo*, 11 April 1897.

30. "Una falda corta de mucho vuelo y camisa adornada con lentejuelas"; Toor, cited in Luna Parra, *Semana Santa*, 137; and further; García Mora, "Iztapalapa," no. 16. Elsewhere in our records those "dressed like Apaches" can be well dressed. See their opulent appearance in certain Huejotzingo Dances of the Apaches in Toor, "Carnavales en los pueblos," 14–15, 18, 20, 22; and in Toor, *Treasury*, pl. 92.

31. And indeed the Excelsior of 1920, after listing various anachronisms, concludes: "pero eso no importa."

32. Presumably for reasons of etiquette, Luna Parra, the editor of *Semana Santa*, omitted this colonialistic passage from the published transcription of this report.

33. Lay activity is unfortunately labelled "religiosity" in Spanish as a whole. This is one reason why ultimately the debate over whether the Iztapalapan play itself is religious or irreligious, for instance, is usually resolved with a negative; see below. My own sense is that the term "pagano-religioso" is analogous to this Spanish term "religiosity," referring to so-called "popular religion," in a context, that is, in which "religion" means only ecclesiastical or clerical activity. For various terms of this type, see Rodríguez, "Las fiestas como modeladores."

34. So strikingly different in tone and content is the concluding paragraph of this article that it must have been written not by the reporter but rather by an editor.

35. Toor, cited in Luna Parra, *Semana Santa*, 135–138, describes the play of 1930 as done for the "primera vez después de nueve años," an assertion confirmed *ad silentium* by *Excelsior* during these same years. Less reliably, an elder is cited in *U:* 1933 saying that the performance had not been done in nine years. To repeat, there is no account of it from 1922 until 1930.

36. *U:* 14 April 1922.

37. 30 March 1923.

38. An interdict was not involved, so theoretically priestly services could be

performed outside the churches. Alas, that was prohibited by long-standing state law. Just the previous year, on the eve of Holy Week 1925, in fact, the state of Mexico reminded its municipal authorities that the 1917 Constitution required religious rites to be held only inside church precincts; Bailey, *Viva Cristo Rey!*, 81, 50.

39. Galván, *Calendario*, at the date; Meyer and Sherman, *The Course of Mexican History*, 587–588; Krauze, *Mexico*, 419–424.

40. Toor, "Semana Santa," 53, with vivid notes written in 1927.

41. (*E:* 15 April 1927). However, the same paper the following day states that the rite of the Adoration of the Cross on Good Friday had filled the city's churches (*E:* 15 April 1927).

42. Ibid.

43. So that "today [1933] it is carried out in the inside of the church. But the figure of Jesus is no longer living, but rather an image."

5. From Dualism to Narrative in the Depression

1. *Fiestas y Costumbres,* 2: 320–326 ("La Representación de la Judea en Ixtapalapa"). Contrary to Rodríguez, *Hacia,* 147–148, the account was actually written c. 1935, long before it was published in 1953. Vázquez has the ceremony of the crucifixion taking place "inside the temple, where one had formed a mountain" (in this often imprecise description, "the temple" appears to be San Lucas); thus this was in fact the venue after the facade of the Santuario ceased to be the locale of the crucifixion, and before the Hill of the Star resumed that role, that is, after 1933 and before 1939; see below for these dates.

2. This was not unique in the postwar world. Several European countries set great store on tourism to rescue their war-scarred economies.

3. C. 1935 Vázquez lists 13 individuals *(personajes)* and 4 groups who dressed for the performances: Jesus, Pontius Pilate, Herod, Caiaphas, Annas, the Virgin Mary, Mary Magdalene, Sts. John and Peter, Joseph of Arimathea, Nicodemus, the Centurion (Longinus), Judas; the priests, the Jews, the Roman soldiers, and the people. Note that the other ten apostles, who had no spoken parts, are not included in the list; *Fiestas y Costumbres,* 2: 322.

4. Not until 1946 do we find a new *camerino* at work, one Martín Cano. He and his descendants would serve in that office down to the present day, and his house remained the center of preparations and tryouts, as well as the place where Jesus was imprisoned the night of Holy Thursday. It may be speculated that like the Canos in the following decade, de la Rosa earlier held the post of *ejidario,* or state official charged with the administration of the common lands

of Iztapalapa, which had been "restored" to the pueblo by the state in October 1916; Krauze, *Mexico*, 353. Indeed, perhaps the house itself was in effect a quasi-official location from these early days. For the Canos, see below.

5. Luna Parra, *Semana Santa*, 135.

6. *Fiestas y Costumbres*, 2: 321.

7. This is very similar to the 1840 description (see chap. 2) of soldiers riding about Tacubaya searching for Jesus. In short, this scene was a vehicle for locals to display their equestrian-military skills.

8. In Luna Parra, *Semana Santa*, 135. In 1931, *Excelsior* refers to "the Señor de Iztapalapa," that is, of the Cuevita, as being venerated there.

9. *Fiestas y Costumbres*, 2: 324.

10. Luna Parra, *Semana Santa*, 137. This could be the Ecce Homo said in 1946 to have been brought to San Lucas from the barrio of Santa Barbara; see chap. 6. If I understand aright, this figure on a litter was not part of the passion narrative, but simply appeared in the procession to be taken into the church.

11. *Fiestas y Costumbres*, 2: 325; Luna Parra, *Semana Santa*, 206.

12. Toor, *Treasury*, 213.

13. Foster, *Empire's Children*, 210.

14. Luna Parra, *Semana Santa*, 137.

15. Ibid.

16. Perhaps this overnight prison of Jesus was the same as it is to this day, that is, the home of the head of the *ejido* of Iztapalapa; see further below. For a photograph of this *aposentillo*, see *E: 1930*. Note also that, again to this day, Jesus is also still shown in prison within the church of San Lucas. This may indicate that at this early date, the conflict between the Iztapalapan lay festival and one sponsored by traditional churchmen and their followers had already erupted. See details of this conflict further below.

17. *Fiestas y Costumbres*, 2: 325.

18. "Con auténtica corona de espinas en la cabeza. Era un mozalbete veinteabrileño, genuinamente indígena, barbilampiño, no se atrevieron los mayordomos de esta representación a colocar sobre la cara joven del indio barbas nazarenas."

19. At this time, Pilate was played by the organizer Santiago Guerra, and in 1939 *Excelsior* noted that he physically resembled a certain retired politician (a former president of the republic?). Is it possible that the (today) well-established Mexico City neighborhood rite of boys throwing quantities of water onto unsuspecting passersby on the morning of Holy Saturday traces in part back to Pontius Pilate's joke of Good Friday? See further below.

20. See the photograph in *E: 1938*. Over the years the acts of Jesus's sen-

tence to death and Jesus's flagellation were performed in one, then the other order.

21. And then continues: "y hasta enclavado en la cruz en condiciones bastante serias, hechos que eran rematadas con la tradicional lanzada del centurio Longinos, que no faltó en la representación de ayer." Note that in the early 1930s, it is possible that the flagellation was carried out at times before the sentencing.

22. *Fiestas y Costumbres,* 2: 324. Upon sentencing, this young Jesus was led off to be whipped.

23. Ibid.

24. Ibid.

25. Ibid.

26. See for instance their usage in the Procession of Silence in the parish of San Angel, Mexico City, beginning in 1963 (*U,* and often thereafter).

27. Vázquez also includes Martha and (her sister) Mary among the *piadosas mujeres; Fiestas y Costumbres,* 2: 325. A band of such women was a part of Jesus's entourage coming out of Galilee. See e.g. Luke 23.27, where Jesus tells them that they and their children will pay for the crucifixion.

28. Prieto, *Memorias,* 2: 11.

29. The latter in *U:* 1946 refers to the indigenous wife of Pontius Pilate.

30. *Fiestas y Costumbres,* 2: 326.

31. The point has previously been made by Rodríguez, *Hacia,* 114–116. I recall first confronting such a seductive-solemn image in 1997 in a religious procession in Parácuaro (Mich.). On a flatbed stood two boys dressed up as friars, surrounded by four young women dressed in ballroom gowns. The contrast was stark. On "Indian Princesses" and "Queens" in native schools in the United States, see Archuleta et al., *Away from Home,* 81–83.

32. Thus those playing Romans in 1944 (*U*) said that they did not mind being an object of scorn, because through playing out their roles they permitted "Christians" to experience their faith; see below.

33. This unfindable word presumably means something like street refuse.

34. From 1935 through 1937, there was no story in either *Excelsior* or *El Universal.* In the following years, up till 1962, *Excelsior* rarely carried a story, the exceptions being 1939, 1946, 1950, 1952, 1954, 1955. *El Universal's* coverage was much more regular over these years.

35. "Actualmente solamente se hace el recorrido de la puerta de la iglesia a un extremo de la población, dando vuelta por las principales calles . . . Entre músicas populares, cohetes y gritos, la comitiva regresó a la parroquia." It is not said where that "end of the pueblo" was.

36. Which certainly refers to the atrium and facade of the Santuario.

37. For Boggs, see chap. 5. Subsequent descriptions seem to uniformly indicate this spot. *El Universal* in 1948 says Jesus carried the cross "to the Cerro, also called the Cerro del Calvario or *de las Tres Cruces.*" In 1957 it speaks of the Cerro, "where are the three crosses," and in 1964 says that the drama culminates "at the promontory of the Cerro de la Estrella, called by locals the Cerrito de la Muerte." Lázaro Cárdenas proclaimed the Cerro a national park; *Catálogo nacional . . . Iztapalapa,* 16.

38. This and the following in Luna Parra, *Semana Santa,* 138.

39. See Trexler, *Church and Community,* 575–613.

40. Ibid.

41. Darley, *The Passionists,* 46.

42. Toor added that adults among themselves would pull each others' ears, saying: "Judas, this is your Glory"; Luna Parra, *Semana Santa,* 138.

43. Let us not be oblivious to this casual assertion that the purpose of the plays was at least in part to make the people hate the Jews.

44. Part of the context of this enthusiasm for tourism is the emergence in these years of the future president Miguel Alemán, who devoted much energy to this sector; Krauze, *Mexico,* 538.

6. Toward a "Less Grotesque" Tourist Passion

1. See below. The newspaper reports in what follows come mostly from *El Universal.* Note the gaps in *Excelsior,* which reported nothing on the festival from 1934–1938, 1940–1945, 1947–1951, and 1953–1960. Beginning in 1961, the paper resumed annual reportage.

2. The Santuario drops out almost completely from the reporting of subsequent years, except for its occasional mention as the goal of a Santo Entierro procession to bury Jesus late on Good Friday. These references were so rare because the crucifixion was increasingly becoming the culmination of the day's events, after which tourists either went home or began feasting. See below.

3. Boggs and Mendoza, "Representación," 139–178. At the same time, Mendoza was preparing publication of the play performed concurrently at nearby Milpa Alta. This appeared in tandem with the Iztapalapan text; Mendoza, "Drama," 249–371.

4. Boggs and Mendoza, "Representación," 143–145, where it is called the *palco* or palace of Herod. The present address of this location is Callejón de Aztecas, no. 7. From this very year 1945 forward, it was owned by the *comisario*

ejidal Martín Cano, who served till his death about 1974 as the chamberlain of the Comité; *E:* 1966.

5. So identified in Luna Parra, *Semana Santa,* 173. He later served as the make-up artist for the passion.

6. Boggs and Mendoza, *Representación,* 142. The point of this was not to see one's girlfriend, not to dance, and not to drink; "Jesus's" account in *E:* 24 March 1967.

7. *E:* 13 April 1979.

8. Boggs and Mendoza, *Representación,* 146. Note on the map that the place of crucifixion is in the foothills of the Cerro de la Estrella.

9. Some Iztapalapans obviously still thought that a statue of Jesus was "more decent" than an actor; see further below.

10. In one of the scattered references to a Santo Entierro procession in this period, Pedro Guillén recalls that in the 1960s the procession of the Santo Entierro featured three allegorical cars: Jesus Praying in the Garden of Gethsemane, the via Crucis, and Judas Hanging. Today (1992), he says, the image of the Señor de la Cuevita, the hooded penitents, and the "virgins Mary and [Mary of] Sorrows" accompany this procession; Luna Parra, *Semana Santa,* 166.

11. The play concludes with "Cayo's" malediction of the Jews and Romans and the sons of their sons for having killed the son of God; Boggs and Mendoza, "Representación," 178.

12. See the interview he gave for the 1992 book coordinated by Luna Parra, *Semana Santa,* 172–176. There he is said to be 83 years old, and thus 36 in 1945. Curiously, in this interview he does not say that he had ever been Jesus, though he is listed as such in Boggs and Mendoza, "Representación," 148.

13. See for example Christian, *Apparitions,* 64.

14. He adds that this is no longer done; Luna Parra, *Semana Santa,* 173–175.

15. Ibid. Epitacio's account goes on to describe the various techniques he developed for the illusions of the play.

16. Note that the organizers, who played the enemies of Jesus, were still much older than the late adolescent Jesuses. This can be observed in the various recent videotapes of the performance, especially Echevarría, *La pasión de Iztapalapa,* and E. Ontiveros, *Memorias de la Pasión.*

17. These clouds rose up with the rising image, thus hiding the mechanisms; Boggs and Mendoza, "Representación," 142, 147.

18. Luna Parra, *Semana Santa,* 166. Guillén says that this representation was stopped in 1965, when the church moved it to (Easter) Sunday.

19. An actual scenic representation of the resurrection on Easter was not tried in Iztapalapa until 1982; *Excelsior,* 9 April 1982. The paucity of Easter repre-

sentations reflects the fact that in keeping with popular Christian customs, the passion of Jesus and not the resurrection brought the festive cycle to an end.

20. See Rodríguez, *Hacia*, 149, and more generally 148–150 for these sentiments.

21. Ibid.

22. This discussion was very loud, and they did not succeed in expelling him from the atrium, the organizer continued; Rodríguez, *Hacia*, 149. Though the name of the church is not given, it was probably San Lucas.

23. Thus the *Excelsior* reporter of 1962 noted that in reading out Jesus's sentence, a soldier "imitated the Gregorian chant," certainly an evocation of a receding past.

24. García Mora, "Iztapalapa," n. 10.

25. Neighboring Milpa Altans used the microphone for their passion by 1947; Mendoza, "Drama," 250. In 1967, *Excelsior* referred to the bad sound coming from the microphones. Soon enough, Jesus had a microphone placed before him: for example, for the seven last words. The identical scene of a modern Spanish woman holding a microphone before Jesus during a fall is shown in Christian, *Local Religion*, 191.

26. The provincialism in this remark is evident. By 1952, Good Friday almost everywhere was well on its way to being viewed as something less than a sacred day. Like the inflated figures for the numbers visiting Iztapalapa on Good Friday, the statement that there was an "infinity of foreigners" must also be taken with a large grain of salt. While the passion play was definitely arousing interest abroad, it took the form of televising the event. As in most developing countries, there is a strong tendency in Mexico to prove that an event is of great importance by referring to foreigners coming "from all over the world," etc. In my various visits after 1996, the same rhetoric of huge numbers and an infinite number of foreigners was abroad, but I found almost no other foreigners besides myself and my friends. The numbers present, as I will show later, were nowhere near those floated by the press and play organizers.

27. Whenever I describe audiences participating in the dynamics of the play, I am of course referring to Iztapalapan witnesses rather than to outside tourists, whom the reporters never identify as participating in these confrontations.

28. Though the sources only hint at this, there can be little doubt that violence done perhaps especially to women by macho drunks was one feature of these raucous events.

29. See Foster, *Empire's Children*, 209.

30. The *Ordo Hebodomadae Sanctae* is contained in an ordinal of Pope Pius XII of 1951, but was officially adopted in 1955; Bernardi, *La drammaturgia*, 383.

31. See for instance Bailey, *Viva Cristo Rey!*

32. *Mutatis mutandis,* kissing the crucified or deposed Jesus remains a standard Holy Week practice elsewhere in Mexico. Like much of this reliturgizing, the reincorporation of the Santuario into the rituals of Good Friday would not last.

33. For a noncanonical "fourth fall," at which Jesus encounters the Wandering Jew, see below, and *U:* 1964.

7. The World Presses In

1. The new market was dedicated by the mayor (regent) Uruchurtu on 12 November 1958; Santoyo Carmona, *Historia y Tradición del Mercado,* 16.

2. See the barefooted pontiff in *E:* 29 March 1959, and the cross-bearing one in *E:* 1971, where it is said that Paul had instituted this practice seven years before.

3. This source says (though the assertion is dubious) that the Taxco passions had started in 1759, when the church of Sta. Prisca was dedicated, were interrupted in the period 1910–1929, and then resumed in 1949. More generally on the politics of reconciliation between church and state in the Alemán years, see Krauze, *Mexico,* 582–583.

4. The heraldic role of Pontius Pilate may in fact have often been played by an important *político.* Beyond the case of Santiago Guerra, note the statement in *E:* 1939 that Pilate looked like an (unnamed) politician.

5. "De eso hace 35 años, cuando volvió la libertad para el culto católico. . . . Años atrás no podíamos hacerlo porque nos hubieran linchado. Quienes pensaban que la iglesia católica se cerraría en México para siempre y ya ve usted, ocurrió todo lo contrario. Hemos vuelto a ganar la calle libremente"; *U:* 1976. Note however that *U:* 1998 says this happened almost fifty years before, or 1948–1949, the same date given in the Taxco report.

6. This is the only specific case of an articulated Nazarene "acting" in a Three Falls representation that I have so far encountered in Mexico. I was fortunate enough to witness this passion play on Good Friday 2001, graciously guided by a member of the Godinez family, which owns the statue; I hope to study it further in another venue. According to an account of 1989, in the *Tres Caídas* fourteen of Jesus's "owners" from the Godinez family carried the litter bearing the statue, whose cross is supported by a live Cyrene on the litter. At the locus of each fall, another six boys, hidden beneath the litter, "moved the articulations of Christ by means of mechanisms, directed by strings and wood pulleys, such that its movements appear natural." Those involved preferred this "Cristo

de Papalotla" to a live Jesus, "considering it offensive for a human to represent Christ as they do at Iztapalapa, D.F." They favored wood to "a sinful mortal." It is said that six generations of this family had been involved in the representation for some 125 years; *U:* 26 March 1989. The following year's account has further information and variations. The six manipulators do their work "in such a way that in the moment the curate of the pueblo announces a fall [of Jesus], they stage [the articulated fall] in such a natural way, as if it were a living thing"; *U:* 13 April 1990. For a much earlier mobile Mary, see Dávila's sixteenth-century description of an articulated statue in the 1582 deposition at Santo Domingo, above, chap. 2. And for the use of more than one articulated statue in nineteenth-century Spanish passions, note the 1816 order of the bishop of Córdoba "que no se representasen al vivo los pasos de la Pasión de nuestro Señor Jesucristo, dando movimiento a las imágenes por medio de muelles o tirando de cuerdas, todo con el objeto de desterrar de dichas procesiones lo que no es conforme a los sagrados ritos y a la gravedad y decoro con que deben celebrarse los actos religiosos"; Aranda Doncel, "Ilustración," 315.

7. See the significant case in Rodríguez, *Hacia,* 149–150. The case of the live passion at Ajusco, which ended with a crucifixion on the Pedregal de la Candelaria, is telling: a native of Iztapalapa moved there in 1967, and since then there had been a representation; *E:* 1975. A market for Iztapalapans who had been involved in that town's representation must have arisen. A reporter covering the passion at Cuajimalpa, after noting that Pérez Escrich's work provided the text for that town's play, said it consisted of "58 sheets dense with text"; *U:* 1973.

8. The competition reached to the very basilica of Guadalupe, Iztapalapa's one national competitor for religious visitors. Its people admitted that the size of its passion performance, started in 1975, was not comparable to Iztapalapa's; *U:* 1979.

9. On this topic, see the excellent study of Bonfil Batalla, "Introducción al ciclo de ferias," (1971), 167–202.

10. For instance, in *U:* 1937. The best work of anthropology is Weigle, *Brothers of Light,* and of history, A. Chávez, "Penitentes." See also the work of Darley, *Passionists,* with documents concerning Sonoran passion plays of the nineteenth century.

11. On this important but largely neglected subject, see the study of Nielsen, *The Great Victorian Sacrilege.*

12. See for instance the case of Poza Rica described further below. After a study of the sources, Rus dismisses the alleged 1868 case of child crucifixion in Chamula; "Whose Caste War?" See also Knab, *A War of Witches,* 178–185. It

would be surprising if no one had ever been nailed to a cross on Good Friday in colonial Mexico and Yucatan, but I have found no systemic evidence of such a practice. In late eighteenth and early nineteenth century New Mexico, live "Cristos" were lashed to crosses, but it is not certain that they were nailed to them; see Weigle, *Brothers of Light,* and immediately below.

13. Recently on Spanish flagellation, Del Río, "Disciplina," and for Italy, Ferlaino, *Vattienti,* studies the practice in Nocera Terinese (Calabria).

14. I observed the San Pedro Cutud ceremonies in Lent, 1998, and have benefited from Nicholas Barker's expertise on this subject; see his "Revival of Religious Self-Flagellation."

15. *Reading* [Pennsylvania] *Times,* 15 April 1995.

16. It did so by repeating a piece from *El Correo del Comerolo* of 26 March 1871 that, pointing to theater's missionary past in Mexico, ostracized priests who had been condemning people going to the theater.

17. "Rabbi" is an honorific oft used by the evangelists to address Jesus, eg. Matt. 26.25.

18. The editorial, written by Francisco de Olaguibel, has much important material on religious theater in the city and its history.

19. The title appears to mimic Pérez Escrich's *El Mártir de Gólgota.*

20. "The woods" refer to the Bosque de Chapultepec and Xochimilco is the town south of center whose canals drew vacationers.

21. He states: "Hoy precisamente, mientras en Iztapalapa transcurre la edición número 156 del Viacrucis, los diferentes canales de la televisión mexicana transmitirán películas que se han vuelto verdaderos clásicos, como ese regio Mártir del Calvario protagonizado por Rambal, y otras historias bíblicas como *Rey de Reyes, El Mando Sagrado, Demetrio el Gladiador y Jesús de Nazareth.* Todavia en la década de los 70, el cine mexicano produjo *El Elegido,* con Katy Jurado y Manuel Ojeda, que si bien no aborda concretamente La Pasión de Cristo, sí recoge el drama y los entretelones de La Pasión de Iztapalapa, tal vez la representación más famosa en el mundo."

22. Perhaps significantly, layouts in the year 2001 seem to reflect some revived attention to ecclesiastical matters.

23. Luna Parra, *Semana Santa,* 168–169.

24. Ibid., 191–192.

25. A church of San Lucas did exist on the spot by 1580; Acuña, *Relaciónes geográficas,* vol. 1, 38–41 (curiously, the name of the man who painted the representation of Iztapalapa in this year was Martín Cano, the name of the mid-twentieth century *ejidatario* whose ancestral home still serves as a staging area for the festival). But the present church structure dates from 1664; *Catálogo nacional . . . Iztapalapa,* 29, which says the church was closed for repairs from 1955–1966.

26. "Un Drama Bíblico."

27. I will not dwell upon the several changes that took place in these first years in this space. For example, in 1969 (U) the Last Supper and the Washing of Feet were done on a platform that was "annexed to the church of San Lucas," whereas by the 1970s the stage for these acts was at the other end of the esplanade. But it is visually important to note that the central market is now hidden from the view of those in the esplanade center—so well that visitors must ask where the town marketplace is.

28. This apocryphal Jew, Samuel Belibeth, was fated to wander because he refused Jesus's request for aid in carrying his cross. In Pérez Escrich, Samuel is a major character, much more so than in the play itself. He is first documented at Iztapalapa in 1945; Boggs and Mendoza, "Representación," 146, 176, and often thereafter. Needless to say, Samuel was a main target of clerically fostered popular anti-Semitism.

29. A decisive shift away from the rental of costumes had also occurred by now. Each player had to buy his or her own clothing, as noted by the U reporter in 1966 and the E reporter in 1967, who helpfully spells out the costs of the outfits of some of the main players. The earlier report tells us that only the horses were now rented by the pageant.

30. To fulfill these vows, we recall, Iztapalapans swore to the Comité to serve in the Good Friday performance a set number of years, as a type of penance, thus affording continuity to the troupe.

31. Jesus assured the reporter in advance that he was up to it, and would "support the weight of the cross without needing any Cyrene to help him." As noted earlier, Simon of Cyrene was the biblical figure who helped Jesus carry the cross.

32. However, already in 1979 the brother of that year's Jesus told a reporter: "Look, here's [this year's] cross. The one of last year weighed something like 70 kilos, but I think that this year it weighs more than 100"; U.

33. See chap. 8, below.

34. See the Spanish evidence in chap. 1. Obviously, the Iztapalapan rumor mill often decided that being Jesus had in fact fostered one's success with young women.

35. Since the newspapers in the years before 1963 do not confirm that a living Jesus did ascend the cross, it may be that this year marked the first in which the spectacle attempted to resume the crucifixion of a live Jesus.

36. On these light crosses made out of corn product, see Orozco, *Los cristos de caña de maíz.*

37. "Una voz autoritaria . . . grita: 'No permitan que retraten a Fidel (Jesús) cuando lo suban a la camilla.' Cerca están los camilleros de la Cruz Roja. En

hombros de media docena de individuos llevan una imagen de cera del Crucificado y la colocan entre Dimas y Gestas. Sobre la camilla está ya Fidel, extenuado, y pensando que el próximo viernes santo volverá a ser Jesús. La gente empieza a bajar, el polvo se hace más denso. La parodia ha terminado"; *E*.

38. In 1965, 160 police helped out around the atrium of San Lucas. In 1966, more than 200 police still could not keep order. The count in 1967 was 270 police, 72 grenadiers, 30 secret agents, 29 mounted police, and even two language police to help foreigners. The numbers have increased further in subsequent years.

39. The route through and around town is given in *Excelsior*'s 1965 account and in that of Good Friday, 1967.

40. Cries recorded in *E: 1999*.

41. The writer clearly thought of this pilgrimage in conjunction with the celebration of the passion.

42. Guillermoprieto, *Looking for History*, 73–86 (Che Guevara).

8. For Sale

1. This is the only occasion in the history of the *Tres Caídas* in Iztapalapa when a newspaper says that the religious orders processed with the laity. We cannot exclude the possibility that in a period of relative calm in church-state relations, it being clear that the lay passion was here to stay, friars of different types if not the secular clergy might have processed, as repugnant as that might appear to established Mexican custom.

2. While San Lucas was formally closed, it was sometimes opened for services at crucial times of the year.

3. The descriptions in both papers are not precise about when "Los Nazarenos" was performed. I have assumed that it was on Good Friday evening, as were almost all such Burial of Christ events. Of what that "play" may have consisted I am not sure. The Guatemalan play of that name by Salomé Jil (José Milla) (1863) could not explain the name "Los Nazarenos"; it is a secular novella largely unrelated to religious themes.

4. I can only imagine that the group at the Santuario were the Penitents and their followers, who were perhaps practicing for, or awaiting, the play of "Los Nazarenos."

5. Rodríguez, "Fiestas como modeladores," analyzes the distinct identities this parallelism fosters, the one anchored in the streets, the other in the church of San Lucas.

6. Obviously, the archaic custom of a private person, like a mayordomo,

keeping a devotional image in his private home, was still very much alive in Iztapalapa. For the Señor de Jerusalén or Señor de las Palmitas, the plaster sculpture of Jesus cum ass used in the Palm Sunday festivity, see *El Sol de México:* 9 April 2001. It was kept in the home of Luis Aguitar (calle de Azitli, 8), its mayordomo or guard for that year.

7. I am not at all suggesting that subdivisions of the town played no previous role in town affairs. Thus at the beginning of the twentieth century, as one sees from plaques on the front of the Santuario, representatives from each of eight "sections" were responsible for collecting funds to raise the tower over that church. According to the 1964 report, inhabitants of the barrios of Santa Barbara, San Miguel, San Pedro, La Asunción, San Ignacio, San Pablo, San Lucas, and San José took part, eight in all.

8. See above, Chapter 2.

9. This will not surprise students of Christian drama. The medieval nativity and magi plays are still commonly referred to as Herod Plays, because that "pagan" figure was the ceremonial center of attention in both Christian stories; see Trexler, *The Journey of the Magi.* The tradition of Pilate as also head of the Comité Organizador has not survived, however. From then until 2001 that head, Jorge Aviles Domínguez, played the role of the herald, never that of Pontius Pilate.

10. He is listed as a merchant and as the director in *E:* 1967. Actually, one Santiago Guerra was principal organizer and Pilate in *U:* 1944, but the longevity of Santiago Guerra Guzmán that we shall presently document, lasting into the 1980s, makes us pause before identifying the two as the same person. The latter was said by *U* to be 50 years of age in 1969 and 60 in 1971. Perhaps the Santiago of 1944 was the son of José and the father of Antonio.

11. In late medieval Florence, Italy (site of my earlier work), in official records the important families (with last names) were rarely identified by their neighborhood, whereas the broad middle and lower classes were usually so identified. The makeup of the Comités will be examined in the next chapter because only in recent years is there enough information about them.

12. I base my judgment on ten years of comparing the crowd estimates of protesters and of the authorities when I demonstrated during the Vietnam War, on my observation of the Iztapalapan passion in 1997, 1998, and 2001, and on studies of newspaper photographs of crowds at the same passions compared to the printed estimates, either by the organizers, by the Delegación, or by the reporters themselves. Thus in a photographic caption in *El Heraldo de México* in 1999 it is said that there were 2,000,000 people on the Cerro for the crucifixion, while the merest glance at the picture itself shows no more than 5,000 peo-

ple there. In personal communications, some Iztapalapan experts, for example Jorge de León Rivera, the town chronicler, and Eduardo Ontiveros, former Delegación coordinator of the spectacle, also threw up their hands at this inflation.

13. Despite serious attempts on my part, I have been unable to identify either the Witold group or the university involved.

14. What is probably meant is that the photographers were prohibited from taking pictures. At this point, incidentally, the delegate, seemingly by way of defending the sale, added to his explanation of the event the fact that 1,500,000 persons had attended the passion in that year.

15. The Delegación had historically voted PRI, and it was generally presumed that the Comité itself was conservatively oriented. But interestingly, the PRI lost Iztapalapa Delegación in 1991. Both newspapers report that during the passion the PRI and PAN openly proselytized again in 1997, in the run up to the mayoral campaign. For the nature of this politicking, see further below.

16. "That's because the *padrecito* is new," the Comité spokesman responded. "He's hardly been here a month. We had problems with his predecessor, Antonio Herrera." It should be pointed out that U identifies Socorro as the rector of the parish of the Annunciation, not of San Lucas. Note also, however, that a rector had in fact done this on the Cerro once before, in 1957; see above.

17. See above.

18. That is, in addition to small donations from the more important shops and the tramway company; E.

19. E. "Hasta hace pocos años," they continued, "los actores eran campesinos y obreros, gente de escasa preparación, pero en los últimos años se ha observado un creciente interés de profesionales y estudiantes por intervenir en la obra." Today, they concluded, Iztapalapa is a world market—for a day.

20. Among the relatively few other expressions of emotion recorded in this decade are: children crying on watching the meeting between Jesus and the Wandering Jew (U: 1976); a man carried away kissing the hem of Jesus on the Way of the Cross (E: 1980); a description of women's weeping increasing until reaching a paroxysm at the crucifixion (U: 1982).

21. "La indiferencia de la masa insensible ya, a fuerza de ver espectáculos sangrientos en los medios masivos de difusión."

22. For such gilded nails, see Toor, *Treasury*, 213.

23. For instance, the Maya employed crucifixions soon after the Conquest, it is said, and in the nineteenth-century Guerra de Castas that practice is said to have continued. See Reifler Bricker, *The Indian Christ*, 19–20; but see Rus, cited above. Also Clendinnen, *Ambivalent Conquests*, 182–189.

24. Toor, "Semana Santa," 57. In her *Treasury* Toor states more cautiously

that "it is said a living Christ was nailed to the cross in some villages"; 212. In 1998, several of my hosts in Mexico City stated in error but with no less certainty that Iztapalapan Jesuses had actually been nailed and had died on the cross. For a recent crucifixion in Northern Ireland, see *Le Monde*, 19 Nov. 2002.

25. Cf. the Zeffirelli video *Jesus of Nazareth*, parts 12 and 13.

9. As the Parents Look On

1. See *U:* 14 April 1963; *E:* 14 April 1974; *U:* 19 April 1987.

2. As I write (2001), Domínguez is the head of the Comité Organizador.

3. This critique is laid out by the Jesuit Francisco Goitia in Luna Parra, *Semana Santa*, 259–261.

4. See Chapter 3, above. Perhaps some assumed the truth of this legend because, in 1995 or after (a decade after it appeared in the press), the National Committee of Sacred Art placed a framed message to that effect inside the Santuario (the message lists Felipe Texeda as the vicar-bishop, and he first appears in this office in 1995).

5. *Excelsior* reports the same collectivistic motivation in Milpa Alta on Good Friday, 1986. "In Payment for Miracles Received, Milpa Alta Also Stages the Passion of Christ," the headline reads, and the following story drives home the lesson: the pageant was a "tribute" to Jesus for having "lightened our punishment" *(penas)*. The same paper in the same year said Iztapalapa's passion was staged as an exhortation to God for a miracle that would bring people out of the economic crisis gripping the nation.

6. It ceased to rain at this moment in the new millennium; see the Conclusion, below.

7. This is not to say that the barrios were not an important civil construction much earlier for other matters. The barrios *(secciones)* had been used early in the twentieth century as units for the collection of money for its opera, as can still be read on this church's towers.

8. Luna Parra, *Semana Santa*, 161. But see the eight *secciones* referred to in the early twentieth century, above, chap. 8, n. 7. A study of barrios in nearby Culhuacán is by Oehmichen, "El Carnaval de Culhuacán"; for the Iztapalapan barrios' part in organizing today's annual pilgrimage to the basilica of Guadalupe, see Garma, "La peregrinación." Atlalilco is most easily identified today as the next subway stop west of Iztapalapa, on the Calzada Ermita-Iztapalapa.

9. The Comité "se va a constituir en asociación civil," with the promise of making each representation better than the previous one; *U:* 24 March. In Mexico, civil associations or companies are relatively small, legally constituted non-

profit organizations registered in the municipalities which house them, which work closely with government. A typical one represents an industrial sector and is associated with an employer organization.

10. Lomelí held the rank of vicar bishop (of the seventh district, that is, the area of Iztapalapa) with the metropolitan clergy. Thus in subsequent Iztapalapan sources, he is not only referred to occasionally as a bishop, but the church that supplied his living, the Santuario, rather than being referred to properly as Lomelí's "liturgical seat," is at times referred to loosely as a "cathedral," even though the Santuario remains under the authority of the rector of the town parish, San Lucas. I avoid such complexities, and continue to refer simply to "the Santuario."

11. Though Nazarenes had been a feature of the passion from the beginning, there is, needless to say, no evidence of a previous corporate existence, nor is it clear why 1895 is said to have been the foundation year of this alleged confraternity or society. Finally, there is no evidence before this time of any particular association of past groups of Nazarenes to this church.

12. See the review by "Gita" in *Variety*, 23 February 1977, 16. The film is based on *El Crucificado* (1959), a play by Carlos Solórzano.

13. In the interest of realism, a pueblo physician in Milpa Alta successfully urged that on Holy Thursday a quarter liter of blood be drawn from the year's Jesus, to be dripped on him the following day; *Reforma:* 1999.

14. It is possible that the spies sent by Judas to find and capture Jesus were customarily young boys; see the eighteen-year-old spies in Tzintzuntzán, Foster, *Empire's Children*, 96.

15. See for instance the latter chapters of Trexler, *Public Life*.

16. Iztacalco's own passion play tradition (see above) had long since been swallowed up by Iztapalapa. Tláhuac is near Culiacán, just south of Iztapalapa. For its well-attended passion play, see *E:* 1986.

17. Unless, of course, one managed to avoid the collector *(el encargado)* and sneaked into the lines without paying for the identifying button *(U:* 1999).

18. As I write, the renters of crosses in Jerusalem have seen their business ruined by the latest outbreak of Israeli-Palestinian violence in Jerusalem; *New York Times*, 11 November 2000, with an illustration.

19. We return to the fate of these enormous numbers of Nazarenes in the conclusion to this work.

20. In traditional Christianity, it had been common for parents of a sick child to promise a supernatural that if the child survived, it would be offered to the church, that is, would be made a priest or nun.

21. Though by now the distinction may have been lost on the Iztapalapans, the Nazarenes or penitents were not, we have insisted, reenactors of historical

figures, but rather contemporary figures regretting their sins before the processional image of their passionate savior.

22. Actually, Pedra Avilés Díaz was Mary in that year.

23. These observers meant more than that it was now less clerical in inspiration; rather, they were pointing to its spectacular profanity, a charge that was as old as the play itself.

24. Dressed in black and also called *jóvenes del pentation,* these volunteers seem to have been toughs brought in to repress disorder; see *U:* 1982 and *U:* 1983, according to which they dedicated themselves to beating up others.

25. The PRI and the PAN, if not the PRD, used the spectacle to their own ends, of course. *La Crónica* in 1997 narrates how the former distributed bottles of water to actors and spectators, while the latter gave out tacos.

26. Boggs and Mendoza, "Representación," 178.

27. Ibid., 176–177.

28. Toor, "The Passion Play at Tzintzuntzán," 21.

29. That decline was to be directly addressed in the newspapers during the Holy Week of 2003. Thus on Good Friday, *E* wrote that "one hoped for 2 million persons; 300,000 came," and that Iztapalapa had been "displaced" by the competition! The other journals repeated this finding.

30. "El drama de la cruz sigue siendo motivo de escándalo para los judíos y locura para los gentiles. Desde siempre, y ahora también, ha existido la tentación de suprimir la cruz"; *E.*

31. An addendum: On Good Friday 2002, the diocese of Mexico City itself staged a passion play at the very entrance of the cathedral! This overwhelming break with tradition confirms my hypothesis of the growing thespianization of the clergy since mid-nineteenth century (*E, U, El Heraldo, Novedades*).

32. The group is so cited, with quotation marks, in *E:* 21 April 2000. Note that while *La Jornada* (13 April 2001) says that all the Nazarenes were male, *E* (14 April 2001) for the first time in our sources refers also to *niñas nazarenas.*

33. See especially *U:* 2000.

Conclusion

1. Clearly, "confusion" of play and reality is not limited to so-called traditional cultures. Further on these mock auctions in I. Berlin, "Overcome by Slavery," *New York Times,* 14 July 2001.

2. See the introduction of Trexler, *Public Life,* for this approach.

3. This frame metaphor was first used as an instrument of social urban analysis in my 1980 *Public Life,* esp. chap. 2.

4. Turner, "The Center Out There," 191–230.

5. A *"reconstrucción"*; *"toda una resurrección histórica, en la que no se perdió ningún detalle de importancia."* Note that this phrase again affirms the centrality of the death rather than the alleged resurrection of Jesus to the Iztapalapans and many other Christian communities.

6. See the works of Halbwachs and Connerton.

7. For all that, only the rare art historian of the passion, such as Webster, has given its enactment much attention; see for example Merback, *The Thief, the Cross and the Wheel.*

8. As the present work shows, resistance, while important, is but one of those messages; compare Harris, *Aztecs, Moors, and Christians.* It definitely is inadequate by itself for studying passion drama. I cautioned against simple bipolar readings of festive motivations while introducing my "From the Mouths of Babes," in Trexler, *Church and Community,* 549.

9. In thinking about the differential fashions of reconstructing the nature of Jesus, I have profited from a reading of Weil, *La condition ouvrière.*

BIBLIOGRAPHY

Acuña, René (ed.), *Relaciones geográficas del siglo xvi: México,* vol. 1 (Mexico City: U.N.A.M., 1986).

Aeschylus. *The Persians* in *Complete Greek Tragedies,* vol. 1 (Chicago: University of Chicago Press, 1953).

AGN. See *Archivo general de la nación.*

Aldrete Cossío, María Teresa. "Semana Santa en San Luis Potosí," in *Semana Santa en Iztapalapa,* Adriana Luna Parra, coord., 63–71.

Allegri, Luigi. *Teatro e spettacolo nel medioevo* (Rome: Editori Laterza, 1988).

Aranda Doncel, Juan. *La Cofradía de la Extirpación y la Semana Santa cordobesa durante los siglos XVII al XX* (Córdoba: Monte de Piedad, 1993).

———— "Ilustración y religiosidad popular en la Diócesis de Córdoba: La actitud de los Obispos frente a las celebraciones de Semana Santa (1743–1820)," in the Acts of the *I Congreso nacional de cofradías de Semana Santa* (Zamora: Ciudad, 1987), 305–318.

Archivo Casa Morelos (Morelia, Mexico), eighteenth century, 648.

Archivo general de la nación (Mexico City), *(AGN), Inquisición,* 1072, 1182.

———— *Historia,* 437.

———— *Misiones,* 25.

———— *Ordenanzas,* 1.

Archivo histórico (Madrid), *Cons. Lib. Gob. 1680.*

Archuleta, Margaret L, Brenda J. Child, and K. Tsianina Lomowaima (eds.). *Away from Home: American Indian Boarding School Experiences, 1879–2000* (Phoenix: Heard Museum, 2000).

Arenas, A. "Elegía del Viernes Florido," *Revista de Revistas* (12–18 April 1943), n.p.

Armella, Virginia (ed.). *Treasures of the Pinacoteca Virrenal: A Pictorial Heritage of New Spain* (Mexico City: Fomento Cultural Banamex, 1993).

Augustine of Hippo. *De sancta virginitate*, in *Patrologia . . . latina*, ed. J.-P Migne, vol. 40 (Paris: Migne, 1887).

Bailey, David C. *Viva Cristo Rey! The Cristero Rebellion and the Church-State Conflict in Mexico* (Austin, 1974).

Baker, Derek (ed.), *Religious Motivation: Biographical and Sociological Problems for the Church Historian* (Oxford: B. Blackwell, 1978).

Bakhtin, Michael. *Rabelais and His World* (Bloomington: Indiana University Press, 1984).

Barker, Nicholas. "Revival of Religious Self-Flagellation in Lowland Christian Philippines," in *Religious Revival in Contemporary Southeast Asia*, eds. Bernhard Dahm and N. Talib (forthcoming).

Bernardi, Claudio. *La drammaturgia della settimana santa* (Milan: Vita e Pensiero, 1991).

Bevington, David. *Medieval Drama* (Boston: Houghton Mifflin, 1975).

Boggs, Ralph S. and Vicente T. Mendoza (eds.). "Representación del drama de la Pasión, en Ixtapalapa, D. F., México (llamado *Las Tres Caídas de Jesucristo*, y representado el Jueves y Viernes Santo en Abril de 1945)," *Anuario de la sociedad folklórica de México* 6 (1945), 139–178.

Bonaventura of Bagnoregio. *Legenda Maior*, in *Analecta franciscana* 10 (Ad Claras Aquas : Ex Typographia Collegii S. Bonaventurae, 1926–1941).

Bonfil Batalla, Guillermo. "Introducción al ciclo de ferias de cuaresma en la región de Cuautla, Morelos, México," *Anales de Antropología* 8 (1971), 167–202.

Brading, David A. *Church and State in Bourbon Mexico: The Diocese of Michoacán, 1749–1810* (New York: Cambridge University Press, 1994).

——— "Tridentine Catholicism and Enlightened Despotism in Bourbon Mexico," *Journal of Latinamerican Studies* 15 (1983), 1–22.

Branch, H. N. (ed.). *The Mexican Constitution of 1917 Compared with the Constitution of 1857* (Philadelphia: American Academy of Political and Social Science, 1917).

Bricker, Victoria Reifler. *The Indian Christ, the Indian King: The Historical Substrate of Maya Myth and Ritual* (Austin: University of Texas Press, 1981).

Bujak, Adam. *Misteria* (Warsaw: Sport i Turystyka, 1989).

Burkhart, Louise. *Holy Wednesday: A Nahua Drama from Early Colonial Mexico* (Philadelphia: University of Pennsylvania Press, 1996).

Bynum, Caroline Walker. "The Body of Christ in the Later Middle Ages," *Renaissance Quarterly* 39 (1986), 399–439.

Calderon de la Barca, Frances. *Life in Mexico during a Residence of Two Years in That Country* (New York: E. P. Dutton, 1931).

Castoreña y Ursúa, Juan, and Sahagún de Arévalo. *Gacetas de México*, vol. 1 (Mexico City: Secretaría de Educación Pública, 1949).

Catálogo nacional: Monumentos Históricos Inmuebles: Iztapalapa (Mexico City: I.N.A.H., 1988).

Cervantes, Fernando. *The Devil in the New World: The Impact of Diabolism in New Spain* (New Haven: Yale University Press, 1994).

———— "The Devils of Querétaro: Skepticism and Credulity in Late Seventeenth-Century Mexico," *Past and Present* 130 (February, 1991), 51–69.

Chávez, Angélico. "The Penitentes of New Mexico," *New Mexico Historical Review* 22 (1954), 97–123.

Chelkowski, Peter J. *Staging a Revolution: The Art of Persuasion in the Islamic Republic of Iran* (New York: New York University Press, 1999).

———— (ed.). *Ta'ziyeh: Ritual and Drama in Iran* (New York: New York University Press, 1979).

Chevalier, François. "Un factor decisivo de la revolución agraria de México: 'El Levantamiento de Zapata' (1911–1919)," *Cuadernos americanos* 113, no. 6 (November 1960), 165–187.

Chimalpahin Cuauhtlehuanitzin, Francisco de San Antón Muñón. *Relaciones originales de Chalco Amaquemecan* (Mexico City: Fondo de Cultura Económica, 1965).

Christian, William A., Jr. *Apparitions in Late Medieval Spain* (Princeton: Princeton University Press, 1981).

———— *Local Religion in Sixteenth-Century Spain* (Princeton: Princeton University Press, 1981).

Clendinnen, Inga. *Ambivalent Conquests: Maya and Spaniard in Yucatan, 1517–1570* (Cambridge: Cambridge University Press, 1987).

Cohen, Gustave (ed.). *Le livre de conduite du Régisseur et le Compte des dépenses pour le mystère de la passion joué à Mons en 1501* (Strasbourg: Librairie Istra, 1925).

Colección de documentos inéditos, relativos al descubrimiento, conquista y organización de las antiguas posesiones españolas de América y Oceania, vol. 13 (Madrid: José María Pérez, 1870).

Connerton, Paul. *How Societies Remember* (Cambridge: Cambridge University Press, 1989).

Constable, Giles. *Attitudes Toward Self-Inflicted Suffering in the Middle Ages.* (Brookline: Hellenic College Press, 1982).

———— *Three Studies in Medieval Religious and Social Thought* (Cambridge: Cambridge University Press, 1995).

Constituciones del Arçobispado de Sevilla, hechas i ordenadas por . . . don Fernando Niño de Guevara, cardenal i arçobispo . . . de Sevilla en el Synodo . . . año domini 1604 (Seville, 1609).

Curcio-Nagy, Linda A. "Giants and Gypsies: Corpus Christi in Colonial Mexico City," in William H. Beezley, Cheryl English Martin, William E. French, eds., *Rituals of Rule, Rituals of Resistance: Public Celebrations and Popular Culture in Mexico.* (Wilmington, Delaware: Scholarly Resources, 1994), 1–26.

Darley, Alex M. *The Passionists of the Southwest, or The Holy Brotherhood, 1893* (Glorieta, New Mexico: Rio Grande Press, 1968).

Dávila Padilla, Agustín. *Historia de la Fundación y discurso de la provincia de Santiago de México de la Orden de Predicadores* (Mexico City: Editorial Académica Literaria, 1955).

Daxelmüller, Christophe. "Der Untergrund der Frömmigkeit: Zur Geschichte und Pathologie religiöser Bräuche," *Saeculum* 47 (1966), 136–157.

Dean, Carolyn. *Inka Bodies and the Body of Christ: Corpus Christi in Colonial Cuzco, Peru* (Durham: Duke University Press, 1999).

De Boor, Helmut. *Die Textgeschichte der lateinischen Osterfeiern* (Tübingen: Niemayer, 1967).

Del Río, María José. "Disciplina: San Vicente de la Sonsierra (La Rioja): Semana Santa de 1992" (unpublished).

———— "Flagelación en San Vicente de la Sonsierra (La Rioja): 'Los Picaos'" (1990) (unpublished).

Delaruelle, Etienne et al. *L'Église au temps du Grand Schisme et de la crise conciliaire (1378–1449)* (Paris: Bloud & Gay, 1964).

Dickson, Gary. "The Flagellants of 1260 and the Crusades," *Journal of Medieval History* 15 (1989), 227–267.

Dinzelbacher, Peter. "Diesseits der Metapher: Selbstkreuzigung und-stigmatisation als konkrete Kreuzesnachfolge," *Revue Mabillon* 68 (1996), 157–181.

Donovan, Richard. *The Liturgical Drama in Medieval Spain* (Toronto: Pontifical Institute of Medieval Studies, 1958).

Drumbl, Johan. *Quem quaeritis: Teatro sacro dell'alto medioevo* (Rome: Bulzoni, 1981).

Egeria: Diary of a Pilgrimage, ed. George E. Gingras (New York: Newman Press, 1970).

Enciclopedia dello spettacolo, 9 vols. (Rome: Casa Editrice Le Maschere, 1954–62).

Encina, Juan del. *Obras dramáticas, I (Cancionero de 1496)* (Madrid: Ediciones Istmo, 1975).

Espinosa, Isidro Félix de. *Crónica de los Colegios de Propaganda Fide de la Nueva España*, ed. L. Caneo (Washington: Academy of American Franciscan History, 1964).

Estrada de Gerlero, Elena. "El programa pasionario en el convento franciscano de Huejotzingo," *Jahrbuch für Geschichte von Staat, Wirtschaft und Gesellschaft Lateinamerikas* 20 (1983), 642–661.

Ferlaino, Franco. *Vattienti: Osservazione e Riplasmazione di una Ritualità Tradizionale* (Milan: Qualecultura, 1990).

Fernández, Enrique. *Cuaresma y Semana Santa en Granada* (Granada, Nicaragua: Tiempo, 1962).

Fischer, Michael M. J. *Iran: From Religious Dispute to Revolution* (Cambridge, Mass.: Harvard University Press, 1980).

Flynn, Maureen. *Sacred Charity: Confraternities and Social Welfare in Spain, 1400–1700* (Ithaca, 1989).

———— "The Spectacle of Suffering in Spanish Streets," in *City and Spectacle in Medieval Europe*, eds. Barbara A. Hanawalt and Kathryn L. Reyerson (Minneapolis: University of Minnesota Press, 1994).

Folda, Jaroslav. "Crusader Liturgical Processions in Jerusalem" (1997) (unpublished).

Foster, George M. *Empire's Children: The People of Tzintzuntzan* (Westport, Connecticut: Greenwood Press, 1948).

Frank, Grace. *The Medieval French Drama* (Oxford: Clarendon Press, 1954).

Gage, Thomas. *A New Survey of the West Indies, 1648* (New York: McBride, 1929).

Galván Rivera, Mariano. *Colección de las efemérides publicadas en el Calendario del más antiguo Galván, desde su fundación hasta el 30 de junio de 1950* (Mexico City, 1950).

García Icazbalceta, Joaquín. *Obras*, vol. 2, part 2 (Mexico City: V. Agüeros, 1896).

García Cubas, Antonio. *El libro de mis recuerdos* (Mexico City: Porrúa, 1986).

García Mora, J. C. "Iztapalapa: Tradicionalismo y Modernización," *Boletín de la escuela de ciencias antropológicas de la Universidad de Yucatán*, 2, 11 (March–April, 1975), 11–27.

Garma Navarro, Carlos. "La peregrinación de Iztapalapa al Tepeyac," in Carlos Garma Navarro and Roberto Shadow (coords.). *Las peregrinaciones religiosas: una aproximación* (Mexico City: UAM, 1994).

Gerbet, Marie-Claude. "Les confréries religieuses à Cáceres de 1467 à 1523," *Mélanges de la Casa de Velásquez* 7 (1971), 75–105.

Gillis, John R. (ed.). *Commemorations: The Politics of National Identity* (Princeton: Princeton University Press, 1994).

González Obregón, Luis. *México Viejo* (Mexico City: Promexa Editores, 1979).

Grendi, Eduardo. "Le confraternite liguri in età moderna," in *La Liguria delle casacce: devozione, arte, storia delle confraternite liguri* (Genoa, 1982), 19–52.

Gretscher (also Gretser), Jakob. *Opera Omnia*, 17 vols. (Ratisbon, 1734–41).

Grijalva, Juan de. *Crónica de la órden de nuestro padre San Agustín de las provincias de la Nueva España* (Mexico City: Porrua, 1985).

Guillermoprieto, Alma. *Looking for History* (New York: Pantheon Books, 2001).

Guzmán, Rodríguez de. *Parecer fiscal, expresión e privilegios, y méritos e justicia de la ven. Tercera Orden de Penitencia de Nuestro Padre San Francisco, sobre ser especial, y singular instituto suyo el exercicio público de la via-Crucis* (Mexico City: Viuda de M. Ribera Calderón, 1714).

Halbwachs, Maurice. *On Collective Memory* (Chicago: University of Chicago Press, 1992).

Hanawalt, Barbara A. and Kathryn L. Reyerson, eds., *City and Spectacle in Medieval Europe* (Minneapolis: University of Minnesota Press, 1994).

Harris, Max. *Aztecs, Moors, and Christians* (Austin: University of Texas Press, 2000).

Hassaurek, Friedrich. *Four Years among the Ecuadorians* (Carbondale: Southern Illinois University Press, 1967).

Henderson, John. "The Flagellant Movement and Flagellant Confraternities in Central Italy, 1260–1400," in Derek Baker (ed.), *Religious Motivation: Biographical and Sociological Problems for the Church Historian* (Oxford: B. Blackwell, 1978).

——— *Piety and Charity in Late Medieval Florence* (Chicago: University of Chicago Press, 1994).

Henker, Michael et al. (eds.). *Hört, sehet, weint und liebt: Passionsspiele im alpenländischen Raum* (Munich: Süddeutscher Verlag, 1990).

Herodotus, *The Persian Wars* (New York: Modern Library, 1942).

Horcasitas, Fernando (ed.), *El teatro náhuatl: épocas novohispana y moderna* (Mexico City: U.N.A.M., 1974).

Iguíniz, Juan Bautista. *Breve historia de la tercera orden franciscana en la provincia del Santo Evangelio de México desde sus orígenes hasta nuestros días* (Mexico City: Editorial Patria, 1951).

Jacobelli, Maria Caterina. *Risus Paschalis: El fundamento teológico del placer sexual* (Barcelona: Planeta, 1991).

Los Judas de Diego Rivera (Mexico City: Culturas Populares, 1998).

Kaplan, Steven. *Farewell, Revolution: Disputed Legacies, France, 1789–1989* (Ithaca: Cornell University Press, 1995).

Klein, Cecelia. "Impersonation of Deities," in *The Oxford Encyclopedia of Mesoamerican Cultures* (New York, 2001), vol. 2:33–37.

Knab, T. J. *A War of Witches* (San Francisco: Harper, 1993).

Knudsen, H. "Passione," in *Enciclopedia dello spettacolo,* vol. 7.

Krauze, Enrique. *Mexico, Biography of Power* (New York: Harper Collins, 1998).

León Rivera, Jorge de. "Benito Juárez," in *Semana Santa en Iztapalapa,* 142–143.

Leyes de Reforma, eds. Flores Gutiérrez and Blas José Alatorre, vol. 2, part 2 (Mexico City: El Constitucional, 1870).

Limata conciliis, constitutionibus synodalibus, et aliis monumentis . . . quibus . . . Toribius Alphonsus Mogroveius, archiepiscopi Limanus, provinciam Limensem, seu Peruanum imperium elimavit, et ad normal SS. Canonum composuit; Omnia fere ex Hispanico sermone latina reddit. . . . Fr. Franciscus Haroldus (Rome, 1673).

Llompart, Gabriel. "Desfile iconográfico y penitentes españoles (siglos XVI al XX)," *Revista de dialectología y tradiciones populares* 25 (1969), 33–51.

Lorenzana, Francisco Antonio. *Cartas pastorales y edictos del illmo. Senor don . . . Lorenzana, arzobispo de México* (Mexico City: Superior Gobierno, 1770).

——— (ed.), *Concilios provinciales primero, y segundo, celebrados en la muy noble, y muy leal ciudad de México, presidiendo el illmo. y Rmo. Señor F. Alonso de Montúfar, en los años de 1555, y 1565* (Mexico City: Superior Gobierno, 1769).

Luna Parra, Adriana (coord.). *150 años, 150 fotos: Semana Santa en Iztapalapa* (Mexico City: El Juglar, 1993).

——— (coord.). *Semana Santa en Iztapalapa* (Mexico City: El Juglar, 1992).

MacLeod, Murdo J. and Robert Wasserstrom (eds.), *Spaniards and Indians in Southeastern Mesoamerica* (Lincoln: University of Nebraska Press, 1963).

Marroquí, José María. *La ciudad de México,* 3 vols. (Mexico City: J. Medina, 1969).

Marrow, James. *Passion Iconography in Northern European Art of the Late Middle Ages and Early Renaissance* (Kortrij: Van Ghemmert Co., 1979).

Meersseman, Giles. *Ordo fraternitatis : confraternite e pietà dei laici nel Medioevo* (Rome: Herder, 1977).

Mendieta, Gerónimo. *Historia eclesiástica indiana* (Mexico City: Porrúa, 1971).

Mendoza, Vicente T. "Drama de la Pasión intitulado: *El drama del Gólgota,* que se representa en la delegación de Milpa Alta, D. F., los días jueves, viernes y sábado de la Semana Santa (años de 1945–1947)," *Anuario de la sociedad folklórica de México* 6 (1945), 249–371.

Merback, Mitchell B. *The Thief, the Cross and the Wheel: Pain and the Spectacle of Punishment in Medieval and Renaissance Europe* (Chicago: University of Chicago Press, 1998).

Meyer, Michael C. and William L. Sherman. *The Course of Mexican History* (New York: Oxford University Press, 1995).

Moreno Navarro, Isidro. *Cofradías y hermandades andaluzas* (Seville: Andaluzas Unidas, 1985).

Motolinía, Toribio. *Memoriales e Historia de los Indios de la Nueva España* (Madrid: Ediciones Atlas, 1970).

Mozo de Rosales, Emilio. *El redentor del mundo: drama sacro en ocho cuadros* (Madrid: J. Rodríguez, 1869).

Munuera Rico, Domingo. *Cofradías y hermandades pasionarias en Lorca* (Murcia: Editora Regional 1981).

Nahmad Sitton, Salomón. "Los días santos entre los Coras de Jesús María, Nayarit," in *Semana Santa en Iztapalapa*, coord. A. Luna Parra, 29–53.

Nielsen, A. *The Great Victorian Sacrilege: Preachers, Politics and* The Passion, *1879–1884*. (Jefferson, North Carolina: McFarland, 1991).

Niemeyer, E. V. "Anticlericalism in the Mexican Constitutional Convention of 1916–1917," *The Americas* 11 (1954), 31–49.

Novísima Recopilación de las leyes de España, vol. 5 (Madrid, 1807).

Oehmichen, Cristina. "El carnaval de Culhuacán: expresiones de identidad barrial," *Iztapalapa* 12, no. 25 (January–June, 1992), 29–42.

Orozco, Luis Enrique. *Los cristos de caña de maíz y otras venerables imágenes de nuestro señor Jesucristo*, vol. 1 (Guadalajara, 1970).

Oviedo, Gonzalo Fernández de. *Las Memorias de . . .* , 2 vols. (Chapel Hill: U.N.C. Department of Romance Languages, 1974).

Pérez Escrich, Enrique. *El Mártir del Gólgota: Tradiciones de Oriente*, vol. 5 (Madrid: F. Martínez García, 1864).

Pérez de Rivas, Andrés. *Historia de los triunfos de N.S. Fe, entre gentes las más bárbaras y fieras del nuevo orbe (Páginas para la historia de Sinaloa y Sonora)*, 3 vols. (Mexico City: Editorial Layac, 1944).

Pérez de Villagra, Gaspar. *Historia de la Nueva México, 1610* (Albuquerque: University of New Mexico Press, 1992).

Pinheiro de Veiga, Tomé. *Fastiginia: Vida cotidiana en la corte de Valladolid* (Valladolid, Fundación Municipal de Cultura, 1989).

Polec, Andrzej and Janusz Plonski, *Kreuzwege in Polen* (Zurich: U. Bär Verlag, 1988).

Prieto, Guillermo. *Memorias de mis tiempos*, vol. 2 (Mexico City: Editorial Patria, 1948).

Puyol, Julio. *Plática de disciplinantes* (Madrid: Tipografía de Archivos, 1928).

———— also in *Homenaje a Bonilla y San Martin*, vol. 1 (Madrid, 1927), 241–266.

Redfield, Robert. "El carnaval en Tepoztlán, Mor.," *Mexican Folkways*, 5, no. 1 (1929), 19–25.

"Representaciones teatrales de la Pasión, Las," *Boletín del archivo general de la Nación* 5 (1934), 332–356.

Rodríguez, J.-M. *Iztapalapa, trono de Nuestro Señor de la Cuevita* (Mexico City, n.d.).

Rodríguez, Mariángela. *Hacia la Estrella con la Pasión y la ciudad a cuestas: Semana Santa en Iztapalapa* (Mexico City: C.I.E.S.A.S., 1991).

———— "Las fiestas como modeladores de identidades y diferenciaciones," *Iztapalapa*, 12, no. 25 (1992), 13–27.

Romeu Figueras, J. "Passione," in *Enciclopedia dello spettacolo*, vol. 7.

Rubin, Miri. *Corpus Christi: The Eucharist in Late Medieval Culture* (New York: Cambridge University Press, 1991).

Rubio, Vicente. *Semana Santa en la ciudad colonial de Santo Domingo* (Santo Domingo: Comisión Dominicana Permanente, 1992).

Ruiz Martínez, Rafael, and Armenta Olvera. *Las capillas del vía crucis en Puebla: su historia* (Puebla: Gobierno del Estado, 1992).

Rus, Jan. "Whose Caste War? Indians, Ladinos, and the Chiapas 'Caste War' of 1869," in Murdo J. MacLeod and Robert Wasserstrom (eds.), *Spaniards and Indians in Southeastern Mesoamerica* (Lincoln: University of Nebraska Press, 1963), 127–168.

Sánchez Gordillo, Alonso. *Religiosas estaciones que frecuenta la religiosidad Sevillana* (Seville, 1982).

Santiago Silva, José de. *Atotonilco* (Mexico City: Ediciones la Rana, 1996).

Santoyo Carmona, Virginia. *Historia y Tradición del Mercado Cabecera Iztapalapa* (Iztapalapa: Late Iztapalapa III, 1996).

Scott, James. *Dominance and the Arts of Resistance: Hidden Transcripts* (New Haven: Yale University Press, 1990).

Shapiro, James. *Oberammergau: The Troubling Story of the World's Most Famous Passion Play* (New York: Little Brown, 2000).

Shergold, N. D. *A History of the Spanish Stage: From Medieval Times Until the End of the Seventeenth Century* (Oxford: Clarendon Press, 1967).

Solórzano, Carlos. *El Crucificado*, in *Crossroads and Other Plays of C. S.* (London: Associated University Presses, 1993).

Stegagno Picchio, L. "Passione," in *Enciclopedia dello spettacolo*, vol. 7.

Stens, María (ed.). *El teatro franciscano en la Nueva Espana: Fuentes y ensayos para el estudio del teatro de evangelización en el siglo XVI* (Mexico City: U.N.A.M., 2000).

Sticca, Sandro. *The Latin Passion Play: Its Origins and Developments* (Albany: S.U.N.Y. Press, 1970).

Taylor, William B. *Magistrates of the Sacred: Priests and Parishioners in Eighteenth-Century Mexico* (Stanford: Stanford University Press, 1996).

Téllez, Gabriel (Tirso de Molina). *Historia general de la orden de Nuestra Señora de las Mercedes*, vol. 2 (Madrid: Provincia de la Merced de Castilla, 1974).

Terrugia, Angela Maria. "In quale momento i disciplinati hanno dato origine al loro teatro?" in *Il Movimento dei disciplinati nel Settimo Centenario dal suo inizio* (Perugia: Deputazione di Storia Patria per l'Umbria 1962), 434–459.

Thurston, Herbert. *Lent and Holy Week: Chapters on Catholic Observance and Ritual* (London, Longmans, Green, 1914).

Toor, Frances. "Carnavales en los pueblos," *Mexican Folkways* 5, no. 1 (1929), 10–49.

——— "La Pasión en Ixtapalapa," *Mexican Folkways* 6, no. 2 (1930), 95–102.

——— "The Passion Play at Tzintzuntzan," *Mexican Folkways* 1, no. 1 (1925), 21–28.

——— "Semana Santa," *Mexican Folkways* 3, no. 1 (1927), 53–60.

——— (ed.). "El Texto de la Pasión, Zintzuntzan," *Mexican Folkways* 1, no. 2 (1925), 27–29.

——— *A Treasury of Mexican Folkways* (New York: Crown Publishers, 1947).

——— "El uso actual de las máscaras," *Mexican Folkways* 5, no. 3 (1929), 127–131.

Torquemada, Juan de. *Monarquía indiana*, 3 vols. (Mexico City: Porrúa, 1969).

Toschi, Paolo. *Le origini del teatro italiano* (Turin: Editore Beringhieri, 1976).

Trexler, Richard C. *Church and Community, 1200–1600: Studies in the History of Florence and New Spain* (Rome: Storia e Letteratura, 1987).

——— *The Journey of the Magi: Meanings in History of a Christian Story* (Princeton: Princeton University Press, 1997).

——— *Public Life in Renaissance Florence* (New York: Academic Press, 1980).

——— *Religion in Social Context in Europe and America, 1200–1700* (Tempe, Arizona: Medieval and Renaissance Texts and Studies, 2002).

Turner, Victor. "The Center Out There: Pilgrim's Goal," *History of Religions* 12 (1972), 191–230.

"Un Drama Bíblico Revivido en Ixtapalapa. A Biblical Drama Reeenacted In Ixtapalapa," *Revista nacional de turismo*, 9 (June, 1964), 64–66.

Vázquez Santa Ana, Higinio. *Fiestas y Costumbres Mexicanas*, 2 vols. (Mexico City: Ediciones Botas, 1940–1953).

Vetancurt, Agustín de. *Teatro Mexicano y los sucesos religiosos*, part 4 (*Crónica de la Provincia del santo evangelio de México*) (Mexico City: Porrúa, 1982).

Varagine, Iacopo da, *Cronaca di Genova dalle origini al MCCXCVII*, ed. G. Monleone, in *Fonti per la storia d'Italia*, 85, part 2 (Rome: Tipografia del Senato, 1911).

Webster, Susan Verdi. *Art and Ritual in Golden-Age Spain* (Princeton: Princeton University Press, 1998).

——— "Art, Ritual, and Confraternities in Sixteenth-Century New Spain: Penitential Imagery at the Monastery of San Miguel, Huejotzingo," *Anales del instituto de investigaciones estéticas* 70 (1997), 5–43.

——— "The Descent from the Cross in Sixteenth-Century New Spain," *The Early Drama, Art, and Music Review* 19 (1997), 69–85.

Weckmann, Luis. *La herencia medieval de México* (Mexico City: Fondo de Cultura Económica, 1994).

Weigle, Marta. *Brothers of Light, Brothers of Blood: The Penitentes of the Southwest* (Santa Fe: Ancient City Press, 1976).

Weil, Simone. *La condition ouvrière* (Paris: Gallimard, 1951).

Young, Karl. *The Drama of the Medieval Church*, 2 vols. (Oxford: Clarendon Press, 1933).

Movies and Videos:

Echevarría, Nicolás. *La pasión de Iztapalapa: Un documental* (Video: Mexico City, 1995).

Gonzalez, Servando (dir.). *El Elegido* (Film: Mexico City, 1977).

Ontiveros, Eduardo. *Memorias de la Pasión: la Representación de la Pasión de Cristo de Iztapalapa* (Video: Mexico City, 1995).

Zeffirelli, Franco. *Jesus of Nazareth* (Video: New Rochelle, c. 1981), parts 12 and 13.

Newspapers:

Excelsior. Mexico City daily.

El Heraldo de México. Mexico City daily.

La Jornada. Mexico City daily.

El Mundo Semanario Ilustrado. Mexico City weekly.

The New York Times. New York daily.

Novedades. Mexico City daily.

La Prensa. Mexico City daily.

Reforma, Mexico City daily.

El Sol de México. Mexico City daily.

El Tiempo. Mexico City daily.

El Universal. Mexico City daily.

INDEX

www.ingramcontent.com/pod-product-compliance
Lightning Source LLC
Chambersburg PA
CBHW021829090426
42811CB00032B/2093/J